HARFORD COUNTY MARYLAND

WILLS

1774–1800

Ralph H. Morgan, Jr.

HERITAGE BOOKS
2011

HERITAGE BOOKS
AN IMPRINT OF HERITAGE BOOKS, INC.

Books, CDs, and more—Worldwide

For our listing of thousands of titles see our website
at
www.HeritageBooks.com

Published 2011 by
HERITAGE BOOKS, INC.
Publishing Division
100 Railroad Ave. #104
Westminster, Maryland 21157

Copyright © 1990, 1994 Ralph H. Morgan, Jr.

All rights reserved. No part of this book may be reproduced or transmitted in any form or by any means, electronic or mechanical, including photocopying, recording or by any information storage and retrieval system without written permission from the author, except for the inclusion of brief quotations in a review.

International Standard Book Numbers
Paperbound: 978-1-58549-166-7
Clothbound: 978-0-7884-8927-3

CONTENTS

	Page
Introduction	v
Author's Notes	vi
Acknowledgments	viii

--###--

Harford County Will Book "AJ-2"	1
Harford County Will Book "AJ-R"	66

---###---

INDEXES

Index of Tract Names and Geographic Locations	A-1
Index of Slaves by First Name	B-1
Index of Slaves by Associated Surname	C-1
Index of Full Names	D-1

INTRODUCTION

Harford County was set off from Baltimore County in 1773 by an act of the Maryland Assembly. The actual formation of the government for Harford County occurred on March 22, 1774, when Henry Harford, Lord Proprietor of the Province, sent his commission to establish the new county seat at Harford Town.[1][2] The maintenance of county government records began at this time.

J. Beale Howard was the first Register of Wills, followed in 1780 by John George Bradford. Abraham Jarrett took office in 1799 and served until 1813.[3] The three ledgers that cover the period from 1774 to 1814 bear his initials, "AJ". In Harford County, the ledgers containing wills are identified by the initials of the Register of Wills for the period covered, except for the first two ledgers. These two ledgers were compiled by Abraham Jarrett who is credited with the systematic recording of the county's wills into ledgers.

This publication covers wills for the period 1774 to 1800 which were recorded in two ledgers identified as "AJ-2" and "AJ-R". Both ledgers have wills grouped by the first letter of the last name. The AJ-2 ledger contains the first part of the alphabet (A-Q), and the AJ-R ledger covers the balance (R-Z), hence the "R" designation.

These ledgers, covering the first twenty-five years of Harford County's history, include wills of many individuals who participated in the Revolutionary War as well as information on their descendants, real estate, slaves, and in a few instances, their ancestors.

The third ledger in the "AJ" series (AJ-C) covers the period from 1800 to 1814, when Abraham Jarrett was himself in office, and will be covered in a second publication.

---

[1] Walter W. Preston, <u>History of Harford County, Md.</u>, (Baltimore:1901), 60.

[2] C. Milton Wright, <u>Our Harford Heritage</u>, (Glen Burnie, Md:1967), 75.

[3] Ibid, 440.

AUTHOR'S NOTES

My initial objective in putting together this volume of abstracts was to include the names of all beneficiaries, executors and witnesses in the wills, along with other information of a genealogical nature that might indicate the existence of an individual's relations. I have also included all slaves and servants mentioned in the wills, many of whom are identified only by first name. In addition to this, information is included on named tracts of land as well as any references to geographic locations both within and outside of Harford County.

The initial source of information for this material was the Harford County Register of Wills record books as recorded on microfilm by the L.D.S. Church in 1948. When these were unreadable, or when questions arose, the original records in Bel Air, Maryland, were consulted.

Each abstract herein has two dates in the upper righthand corner, these being the date on which the will was signed and the date when it was first recorded with the Register of Wills. In some instances the date of signing or a part thereof was left out. If the day was left blank on the will, that will be noted by several underscores in front of the date (e.g.: __ Nov 1789). If the will contains no date of signature, that will be so noted. For uniformity, all dates have been shown in the day/month/year format (DD MMM YYYY).

Throughout this book, surnames are capitalized. If a surname is not indicated and can not reasonably be deduced, the probable surname is indicated in parentheses with a question mark, eg: William (SUTTON ?).

If a surname has been listed in the will with multiple spellings, the variations are indicated in parentheses, eg: Benjamin RICHARDSON (or RICHENSON). Where females of a family have been listed by first name only and it is probable that they may be married, but no married name is given, the surname of birth is shown in parentheses, e.g.: Hannah (nee RIGBIE).

Names of slaves in the wills were usually listed only as a single first name. A notation is shown if they are set free in the will, e.g.: Negro man Jack - set free. If a slave is bequeathed, the recipient is indicated, followed by a dash (-), followed by the slave(s), eg: John PRIGG - Negro man William.

Abbreviations used in the abstracts include:

a.	acres	pur.	purchased
adj.	adjoining	rem.	remaining/remainder
ex.	executor/executress	unspec.	unspecified
inc.	including/included	wt.	wutness
incr.	increase		

Directions:
```
N   North/northern      NE  northeast/northeastern
S   South/southern      NW  northwest/northwestern

E   East/eastern        SE  southeast/southeastern
W   West/western        SW  southwest/southwestern
```

In order to conserve space, several unrelated individuals in a will may be listed on a single line of text, in which case they will be separated by a pair of vertical bars, eg: R. DALLAM || W. OSBORN. Also, related individuals have often been grouped to conserve space, such as in the listing of all sons together and all daughters together. The order in which individuals are listed in an abstract should not be construed as necessarily the same order that is contained in the will.

Four sets of indexes are provided following the abstracts. These include:

1. Index of Named Tracts and Geographic Locations - includes all named tracts as well as towns, counties, states, countries, rivers, and streams mentioned.

2. Index of Slaves by First Name - includes first name with all associated surnames and description.

3. Index of Slaves by Associated Surname - listed by surname of both the bequestor and the recipient; identifies whether slave was manumitted in the will (if applicable).

4. Index of Full Names - lists all persons mentioned in the wills, including beneficiaries, executors, witnesses and others.

ACKNOWLEDGEMENTS

I wish to acknowledge the extensive assistance that I have received from my wife, Joni P. Morgan, in this project. She has spent long hours straining to help read faint microfilms, labored through the proofreading of a number of versions of the abstracts themselves and helped in the cross checking of a number of cycles of the indexes.

I also want to thank Henry C. Peden, Jr. for his proofing of this book. He had recently been working independently on a similar abrstract, and graciously agreed to compare his work with my final copy. As a result of this effort, coupled with his familiarity with the Harford County source data, he has greatly aided in assuring the accuracy of this book. His assistance is especially appreciated.

Dedicated to my aunts
Elizabeth Morgan Stover
and
Carrie Morgan Forsythe

WILL BOOK "AJ-2"
HARFORD COUNTY, Md.

AJ-2-001   BENJAMIN AMOS   11 Apr 1775/ 29 May 1775
To: Youngest son, Zechariah (or Zachariah) AMOS - tract 100 a. with
    dwelling & orchard
    Wife, Sarah AMOS - use of 20 a. & dwelling
    Sons, Benjamin, John, & Elijah AMOS - rem. of land
    Daughter, Anne AMOS - Negro wench Bess
    Daughter, Susannah AMOS - Negro wench Peg
    Daughter, Elizabeth AMOS - Negro boy Ignatius
Ex: Wife: Sarah AMOS
Wt: William ROBINSON; Samuel CALWELL; Daniel O'LEARY

AJ-2-002   **William AMOSS** of Joshua   12 Sep 1783/ 21 Oct 1783
To: Wife, Mary AMOSS
    Children, Aquilla, Mary, William, Martha, & James AMOSS - tract
    41 a. Joshua's Choice where I live, leased tract 40 a.
    Addition to Joshua's Choice, leased tract 17 a. Amos Fancy
    given by my father
    To be sold - tract 100 a. Joshua's Forest, tract 54 a. Joshua's
    Meadow & contiguous lease
Ex: Wife, Mary AMOSS; Relation, Mordecai AMOSS, Esq.
    Relation, Frederick AMOSS
Wt: John DAVIS; Daniel McCOMAS of Daniel; John COX

AJ-2-004   **John ALLENDER**   20 May 1786/ 28 Nov 1786
To: Wife, Lucina ALLENDER (or ALLINDER) & family
Ex: Wife, Lucina ALLENDER
Wt: William GRAVES; Joseph PHIPS; Deborah ALLENDER

AJ-2-005   **Lucina ALLENDER**   27 Oct 1788/ 17 Mar 1789
To: Son, John ALLENDER (or ALLINDER)
    Son, Nicholas ALLENDER - Negro man Ceasar
    Daughter, Margaret WANE & her 3 children, John, Sarah, & Lucina
      WANE - Negro man old Ned, Violett, Jenny, Dinah & her 2 sons
      James & Daniel, Negro boys Ned & black Jack, Chloe & her son
      York
    Grandson, John WANE - Negro boy black Jack upon death of
      Margaret WANE
    Granddaughter, Sarah WANE - Negro woman Chloe & son York upon
      death of Margaret WANE
    Granddaughter, Lucina WANE - all other Negroes upon death of
      Margaret WANE
Ex: Sons, John & Nicholas ALLENDER
Wt: John RUMSEY; Mary DAVIS; Samuel Groom OSBORN

AJ-2-007   **James ARMSTRONG**   30 Jun 1790/ 11 Sep 1790
To: Daughter, Jane HUSTON; Son-in-law, James HUSTON
    Children, Agness, Loving, Elizabeth, & Esther (nee ARMSTRONG)
    Children, Sary, Mary, & Anna KANADAY
Ex: Wife, Laving (or Levina) ARMSTRONG
Wt: Samuel SMITH; Andrew STEVENSON; James MACON (or MADON ?)

AJ-2-008　**William ALLEIN**　　　　　　　29 Sep 1790/ 6 Sep 1791
To: Little son, Jimmy ALLEIN - property in America; property in
　　County Derry, Parish of Dunboe at Dunbo Mill near Colerain,
　　Ireland left by my father
　　Friend, James OSBORN
Ex: James OSBORN
Wt: George LITTLE; John RYAN

AJ-2-009　**William ANNAN**　　　　　　　22 Sep 1785/ 5 May 1791
To: Mrs. Frances COPLAND - my Bible ‖ Joseph STILES
　　Gen. PUTNAM - all I have coming from the state of Boston
　　Jane LUCKY, wife of William LUCKY
　　Brothers, Daniel & James ANNAN; Sister, Peggy ANNAN
Ex: George PATTERSON; brother, Daniel ANNAN
Wt: James BELL; James MADDEN

AJ-2-010　**Catherine ANDERSON**　　　　　19 Mar 1797/ 23 Jan 1798
To: Son, Hugh ANDERSON - tract 141 a. *Hugh's Inheritance*, tract 204
　　a. part of *Andersons Lot*; Negro boy Ben
　　Daughters, Mary RENSHAW & Elinor CLARK, wife of John CLARK
　　Daughter, Elizabeth ANDERSON - Negro boy Jim
　　Daughter, Ann ANDERSON - tract 54 a. part of *Andersons Lot*
　　　adj. Widow STOVINGTON's, the old wagon road, & Daniel
　　　THOMPSON's land; Negro girl Hannah
　　Negro woman Dinah - freedom
Ex: Son, Hugh ANDERSON
Wt: Robert BRYARLY; Thomas WEST; Enos WEST

AJ-2-012　**Benjamin BIDDLE**, yeoman　　　12 Nov 1779/ 18 Apr 1780
To: Daughters, Augustine & Nancy (nee BIDDLE) (both under age 16)
　　Son, John BIDDLE ‖ Brother-in-law, James BROCK
　　Son, Richard BIDDLE (under age 16) - Negro boys Samuel & Isaac
　　Wife, Karenhappuch BIDDLE - Negro woman Matilda
　　Negro man Bash & Negro girl Lucy - divided between 2 sons
Ex: Wife, Karenhappuch BIDDLE; James CURRY
Wt: Robert CLARK; Jesse BIDDLE; James CURRY

AJ-2-014　**Daniel BOND**, farmer　　　　　24 Jul 1779/ 11 Jul 1780
To: Sons, Thomas Scott & Joshua BOND - tract *Iles of Caparee*
　　Son, Zacheus Onion BOND - Negro boy George
　　Daughter, Alsannah BOND - Negro boy Davey, Negro girl Dinah
　　Daughter, Hannah BOND
　　Wife, Patience BOND - Negro man Guy, Negro woman Fan
　　Daughter, Elizabeth BOND - Negro man John, Negro girl Rose
Ex: Wife, Patience BOND; son, Thomas Scott BOND
Wt: Joshua MILES; Cornelius GARRISON; John MAULSBY - Quaker;
　　Richard HUTCHINGS

AJ-2-016　**John BULL**　　　　　　　　　4 Sep 1782/ 28 Dec 1782
To: Second son, John BULL - part of 2 tracts *Ruffs Chance & Howards
　　Harbour* adj. Henry WATERS' land
　　First son, Richard BULL - rem. of land & dwelling
　　Son, William BULL ‖ Son, Jacob BULL
　　Daughters, Hannah, Mary, Ann, & Frances BULL

Negroes (names unspec.) - set free according to manumission
document
Ex: Wife (name unspec.)
Wt: Henry RUFF; Frederick FRALEY; Benjamin SEDGWICK; John FORWOOD

AJ-2-017   Ann BRIERLY   30 Apr 1788/ 10 Jun 1788
To: Son, Thomas BRIERLY - tract *Leases Herbitation (or Habitation)*
    lying in His Lordships Reserve
    Grandson, George WORSLEY || Sons, George & Robert BRIERLY
    Granddaughters, Charlotte, Sophia, & Ann WORSLEY
Ex: Son, Robert BRIERLY
Wt: Nathaniel KINGSTON; James MEADS, Jr; Daniel TREDWAY

AJ-2-018   William BOARDMAN (or BOARDSMAN) 7 Dec 1778/ 19 Dec 1778
To: Wife, Catharine BOARDMAN
    Only daughter, Ann BOARDMAN (under age 16)
Ex: Wife, Catharine BOARDMAN; John STEVENSON
Wt: John ARCHER; Susannah WALDRON (or WALDRUM)

AJ-2-019   James BROWN   14 Sep 1774/ 18 Oct 1774
To: Daughter, Mary BROWN || Son-in-law, John YOAKLY
    Sons, James, John, & Thomas BROWN
    Daughters, Elizabeth, Hannah, Martha, & Mary (nee BROWN)
Ex: Son, James BROWN
Wt: Jacob CAMBESSS; James McCARTY; Abraham SPRUSBANKS (or
    SPRUCEBANKS)

AJ-2-021   John BOND   18 May 1790/ 23 Dec 1791
To: Sons, Samuel, John, William, & Thomas BOND
    Grandsons, John BOND (minor), son of Thomas BOND - tract part
    of *Bonds Forest* where I live adj. Jacob RUSH's land, William
    SMITH, Esq. land, Old Joe's Spring Branch, Hog Pen Branch,
    the Falls, Maple Ford Branch, Enoch WILLIAM's land, &
    Benjamin LANCASTER's land, half of tract *Fountain Copper
    Mines* & half of adj. Resurvey, 1/3 of copper mine in
    Frederick Co., half of lots on W side of Thames St., Fells
    Point, Baltimore Town
    Grandson, Thomas BOND, son of Thomas BOND - other half of above
    Grandson, William BOND, son of Samuel BOND
    Daughter, Alisana KELL, wife of Thomas KELL - plantation where
    she lives being 2 tracts *Second Thought* & *Second Thought
    Improved*, tract part of *Bonds Pleasant Hill* adj. *Prospect*
    & Captain Thomas KELL's land
    Daughter, Hannah JOHNS, wife of Aquilla JOHNS
    Daughter, Susanna HUNT, wife of Phineas HUNT
    Daughter, Alisana LOCKWOOD
    Daughter, Pamela MOORE, wife of William MOORE of Baltimore Town
    - house in Fells Point *Coffee House*, lot with house built
    by Henry Wells CARVER on east side of Thames Street
    Grandsons, John BOND, son of William BOND - tract part of *Bonds
    Forest* where William BOND lives, land between two branches,
    viz. the *Overshott*, Old Joe's Spring Branch, & over the
    Falls

       Grandson, Edward Fell BOND, son of William BOND - tract 100 a.
            part of *Bonds Forest* where STANDIFORD's live with house &
            orchard, tract 65 a. where Amos JONES lives
       Grandson, John Bond KELL, son of Thomas KELL - tract 100 a.
            Bond Pleasant Hills where Jonathan ADY lives
       Friend, Isaac EVERTT - tract 100 a. part of *Bonds Forest* where
            he lives adj. Old Joe's Spring Branch, Hog Pen Branch, &
            over the Falls
Ex: Son, Thomas BOND; Son-in-law, Capt. Thomas KELL
Wt: George RUSH; Enoch WILLIAMS; Benjamin LANCASTER, Jr. (Quakers)

AJ-2-024   **Morris** (or **Maurice**) **BAKER**   15 Feb 1774/ 19 Mar 1774
         of Baltimore Co.
To: Wife, Christian BAKER - Negroes Coffee, Dinah, Suck, Tamer, &
         George
    Son, William BAKER - Negro Coffee, after Christian's decease;
         Negro boy Tom
    Son, Grafton BAKER - Negro Tamer, after Christian's decease;
         Negro Barnett
    Son, John BAKER - Negro Dinah, after Christian's decease; Negro
         boy Oliver
    Son, Nathan BAKER - Negro George, after Christian's decease;
         Negro girl Easter
    Son, Charles BAKER - Negro wench Phillis
    Son, Morris BAKER - 3 tracts *Preston's Deceit*, *Sam Halls*, &
         Other Centre; tract *Antioch*; Negroes old Tom & Bess
    Daughter, Hannah BAKER; Daughter, Margaret GARRETT
    Daughter, Mary GARRETT - Negro boy Ceasor
    Daughter, Rhoda THOMAS - Negro girl Vilette
    Daughter, Rachel BAKER - Negro boy Ben
    Daughter, Martha WHITAKER - Negro girl Beck
    Daughter, Ann BAKER - Negro girl Patience
Ex: Wife, Christian BAKER; Son, Charles BAKER; Son Morris BAKER
Wt: Thomas BOND; Daniel MACCOMAS, son of William; Richard HOLLOWAY;
         Theophilus BAKER (Quakers)

AJ-2-027   **John BOYCE**, of Baltimore Co.   7 Jul 1783/ 30 Nov 1786
To: Three sisters, Rebecca SAPPINGTON, Eleanor COWAN, & Ann BOYCE
    Brother-in-law, Alexander COWAN
    Nephew, Roger Boyce COWAN (under age 21) - Negroes Dembo & Tom
    Brother, Roger BOYCE - tract 620 a. *Bears Neck* in Baltimore Co.
Ex: Brother, Roger BOYCE
Wt: Alexander FRAIZER; William PINKNEY; James DASHIELL

AJ-2-028   **Edmund BULL**   8 Mar 1776/ 15 Jun 1776
To: Sons, Jacob & John BULL (both under age 21) - all lands part
         of *His Lordships Reserves*
    Wife, Susannah BULL - Negro wench Bell & boy Frank
    Daughters, Rachel, Esther, & Mary BULL
Ex: (None named)
Wt: John LOVE; William MILES; William PRESTON; James PRESTON;
         Margaret M. LOVE
                                        Codicil: 8 Mar 1776/ 15 Jun 1776
    Dropped wife from will if she remarries.

AJ-2-029   **Thomas BRICE**   10 Oct 1775/ 16 Apr 1776
To: Wife, Elisabeth BRICE
    Daughters, Mary, Christian, & Margeret BRICE (all under age 16)
Ex: Wife, Elisabeth BRICE
Wt: Thomas JOHNSON; Christian NORRIS; James BRICE

AJ-2-030   **Thomas BUSSEY**   16 Sep 1775/ 2 Oct 1775
To: Wife, Susana BUSSEY ¦¦ Unborn child
    Daughters (names unspec.)
    Sons, Edward & Thomas BUSSEY - dwelling plantation
Ex: (None named)
Wt: Abraham JARRETT; John TAYLOR; Martha GARRETT; John LONDON

AJ-2-031   **Lt. Joseph BUTLER**   Verbal: 27 Aug 1776/ 17 Oct 1777
           of Col. SMALLWOOD's Company at Long Island, New York
To: Brother or half-brother (name unspec.); Miss Sarah HALE
Ex: John PATTERSON
Wt: Capt. Joseph FORD; Ens. PRAUL

AJ-2-031   **David BENFIELD**   24 Jan 1779/ 17 May 1779
To: Wife, Hannah BENFIELD - my plantation
    Mother, Mary BENFIELD ¦¦ Father-in-law, Thomas ELLIOTT
    Sister-in-law, Mary, wife of William BENFIELD, now living in
       Oxfordshire, England at Great Barrington near Burford
    David BENFIELD, son of William & Mary BENFIELD
    Trustees: Robert AMOSS, Esq. & Aquilla THOMPSON, Genl.
    Christopher DAWSON ¦¦ John ADAMS ¦¦ Henry FARVET (or FAWCET ?)
    John BROWN, late of Oxford
    John WAYNE ¦¦ Samuel DAY ¦¦ Sarah WOODMAN ¦¦ William WOOD
Ex: Wife, Hannah BENFIELD; Robert AMOSS; Aquilla THOMPSON
Wt: George Hughes WORSLEY; Solomon BROWN; John BROWN

AJ-2-033   **Robert BRYERLY**   (Undated)/ 9 Feb 1779
To: Nephew, Robert BRYERLY, son of brother Thomas BRYERLY - tract
       Bonds Last Shift
    Wife (name unspec.) - Negro wench Hager
    Nephew, John BRYERLY, son of brother Hugh BRYERLY
    Nephew, Robert BRYERLY, son of brother John
    Sister, Isabella ARMSTRONG
    Ann HUGANS, daughter of Jacob HUGANS
    Male children (names unspec.) of my brothers
       John, Hugh & Thomas BRYERLY
Ex: Thomas BRYERLY; William WEBB
Wt: Barnerd PRESTON of Daniel; Thomas JOHNSON, Jr; Samuel ASHMEAD

AJ-2-034   **Garrett BROWN**   25 Jul 1786/ 27 May 1788
To: Children of my brother, Freeborn BROWN
Ex: Brother, Freeborn BROWN
Wt: James BELL; Thomas CURRY; John ARCHER

AJ-2-035   **Robert BELL**   14 May 1779/ 1 Jun 1779
To: Brother, David BELL; Wife, Sarah BELL
Ex: Wife, Sarah BELL
Wt: Martha SIKLAR (or SIKLER); William HILL; Rev. John CLARK

AJ-2-036 Robert BISHOP   11 Dec 1779/ 21 Feb 1780
To: Daughter-in-law, Hannah DAY
Ex: Daughter-in-law, Hannah DAY
Wt: Mark Brown SAPPINGTON; John Beale HOWARD; John WANE; Lucin (or
    Lucenia) ALLENDER; Ann JARVIS

AJ-2-037 John BARTON   4 Jan 1773/ 6 Aug 1777
To: Wife, Ann BARTON
    Son, John BARTON - tract where I live adj. Robert BISHOP's
      Quarter or Plantation on *Myladies Manner (My Lady's Manor)*,
      Daniel POCOCH's land, Elliott's Run, the Great Road, & the
      Spring Branch by MORGAN's hog pen
    Sons, William, & James BARTON - rem. of land
    Daughters, Elizabeth BARTON, Jemima POCOCK & Kesiah CLARK
    Daughter, Alisanna BARTON - Negro girl about 3 months old named
      Lintey & her incr.
Ex: (None named)
Wt: Daniel POCOCK; James LEWIS; William BOSLEY

AJ-2-038 Elizabeth BOND   8 Sep 1782/ 28 Feb 1783
To: Sister, Sarah MORRIS - Negro girl Bell, 12 years of age
    Sister, Ann BOND - Negro boy Abraham, to be free at 21; Negro
      woman Amey, free 12 months after my decease
    Sister, Amelia BOND ¦¦ Brother, James BOND
Ex: Brother, Buckler BOND
Wt: William BOND, son of Joshua; Ann WRIGHT

AJ-2-040 Jacob BOND   2 Oct 1780/ 30 Nov 1780
To: Son, Jacob BOND
    Son, Ralph BOND - tract 200 a. part of *Osborns Lott* left by my
      father, tract 100 a. *Harrises Trust*, tract 150 a. *Ables
      Lott*, bond from Graham & Stewart for 18 a. tract *My Lords
      Gift*, bond from Isaac WEBSTER for tract 12 1/2 a., bond from
      Daniel SCOTT for tract 10 a. *Scotts Modesty*, caution of land
      adj. *Bonds Forest*, *Bond Pleasant Hill*, & *Clarksons Purchase*
    Daughter, Sarah PRESTON; Grandson, Walter PRESTON
    Son, Dennis BOND - tract part of *Poplar Neck* deeded by my
      father, tract 20 a. part of *Joshua's Meadow Enlarged* left
      by brother Joshua, tract 16 a. *Clarksons Purchase* bought
      from John GREEN, caution of vacant land adj. *Joshua's
      Meadows Enlarged*, caution of vacant land adj. *Bonds Forest*,
      half of caution of vacant land adj. *Bonds Pleasant Hills*,
      half of caution of land adj. *Clarksons Purchase*; Negro old
      Tony & his wife Phillis
    Single daughters, Ann, Priscilla, Martha, & Charlotte BOND
    Non-beneficiary: Thomas BOND, son of Barnett BOND
Ex: Sons, Dennis & Ralph BOND
Wt: John BOND; William BOND, son of Joshua; James BOND, of Joshua

                                         Codicil: 8 Nov 1780/ 30 Nov 1780
    (No change in beneficiaries)
Wt: William BOND, son of Joshua; Thomas DRUMMOND; Ann BOND

AJ-2-044　**Nathan BOND**　　　　Feb or Mar, 1782/ 15 Oct 1782
To: Brothers, Samuel & Thomas BOND
　　Thomas KELL, Jr ¦¦ Capt. Thomas KELL
Ex: Capt. Thomas KELL
Wt: (not witnessed)

Written by Nathan's brother, Thomas BOND when they were together at William MOORE's house in Baltimore Town. Nathan felt he would die at Capt. Thomas KELL's residence in Baltimore and not return to Harford Co.

15 Oct 1782 - Thomas BOND, son of John, relinquished rights to all above legacies.

AJ-2-045　**Margaret BRYARLY**　　　13 Oct 1781/ 1 Dec 1781
To: Sons, Thomas & Hugh BRYARLY ¦¦ Daughter, Ann HUGGINS
　　Daughter, Elizabeth ARMSTRONG - Negro boy Roger
　　Grandson, Thomas BRYARLY, son of John
　　Grandson, Robert BRYARLY, son of Hugh
　　Granddaughter, Margaret BRYARLY, daughter of Hugh
Ex: Son, Hugh BRYARLY
Wt: William COALE; Robert BRYARLY; Mary WATSON

AJ-2-046　**Joshua BROWN**　　　　22 Nov 1788/ 9 Feb 1789
To: Wife, Mary BROWN ¦¦ My children (names unspec.)
Ex: Wife, Mary BROWN; Brother, John Thomas BROWN; Henry WEATHERALL
Wt: Aaron FIELD; Isaac WHITAKER; Thomas BROWN; Sarah BROWN

AJ-2-047　**Thomas BROWN** of Primrose Hill　6 Apr 1785/ 20 Jun 1785
To: Wife, Mary BROWN
　　Sons, Jacob & William BROWN (both under age 21)
　　Daughters, Elizabeth, Fenton, Ann, & Mary BROWN (all under age 16)
Ex: Wife, Mary BROWN; Brother, John BROWN; Roger MATHEWS
Wt: Benedict Edward HALL; Francis LOVETT, P.M. (or Francis Lovitt PITT ?); Mitchell STEWART

AJ-2-049　**Mary BRUSEBANKS**　　　11 Oct 1784/ 13 Nov 1784
To: Daughter, Blanche BRUSEBANKS
　　Two small children, her brother & sister (names unspec.)
Non-beneficiary: Husband, Abraham BRUSEBANKS, deceased
Ex: Daughter, Blanche BRUSEBANKS
Wt: John JOHNSON; Benjamin BODY; James REARDON

AJ-2-050　**William BROWNING**　　　21 Sep 1798/ 14 Dec 1798
To: Three children, Perygrine, Ann, & Martha BROWNING
　　Sister, Martha BROWNING
Ex: Brother, Wilson BROWNING
Wt: John Hammond DORSEY; James HILL, Sr.

AJ-2-051　**John BROWN**　　　　　21 Jan 1786/ 7 Mar 1786
　　　　of Bush River Upper Hundred
To: Wife, Jean BROWN & son Robert BROWN - half of land
　　Sons, John, & William BROWN - other half of land
　　Daughters, Hanna, Marget, & Sara BROWN

Grandchildren, John Brown SMITH, John DAVISON, John & Jean
   BLACK
   John SMYTH ‖ Ealce DAVIDSON ‖ Mary BLACK
Ex: Wife, Jean BROWN; Son, John BROWN
Wt: Hugh BAY; John VANCE; John BAY

AJ-2-053   **Thomas BOND**   25 Oct 1787/ 9 Sep 1788
To: Daughter, Ann CLEMMENTS ‖ Heirs of daughter Elizabeth HOWARD
    Heirs of daughter Sarah HOWARD
    Son, Daniel BOND
    Son, Thomas BOND - tract part of *Iles of Capere* where he lives
       adj. *Thomas's Orchard* & *Lady Baltimore's Manner*, all other
       lands
    Three grandsons, Thomas Scot BOND, Joshua BOND, & Zachius Onion
       BOND, sons of Daniel BOND - rem. part of *Iles of Caparee*
    Daughters, Hannah McCOMAS & Martha SMITH
    Granddaughter, Sally Charity BOND; Wife, Elizabeth BOND
Ex: Wife, Elizabeth BOND
Wt: James McCOMAS; William WILSON; Joseph BURGES

AJ-2-055   **Sarah BROWNE**   9 Aug 1780/ 22 Sep 1780
To: Sons, John, Freeborn, & Thomas BROWNE
    Grandson, Joshua BROWNE, son of John BROWNE
    Grandson, Thomas Freeborne BROWN, son of daughter Sarah
       THOMPSON - Negro boy Ned
    Granddaughter, Amelia Freeborn BROWN, daughter of daughter
       Sarah THOMPSON - Negro boy Limus, & mulatto girl Chaney
       BRADFORD
    Daughter, Sarah THOMPSON, wife of John THOMPSON - Negro women
       Murrier & Dutches
    Son, Garrett BROWNE - mulatto girl Abigal BRADFORD, mulatto boy
       Nathan BRADFORD
    Negro man Jack - freedom
    Mulatto woman Jane BRADFORD - freedom, with youngest child
Ex: Son, Garrett BROWNE
Wt: Samuel GRIFFITH; William MURPHY; John MICHAEL

AJ-2-056   **Enoch BRADIN (or BREDIN)**   13 Jul 1791/ 19 Jul 1791
To: Sons, Robert & Thomas BRADIN
    Poorest children of the school I last teached
    James McCANDLESS of York Co, Penn.
Ex: William SLADE of Ezekiel
Wt: David BELL; Samuel PATTERSON; John LONG, Jr.

AJ-2-057   **Clemency BILLINGSLEA**   14 Jun 1794/ 2 Sep 1794
To: Grandson, Benjamin SMITHSON, & granddaughter, Mary SMITHSON,
       son & daughter of daughter Sarah
    Granddaughter, Elizabeth PRESTON, daughter of son Martin
       PRESTON
    Granddaughter, Clemency SCOTT, daughter of daughter Mary SCOTT
    Grandson, Benjamin PRESTON, son of daughter Mary PRESTON
    Children of son Martin PRESTON, Clemency, James, Martha,
       Benjamin, & Scott PRESTON
    Son, Bernard PRESTON
    Daughter, Clemency PRIBBLE, wife of Stephen PRIBBLE

```
     Daughter, Sarah ALDERSON, wife of Thomas ALDERSON
     Daughter, Mary SCOTT, wife of Aquilla SCOTT of Aquilla
Ex:  Son, Bernard PRESTON
Wt:  Joseph H. PRESBURY; Aquilla DURHAM; Walter BILLINGSLEA
```

AJ-2-059   **Christian BAKER**   8 Feb 1792/ 15 Jan 1793
```
To:  Daughter, Ann DENNEY, wife of Michael DENNEY - Negro girl
       Darkus
     Grandson Grafton BAKER, issue of son Maurice BAKER
     Daughter, Hannah EVERIT, wife of Samuel EVERIT
     Sons, Nathan, Charles, & William BAKER
     Son, John BAKER - Negro girl Betty, Negro boys James & Isaac,
       Negro girl Sall (all born of Negro woman Dinah)
     Son, Grafton BAKER - Negro boy Archibald
     Daughters, Mary MORROW, Rachel PENDIGRASS, Martha WHITAKER, &
       Margaret GARRETT
Ex:  (None named)
Wt:  John LOVE; Joseph ROBINSON; John ADAMS
```

AJ-2-060   **Susannah BULL**   10 Oct 1784/ 13 Nov 1792
```
To:  Sons, John & Jacob BULL ¦¦ Daughters, Easther, & Mary BULL
Ex:  (None named)
Wt:  Corbin PRESTON; William PRESTON; John PRESTON
```

AJ-2-061   **Abraham SPRUSEBANKS**   22 Aug 1781/ 15 Jan 1783
```
To:  Wife, Mary SPRUSEBANKS
     Sons, Francis, Jackson, Benjamin, & Abraham SPRUSEBANKS
     Daughters, Blanche, Jean, Martha, Ann, & Mary SPRUSEBANKS
Ex:  Wife, Mary SPRUSEBANKS
Wt:  Freeborn GARRETTSON; William WATTERS; Archabel JOHNSON
```

AJ-2-062   **William BULL**   17 May 1790/ 4 Jan 1791
```
To:  Wife, Sarah BULL - plantation where we live, half of tract
       Beaver Dams
     Son John BULL - tract part of Robinsons Outlett on N side of
       Bread & Cheese Branch & adj. lands on N side of Bread &
       Cheese Branch
     Son, William BULL - tract Cecils Adventure, tract part of
       Robinsons Outlett on S side of Bread & Cheese Branch, tract
       Partners Hills
     Sons, Walter, Billingslea, & Elisha BULL
     Daughters, Sarah & Rachel BULL - lot in Baltimore Town
Ex:  Wife, Sarah BULL
Wt:  William AMOSS; William AMOSS, Jr.; Thomas WILSON (Quakers)
```

AJ-2-064   **John BROWNE**   4 Jan 1783/ 23 Apr 1783
```
To:  Eldest son, Joshua BROWNE - tract Bonds Inheritance where he
       lives
     Eldest daughter, Elizabeth BROWNE - Negro girl Floria
     Youngest daughter, Martha BROWNE - Negro girl Dinah
     Youngest son, John Thomas BROWNE - tract Oakington Agreeable
       Settled where I live; Negro men Chance, & Bob, Negro boy
       Isaac, & Negro girl Dip
Ex:  Wife, Sarah BROWNE; Son, Joshua BROWNE
Wt:  Thomas ASHLEY; John BECK; John REESE; Ann KERNS
```

                                    Codicil: 4 Jan 1783/ 23 Apr 1783
To: Daughters (names unspec.)
Wt: Thomas ASHLEY; John BECK; John REESE; Ann KERNS

AJ-2-066   **John Thomas BROWN**   9 Feb 1794/ 21 Mar 1794
To: John Brown BAYLES (under age 21), son of brother-in-law
       Augustine BAYLES - plantation on Gunpowder River
    Nimrod BAYLES, son of Augustine BAYLES ¦¦ Augustine BAYLES
    Mary BROWN, widow of Joshua BROWN
    Elizabeth BROWN, daughter of Mary BROWN - Negro man James
    John BROWN, son of Mary BROWN - Negro Bobb
    Mary BROWN, daughter of Mary BROWN - female Negro Dipp
Ex: Brother-in-law, Augustine BAYLESS
Wt: Jacob FORWOOD; Roger BOYCE (Roger Boyce COWAN ?); Stephen
       KIMBLE; Thomas SHAY

AJ-2-067   **Amos BARNES**   5 Sep 1797/ 21 Oct 1797
To: Eldest son, John BARNES - half of lot part of *Rupalta* adj.
       River Susquehanna; Negro boy Isaac
    Son, Garrett BARNES (minor) - W end of above lot; Negro boy Ben
    Daughter, Sarah BARNES (minor) - Negro boy Bill
    Non-beneficiary: Brother, Ford BARNES
Ex: Brother, Bennet BARNES; John MICHAEL
Wt: Hosier BARNES; John MICHAEL; Joshua WOOD

2 Oct 1797 - John MICHAEL renounced his right of executorship.

AJ-2-069   **Nathaniel BRYARLY** (or **BRIARLY**)   4 Jul 1794/ 12 Aug 1794
To: Brother, John BRYARLY
    Sister, Sophia NORTON, wife of Stephen NORTON
Ex: Brother-in-law, Stephen NORTON
Wt: Samuel WILLITS; John COX

AJ-2-070   **Samuel BIRCKHEAD**   13 Dec 1785/ 9 Sep 1786
To: Wife, Elizabeth BIRCKHEAD - all lands & dwelling except 150 a.
    Son, Mathew BIRCKHEAD - above lands after wife's death
    Sons, Francis, Nehemiah, & Thomas Howel BIRCKHEAD
    Daughter, Elizabeth BIRCKHEAD - Negro boy Cato, Negro man Clem,
       & Negro girl Lid
    Daughter, Ann BIRCKHEAD ¦¦ Daughter, Margret BIRCKHEAD, now
       married
    Grandson, Samuel BIRCKHEAD, son of son Seaborn BIRCKHEAD,
       deceased
    Two granddaughters (names unspec.), daughters of son Seaborn
       BIRCKHEAD, deceased
    Heir of son Seaborn BIRCKHEAD, deceased - tract 150 a.
Ex: Sons, Thomas Howell BIRCKHEAD & Francis BIRCKHEAD
Wt: Henry WETHERALL; Archibald JOHNSON; Samuel Groome OSBORN

AJ-2-071   **William BOND**, son of Joshua   29 Nov 1787/ 21 Oct 1788
To: Sisters, Sarah MORRIS & Pamelia BOND
    Niece, Sally Charity BOND, daughter of brother Buckler BOND
    Susannah MORRIS ¦¦ Samuel DAY ¦¦ Nephew, William Bond MORRIS
    Brother, Buckler BOND - tracts 200 a. *Morgan's Lott* & *Rangers
       Range*

```
          Brother, James BOND - all rem. real estate
     Ex:  Brother, James BOND
     Wt:  John LYNCH; Isaac GUYTON; Dennis BOND
```

AJ-2-074   **Ann BOND**   18 Jan 1783/ 1 Jun 1784
```
     To:  Sister, Sarah MORRIS - Negro girls Letticia & Jane, to age 18
          Sister, Amelia BOND ¦¦ Nephew, William Bond MORRIS
          Brother, William BOND - Negro boy James, until age 21
          Non-beneficiaries: Brothers, Buckler & James BOND
     Ex:  (None named)
     Wt:  Buckler BOND; Ann ABBIT; Sarah MAULSBY
```

AJ-2-076   **Hugh BRYARLY**   20 Feb 1798/ 8 Oct 1799
```
     To:  Daughters, Ann ROWLS & Mary WARE
          Daughter, Margaret DAWSON - Negro boy Nat, to be free at 32
          Son, Robert BRYARLY ¦¦ Negro woman Nell - freedom
          Young Negroes Hannah, Nat, Cisiah, Willis, & Phill - free at
               age 32
          Robert BRYARLY, son of brother Thomas
     Ex:  Robert BRYARLY, son of brother Thomas; Son-in-law, Thomas WARE
     Wt:  Giles THOMAS; John CLENDINEN; William CREAL

                                Codicil: 5 Aug 1799/ 26 May 1801
     To:  Son, Robert BRYARLY ¦¦ Grandson, Thomas DAWSON
     Wt:  Joseph ROBINSON; William GRIFFEN; Thomas ROBINSON
```

AJ-2-079   **Benjamin CULVER**   12 Apr 1774/ 21 May 1774
```
     To:  Heirs of late daughter, Elizabeth BARNES, late wife of James
               BARNES - tract 100 a. part of Culvers Entrance
          Daughter, Lydia WILSON - tract 25 a. Margarets Purchase, tract
               25 a. part of Culvers Entrance
          Daughter, Sarah WHITE
          Son, Robert CULVER - tract 202 a. part of Culvers Entrance
          Son, Benjamin CULVER - tract 202 a. part of Culvers Entrance
     Ex:  Wife, Ann CULVER; Sons, Robert & Benjamin CULVER
     Wt:  Thomas SHEARER; Charles GILBERT; Geofrey WATTERS
```

AJ-2-081   **Dennis CANE**, weaver   25 Jul 1775/ 2 Aug 1796
```
     To:  Wife (name unspec.), son, James CANE & 2 youngest sons (names
               unspec.) - lease of this land where I live
          Daughters, Ann, & Jsab (Isab ?) CANE
          Daughter, Mary CANE ¦¦ Son, Mathew CANE
          Servant woman (name unspec.) - to be sold
     Ex:  Wife (name unspec.); Son, James CANE
     Wt:  John CRETIN; Phillip QUINLAN; Charles MOORE
```

AJ-2-082   **Silina CLARK**   10 Jun 1775/ 18 Oct 1777
```
     To:  Sons, Robert, William, George, & David CLARK
          Daughters, Frances RENSHAW, Hannah AMOS, Sarah FORWOOD, Mary
               JOHNSON, & Hester JOHNSON
          Daughter, Elizabeth COLEGATE - Negro man Jack
          Granddaughter, Sarah JOHNSON, daughter of Thomas JOHNSON
          Granddaughter, Sarah PRESTON
          Granddaughters, Frances & Silina RENSHAW
```

Granddaughters, Rachel & Elizabeth, daughters of son Robert
    CLARK
  Daughters, Ann JOHNSON & Silina MacCOMAS
Ex: (None named)
Wt: Edmund BULL; Susannah BULL

6 Aug 1776 - Rewittness needed, Edmund BULL now deceased.
Wt: John LOVE; Jacob BOND; Bernard PRESTON

AJ-2-084   **John CARROLL**   7 Mar 1778/ 8 Aug 1778
To: Mother, Ann CARROLL
    Sister, Hannah CARROLL ¦¦ Brother, James CARROLL, Junr.
Ex: Brother, James CARROLL, Junr.
Wt: Daniel MACCOMAS (or McCOMAS); James DEELEY (or DULEY)

AJ-2-085   **William CROOKS**   30 Dec 1776/ 7 Sep 1778
To: Wife, Mary CROOKS - Negro woman Phillis
    Daughter, Rosanna (nee CROOKS) - tract 50 a. adj. *Cley Hill
      Inlarged* & the *Second Runn*
    Sons, Henry, Thomas, & Robert CROOKS - all other lands
    Daughters, Jennet, Mary, & Margaret (nee CROOKS)
    Grandson, William CROOKS, son of son Henry
    Grandson, James DAGLE ¦¦ Grandson James CROOKS
Ex: Wife, Mary CROOKS; Son, Henry CROOKS
Wt: William HOPKINS, Sr. Called to wit: Henry GUFFEE; James BARNETT

31 Dec 1776 - William CROOKS died before signing his will.

AJ-2-087   **Aquila CLARK**   7 Sep 1779/ 22 Oct 1779
To: Brother, Robert CLARK ¦¦ Brother, Thomas CLARK
    Sister, Sarah LION ¦¦ Mother, Elizabeth CLARK
    Sister, Elizabeth HITCHCOCK, married
    Sisters, Martha CARROL & Charity HITCHCOCK
Ex: Mother,Elizabeth CLARK; Sisters, Martha CARROL & Charity
      HITCHCOCK
Wt: David DURHAM; Sarah DURHAM; William NORRIS

AJ-2-088   **John COOK**   18 Jan 1780/ 3 Mar 1780
To: Daughters, Mary HUTCHISON, Jane STERLING, Lydia BLACK, Sarah
      COOK, & Agnes COOK
    Sons, John & James COOK
    Granddaughters, Sarah & Lydia COOK, daughters of son John
    Wife, Mary COOK ¦¦ Sons, Samuel & Mathew COOK
Ex: Wife, Mary COOK; James CLENDENING; William JOHNSTON
Wt: James WILGUS; Joseph ROBINSON; Nathan EVANS (EVENS ?)

AJ-2-090   **Richard CHANEY**   3 Jun 1781/ 7 Jun 1781
To: Niece, Eleanor ELLEET (or ELLIOT) ¦¦ Brother, Thomas CHANEY
Ex: (None named)
Wt: Samuel SUTTON; Abraham CORD; Bond James KEMBERLAND

AJ-2-090   **John COWEN**   (Undated)/ 14 Aug 1781
To: Son, Benjamin COWEN - tract 50 a. *Woods Close*
    Eldest son, William COWEN ¦¦ Wife, Elizabeth COWEN (nee WOOD)
    Daughter, Hannah, wife of James SEAL

Non-beneficiary: Mother-in-law, Elizabeth WOOD
Ex: Wife, Elizabeth COWEN; Son, Benjamin COWEN
Wt: Kent MITCHEL; Daniel ANDERSON; James MITCHELL; Enuch WEST

AJ-2-092   **William COX**   13 Apr 1781/ 16 May 1782
To: Wife, Mary COX
    Son, John COX - Merchant Mill where he lives, tract 20 a.
      bought from Smith, Dallam & Smith, & small plantation *Peeled
      Egg* bought from Patrick McQUIRE, all on Deer Creek 18 m.
      from my dwelling plantation, and *Merchant's Mill* (brewery)
    All my children - estate in England near Staines in Middlesex
      & Egham Hithe in Surry which was part of wife's inheritance
      to be divided equally under power of attorney to Thomas
      FINCH, Sr. & Thomas FINCH, Jr.
    Son, William COX, Jr. - tract 140 a. parts of *West Wood* & *Wests
      Beginning Improved* with houses, grist mill, malt house, crew
      house & saw mill, tract 3 3/4 a. part of *Aquillas
      Inheritance* conveyed from William WILSON, Senr., deceased,
      tract 40 a. part of *Margrets Mount* bought from Samuel LITTEN
    Son, Isreal COX (minor)- plantation *Murdaugh's Chance* & tract
      40 a. *West Wood* or *New West Wood* both under tenure to James
      ELLIS; vacant land in resurvey of lands bought of Gregory
      & Samuel FARMER lying S of main road & adjoinging *Murdaugh's
      Chance*, tract 40 a. parts of *West Wood* & *Wests Beginning
      Improved* at S end
    To be sold - tract 23 3/4 a. *Cox's Chance* on N side of Deer
      Creek
    Daughters, Sarah PUSEY, Mary Bains BROWN, & Mercy & Rachel COX
    Granddaughter, Elizabeth HAWKINS, daughter of daughter
      Elizabeth HAWKINS, deceased wife of Richard HAWKINS
    Daniel DULANEY || Widow GREENLEAF in Philadelphia
Ex: Wife, Mary COX; Sons, William COX, Jr & John COX
Wt: James WALKER; Nathaniel BAYLES; William CHAPPELL

AJ-2-096   **John CAMPBELL, Jr.**   27 Dec 1783/ 4 May 1784
To: Wife, Hannah CAMPBELL || Aged father, John CAMPBELL
    Brother, James CAMPBELL
    Son, Benjamin CAMPBELL - rights to some certificate lands
Ex: Wife, Hannah CAMPBELL; William McCOMAS
Wt: James McCOMAS of Aquilla; John NORRIS; William McCOMAS; John
    COX

AJ-2-097   **William COALE**   5 Jan 1782/ 26 Aug 1784
To: Oldest son, Phillip COALE - tract 200 a. at E end of my
      plantation
    Sons, Skipwith & William COALE - residue of my plantation to
      be divided equally, Skipwith to have part with dwelling
      house
    Daughters, Sarah & Ann COALE, & Susannah RODGERS
Ex: Sons, Phillip, Skipwith, & William COALE
Wt: Joseph WARNER; John WILSON; Joseph Jacob WALLIS

AJ-2-099   **Robert COLLINS**   24 Sep 1785/ 4 Nov 1785
To: Wife, Jemima COLLINS - tract 100 a. *Park Hill* (or *Pork Hill
      ?*) adj. *Saint Albins*, tract 12 a. part of *Surveyor's Point*

```
        Robert, Caleb, Martha, & Jemima BENNETT
Ex: Wife, Jemima COLLINS
Wt: Bennet BUSSEY; Richard ROBINSON; Jesse HANWAY
```

AJ-2-100 Mordecai CRAWFORD　　　　　　　20 Jul 1785/ 10 Sep 1785
```
To: Wife, Susannah CRAWFORD - Negro woman Gain, Negro boy David,
        Negro boy Ned, & Negro girl Hager
    Son, Mordecai CRAWFORD - Negro boy Ned, after wife's death
    Son, John CRAWFORD - Negro boy David, after wife's death
    Son, James CRAWFORD - Negro boy Tom & tract Mary's Delight
    Daughter, Ruth CRAWFORD - Negro girl Hager, after wife's death
    Son, Seaborn CRAWFORD - Negro boy Moses
    Daughter, Susannah DAVIS - Negro girl Dinah
    Daughter, Hannah GORRAL - Negro girl Margret
    Daughters, Sarah HAWKINS & Margret WILLIAMS
Ex: Wife, Susannah CRAWFORD; Son, James CRAWFORD; William WILSON
Wt: Elizabeth WILSON; Benjamin WILSON; James CRAWFORD (Quakers)
```

AJ-2-103 Samuel CROCKETT　　　　　　　　24 Jun 1785/ 9 Aug 1785
```
To: Brother, Benjamin CROCKETT - Negro woman Ester & her 3 children
    Cousin, William WEBB, son of William WEBB, deceased
Ex: Cousin, John CROCKETT - merchant in Baltimore
Wt: Samuel WEBB, Junr; James McDANIEL; Hannah SCOTLAND
```

AJ-2-104 George COPELAND　　　　　　　　27 Mar 1785/ 25 Oct 1785
```
To: Wife, Frances COPELAND || Child my wife is now pregnant with
    Oldest son, John COPELAND - dwelling plantation pur. of David
        MAGEE, tract pur. of James MOORE except part leased to
        Doctor William ARMIN
    Daughters, Mary & Sarah COPELAND
Ex: Wife, Frances COPELAND; Brother, John COPELAND
Wt: Nathan GALLION; Henry RUFF, Jr.; John ARCHER
```

AJ-2-106 William CORBIT, farmer　　　　　8 Dec 1785/ 10 Jan 1786
```
To: Sons, John & James CORBIT - two tracts 119 a. Valentine's
        Choice & Netter Wills Addition
    Son, Samuel CORBIT - plantation 142 a. where I live
    Son, Lewis CORBIT || Granddaughter, Mary LONG
    Daughters, Catharine RUFFCORN (RUFF ?) & Phebe DUNGHAM
Ex: Son, Samuel CORBIT; James CLENDINEN
Wt: James VERNAY; Catharin ANDERSON; Walter BILLINGSLEA
```

AJ-2-107 Alexander CRAWFORD　　　　　　　2 Jun 1786/ 26 Jul 1786
```
To: Five children, Margret, George, Thomas, Francis, & Alexander
        CRAWFORD - land pur. over the mountains on the waters of
        Whealing
    Wife, Frances CRAWFORD
    To be sold - house & lot at Eden Town
Ex: Wife, Frances CRAWFORD
Wt: Daniel McFILTON (or McJILTON); John CARRS (or CARR); Hannah
        COPE (or COOP)
```

AJ-2-109 Mary COX　　　　　　　　　　　　1 Aug 1790/ 17 Sep 1790
```
To: Son, John COX & four daughters, Sarah, Mary, Mercy, & Rachel
        COX - property in Great Britain
```

     Sons, William & Israel COX
     Granddaughter, Elizabeth HAWKINS, daughter of daughter
          Elizabeth HAWKINS, deceased
Ex: Son, John COX; John WILSON
Wt: Gerrard HOPKINS; Joshua HUSBAND; Frances HOPKINS

AJ-2-110   Phillip COALE   4 Apr 1791/ 14 Sep 1791
To: Wife, Ann COALE
     Children, Cassandra, Francis, Sarah, Richard, Ann, Elizabeth,
          William, & Phillip COALE
Ex: Wife, Ann COALE; Brother-in-law, Richard DALLAM
Wt: Anna COALE, Junr.; John WILSON; John DALLAM

AJ-2-111   James CARROLL   17 Apr 1792/ 12 Jun 1792
To: Son, Benjamin CARROLL - tract part of *Barton's Chance*, & tract
     Expectation
     Sons, James, & Peter CARROLL
     Four daughters, Elizabeth SMITH, Eleanor PRICE, Ann SWITZAR,
          & Hannah COVENHAVEN
     Grandson, Parker CUNNINGHAM, son of daughter Sarah CUNNINGHAM,
          deceased
Ex: Son, Benjamin CARROLL
Wt: Joseph NORRIS, Junr.; Henry Davis NORRIS; Mordecai DAWES
Verified by: Robert SAUNDERS; Henry NORRIS; George CUNNINGHAM;
     Samuel STEWART; Ann CARROLL, widow of James

AJ-2-115   Elizabeth CARROLL   28 Apr 1792/ 23 Jun 1792
To: Daughter, Rachel KITELY - house & 1/2 of lot where I live, if
     without heirs then divided among grandchildren
     Daughter, Rebecca NORRIS
     Granddaughter, Elizabeth MURPHY - house & 1/4 lot
     Grandson, Charles NORRIS - 1/4 lot on SW corner
     Granddaughters, Providence & Elizabeth KITELY- 1/4 lot each
     Granddaughter, Mary KITELY
     Negro man Joe - free ¦¦ Negro woman Hannah - free
Ex: Daughter, Rachel KITELY
Wt: Joseph TOY; Christian WASKEY; Elijah BLACKSTON

AJ-2-116   John CRETIN   10 Nov 1783/ 22 Mar 1784
To: Son, John CRETIN - dwelling plantation
     Sons, James, & Patrick CRETIN ¦¦ Miles McGOUGH
     Wife (name unspec.) ¦¦ Granddaughter, Bettsey CASKREY
     Negroes Joe, Tom, Sam, Rachel & son, & Bett - divided between
          wife & 3 sons
Ex: Parish priest (name unspec.); Dr. John ARCHER; Ignatius WHEELER
Wt: Edward FLANAGAN; Bernet RYELEY (or Barnet or Barney RILEY);
     Francis CASKERY (or CASKREY)

1 May 1784 - Elizabeth CRETIN renounced this will.

AJ-2-118   John CRAIG,   25 Aug 1793/ 20 Jan 1794
     formerly a soldier for 5 years in the Continental Army
     under General Moses HAZEN in Congress Own Regiment
To: Wife, Ann CRAIG

Ex: Wife, Ann CRAIG
Wt: Isaac MASSEY; Aquilla MASSEY; Thomas JAMES

AJ-2-120 **Isabella CRISWELL**   19 Jul 1794/ 22 Sep 1795
          widow to William CRISWELL, deceased, of Deer Creek
          Hundred
To: William Criswell EDGAR - my Negro lad Jo ¦¦ Eliner C. EDGAR
    Isabella CRISWELL ¦¦ James CRISWELL ¦¦ Elizabeth CRISWELL
    Daughter, Mary CRISWELL ¦¦ Daughter-in-law, Mary EDGAR
    Brother-in-law, John McADOO
Ex: Joseph MILLAR
Wt: James DAGG; Arthur McGIRR

AJ-2-121 **Susanna CRAWFORD**   16 Oct 1793/ 9 Jan 1797
To: Son, Mordecai CRAWFORD
    Negro woman Jane & her offspring - freedom
Ex: Son, Mordecai CRAWFORD
Wt: John WILSON; Sarah WILSON; Benjamin WILSON

AJ-2-122 **Benjamin CROCKETT** (or **CROCHETT**) 13 Oct 1796/ 8 Nov 1796
To: Aunt, Sarah McMATH
Ex: William McMATH
Wt: John JACKSON; Thomas Pycraft PRESBURY; John BARNS

AJ-2-123 **John COOK**   4 Dec 1797/ 22 May (1797 ?)
To: Mother, Sarah COOK ¦¦ Sister, Ester COOK
    Three children in my mother's care, Milcah, Jeaims, & Nansey
    William WELLS, Junr.'s children (names unspec.)
    Ester COOK's children, if she should marry & have any
    Robert BODKES ¦¦ Thomas ROGENS (or ROGERS ?)
    Non-beneficiaries: Father, deceased; Brother, James COOK,
      deceased
    John WELLS, son of William WELLS, Junr.
    To be sold - ferry & all land belonging to it
Ex: Stephen NORTON; John STREET; Solomon PERKINS
Wt: James WILSON: Robert MORGAN; Elisha DAY

AJ-2-124 **John COVENHOVEN**   28 Mar 1797/ 13 Jun 1797
          (or **COVENHAVEN**)
To: Wife, Hannah COVENHOVEN - tract 10 a. part of *Homer Resurveyed*
      where I live bought of Col. Richard DALLAM
    Daughters, Gainer & Betsey COVENHOVEN (both minors)
    Son, Jacob COVENHOVEN (minor) - tract 10 a. upon wife's death
    Col. Richard DALLAM
Ex: Brother, Jacob COVENHOVEN; Brother-in-law, Jesse DUNCAN (or
      DUNGAN ?)
Wt: John DUTTON; Joseph BURGES; Ady EVERITT

AJ-2-126 **Donn CONNOLLY**   20 Feb 1791/ 25 Mar 1800
To: Sons, John & Donn CONNOLLY - plantation
    Wife, Mary CONNOLLY ¦¦ All my daughters (names unspec.)
    Trustees: Rev. Sylvester BOARMAN, James CRETIN
Ex: (None named)
Wt: Benjamin TOLAND; George AMOSS; James HUDLY

AJ-2-128   James CLENDINEN   30 Sep 1795/ 8 Dec 1795
To: Sons, John, David, & Adam CLENDINEN
    Daughters, Jane, Elinor, & Mary CLENDINEN
    William ADY - tract part of *Friends Discovery* previously sold
    Trustees: Samuel BAYLIS, Thomas HOPE, James VARNEY
Ex: Sons, John & David CLENDINEN
Wt: David PETE; James JOHNSON; William JOHNSON

AJ-2-130   John CUMMINS   5 Apr 1800/ 10 May 1800
To: Wife, Cassandra CUMMINS - Negro girl Cloe
Ex: Wife, Cassandra CUMMINS
Wt: Archer HAYS; Arthur MONAHON; George WOOLSEY

AJ-2-134   Daniel DURBIN   17 Jan 1774/ 23 Mar 1774
To: Son, Thomas DURBIN - tract 60 a. *Durbins Beginning* where I live
    Daughter, Avarilla DURBIN - tract 50 a. *Obediahs Venture*, &
       tract 50 a. part of *Improved Venture* conveyed by James
       RITCHARDS
    Charles GILBERT - tract 3-4 a. part of *Improved Venture*
    Representatives of Robert ADAIR, deceased - tract *Durbins
       Chance* previously sold to him
    Non-beneficiary: Charles GILBERT - guardian of son, Thomas
Ex: Daughter, Avarilla DURBIN
Wt: Amos GARRETT; Nicholas BAKER, Junr.; Kent MITCHELL, Junr.

AJ-2-136   William DAVIS, planter   3 Mar 1772/ 20 Apr 1774
              of Baltimore Co.
To: Wife, Elizabeth DAVIS - all my Negroes (names unspec.)
    The children (names unspec.) equally after wife's death
    William HAWKINS, son of Robert HAWKINS & Martha - hunting gun
       called "Jackson"
Ex: (None named)
Wt: Maurice BAKER; Elizabeth SAUNDERS; John CARROLL; Richard
    HOLLOWAY

AJ-2-137   Stephen DEACON   1 May 1775/ 12 Jun 1775
To: Servant boys, Thomas FOX & John WRIGHT - set free December 25th
       next
    Thomas PRESBURY || Judah LEGOE || Michael WEBSTER
    John CAUSLEY || James CAUSLEY || Richard HILL
    Billingsley ROBERTS || Nathan WHITEHEAD
    William SMITH || Amos LAZZEL, alias SMITH
    Alexander VALENTINE || Martha VANHORN
    Elizabeth BENNETT || Hannah HENDEL
Ex: William SMITH
Wt: Billingslea ROBERTS; Thomas PRESBURY; John McCORMICK

AJ-2-139   William DOUGHERTY, planter 30 Sep 1777/ 8 Nov 1777
              of Baltimore Co.
To: Sister, Ufan LONEY, wife of Moses LONEY - tract & plantation
       left by my father William DOUGHERTY
Ex: Brother-in-law, Moses LONEY
Wt: John Lee WEBSTER; Abraham TAYLOR; William Gray DUZAN

AJ-2-140   **Thomas DORNEY**   19 Nov 1770/ 1 Nov 1777
To: Son, Thomas DORNEY, & his wife Mary - all my land
    Son-in-law, Thomas HILL, & his wife Marthew (Marther ?)
    Son-in-law, James SPENCER, & his wife Batricks
    Son-in-law, William GROVES, & his wife Sarah
Ex: Son, Thomas DORNEY
Wt: John DAY, son of Edward; William ENSOR; James COSLEY

AJ-2-141   **Hugh DORAN**   8 Apr 1778/ 13 Jun 1778
To: Wife, Margret DORAN - all Negroes (names unspec.)
    Son, John DORAN - tract *Clear Fountain* in Pennsylvania & tract
       Little Worth adj. it, tract 200 a. in York adj. William
       LEPPER's land in William MATHEWS hands
    Son, Patrick DORAN || Daughters, Mary & Catharine DORAN
    Sons, Edward, Thomas, Nicholas, Francis, & Phillip DORAN
    Daughter, Margaret DORAN
Ex: Wife, Margaret DORAN
Wt: Thomas BLEANY; Thomas WHEELER; George VOGAN

AJ-2-142   **John DALE**   2 Apr 1778/ 4 Jul 1778
To: Wife, Mary DALE
    Daughter, Mary ORR || Grandson, John Dale ORR
    Children of Mary ORR (names unspec.)
    Grandson, Richard Colegate DALE - Negro Ben
    Granddaughter, Nancy DALE - female Negros Dinah & Prescilla
    Brother, William DALE || Nephew, Joseph DEMSTER
Ex: James CLENDINEN
Wt: James AMOS, Senr.; Joshua AMOS; Hannah AMOS

                              Codicil: 2 Jul 1778/ 21 Aug 1778
To: Daughter Mary's children (names unspec.)
    Richard Colgate DALE
    Scratch out Ben's name as he is sold to Dr. BENFIELD
Wt: Joseph McCLASKEY; Agness McCLASKEY; James ORR

AJ-2-144   **Mordecai DURHAM**   __ Apr 1777/ 7 Feb 1778
To: My brothers & sisters (names unspec.)
Ex: Brother, Samuel DURHAM
Wt: James PRESTON; Frederick FRALEY; Patric TIERNEY

AJ-2-145   **David DICKSON**   19 Oct 1778/ 19 Dec 1778
To: Wife, Jennet DICKSON || Children, Robert & John DICKSON
    Brother, Benjamin DICKSON
Ex: Wife, Jennet DICKSON; John McADOW
Wt: Alexander HANNA(or HANNAH); John ARCHER

AJ-2-146   **Josiah DYER**, Quaker   26 Jan 1780/ 1 Jun 1780
           of Bucks Co., Penn.
To: Wife, Hester DYER || Sons, Joseph, Josiah, & John DYER
    Children, Thomas, Mary, Hester, Elizabeth, Phebe, & Rachel
    Phebe's children (names unspec.)
Ex: Eldest sons, Joseph DYER of Harford Co. & Josiah DYER of Sussex
    Co, N.J.; Daughter, Hester BRADSHAW
Wt: Isaac DAWES; Benjamin DAWES; Isaac DAWES, Junr

AJ-2-148   **Benjamin DEBRULAR**   7 Aug 1775/ 7 Dec 1780
To: Daughter, Elizabeth WILSON || Wife, Samelia DEBRULAR
Ex: Wife, Samelia DEBRULAR
Wt: William SMITH; George YORK, son of William

AJ-2-149   **George DAUGHTERY**   18 Aug 1783/ 24 Jan 1784
To: Son, John DAUGHERTY - all my lands in Harford County; Negro boy
    Shedrach
    Daughter, Mary Ann DAUGHERTY - Negro woman Nan, Negro girl Jean
Ex: Freeborn GARRETTSON, Junr.
Wt: James GARRETTSON; Jonas STEPHENSON; Patrick O. McCLAIN

AJ-2-150   **John DAY**, son of Edward   16 Dec 1782/ 7 Feb 1784
To: Eldest son, John DAY - plantation 514 a. part of *Maxwell's
    Conclusion* where I live, tract 73 a. *Days Double Purchase*;
    tract part of *Days Privilege*; my family Bible marked "John
    DAY 1760", my fine bullet gun marked "John DAY March 20,
    1756"; Negro man Tom, Negro girl Rachel
    Second son, Nicholas DAY - tract 100 a. *Holmwood* & tract *Days
    Meadows* in Gunpowder Neck; Negro boy Jacob, Negro girl
    Frank, Negro man Peter
    Son, Edward DAY (under age 21) - Negroes Phoebe & her incr.,
    & Sam & Nan
    Daughter, Mary HYNSON - all my Negroes now in her possession
    Son-in-law, Robert CRUIKSHANKS, & his wife Avarilla, my
    daughter - all my Negroes now in their possession
    Daughter, Sarah DAY - Negroes Peg, Will, Fie, big Jem, & their
    incr.
    Daughter, Charlotte Elizabeth DAY - Negroes Nell & her
    incr., & Samson
    Nephew, William ALLENDER, son of Avarilla ALLENDER - tract
    Arthurs Lott in the fork of Gunpowder in Baltimore Co.
    Niece, Sarah ALLENDER, daughter of sister Jane ALLENDER - Negro
    woman Fann
    Niece, Mary ALLENDER, daughter of sister Jane ALLENDER - Negro
    boy Joe
    Non-beneficiaries: Col. Benjamin RUMSEY - guardian of son
    Nicholas & daughter Charlotte Elizabeth; Col. Alexander
    COWAN - guardian of son Edward & daughter Sarah
Ex: Col. Benjamin RUMSEY; Col. Alexander COWAN
Wt: Lambert WILMER; Thomas STRONG; Thomas DORNEY; John LEE

AJ-2-153   **John DORSEY**   13 Apr 1785/ 13 Jun 1785
To: Half-sister, Mary DORSEY (single & under age 18) - mulatto girl
    Averilla & Negro boy Harry, both the offspring of Negro
    woman Rachael
    Brother, Greenbury DORSEY || Housekeeper, Mary COX
    Sons, Greenbury DORSEY, Leonard DORSEY, & Doctor John DORSEY
Ex: Sons, Greenbury, Leonard, & Doctor John DORSEY
Wt: John HAY; John SEWELL; Jacob MAXWELL; Samuel Groome OSBORN

AJ-2-155   **Anthony DREW**   8 Feb 1786/ 23 Feb 1786
To: First son, George DREW - Negroes old Easter & Abraham
    Second, 3rd & 4th sons, Henry, James, & Anthony DREW - tract
    part of *Drews Inlargement* divided equally by friends Henry

```
              VANSICKLE & James OSBORN
         Daughter, Hannah DREW - Negro girl Sall
         Daughter, Mary DREW - Negro girl Poll
         Son, James DREW - Negroes Hary & yallow Jim
         Daughter, Sarah DREW - Negroes Hannah & Dinah
         Son, Henry DREW - Negroes Clenes & Sim
         Son, Anthony DREW - Negroes Hager & Joe
         Wife, Sarah DREW
    Ex:  Wife, Sarah DREW; Son, Henry DREW
    Wt:  Henry VANSICKLE; Archibald BETTY (or BEATTY); James OSBORN
```

AJ-2-156   Cornelius McDONALD, yeoman   26 Jan 1786/ 11 Jan 1787
    To: Son, John McDONALD
         Daughter, Mary McCALLA, wife of Andrew McCALLA
         Daughter, Ann TURNER, wife of Andrew TURNER
         Servant, William OLDUM - freedom
    Ex: Son, John McDONALD; Son-in-law, Andrew McCALLLA; Son -in-law,
           Andrew TURNER
    Wt: Francis HENDERSON; John BELL; Andrew HENDERSON

AJ-2-158   Henry DREW   14 Feb 1787/ 22 Mar 1787
    To: Brother, Anthony DREW - tract left by my father; Negro boy Sim
         Sister, Hannah KENARD
         Sister Mary's 2 little children (names unspec.) which she
           had by John REED
         Sister, Sarah THOMPSON, wife of David THOMPSON - Negro boy
           Clenas
         Nephew, Henry DREW, son of James
         Brothers, George & James DREW
    Ex: Brother, Anothony DREW; Brother-in-law, David THOMPSON
    Wt: George CHAUNCY; James OSBORN; William POWELL

AJ-2-159   Samuel DURHAM   6 Jul 1786/ 27 Feb 1787
    To: Son, Samuel DURHAM - all my real estate
         Sons, Thomas, Aquilla, Loyd, Lee, & Joseph DURHAM
         Granddaughter, Ann (DURHAM ?) || Grandson, William (DURHAM ?)
         Three daughters, Susannah, Eleanor, & Charlotte (nee DURHAM)
    Ex: William SMITHSON; Son, Samuel DURHAM
    Wt: John JERVIS; Aquilla DURHAM; John GREEN

AJ-2-161   Thomas DURBAN   Verbal: 10 Dec 1787/ 26 Feb 1788
    To: Frances CARTY || James NICHEAS (or NICLEAS ?)
    Ex: (None named)
    Wt: Sinah DURBAN (or Cina Lee DURBIN); Elizabeth CARTY; Rachel
           DURBAN

AJ-2-162   Samuel DURBIN   5 Feb 1788/ 26 Jan 1789
    To: Wife, Cassandrew DURBIN || Step-daughter, Marget WALER
         Children, John & Mary DURBIN
    Ex: Brother, Daniel DURBIN
    Wt: John Hale HUGHS; Mary STEPHENSON; William Skipwith COALE

         Widow, Cassandra DURBIN, quitted her claim by letter some
           months before probate was taken.

AJ-2-163 **Simon DENNY**   3 Jan 1786/ 23 Jun 1786
To: Wife, Margaret DENNY - all my lands in Harford Co.; Negro girl
    Dinah
    Daughters, Rebekah & Margret (nee DENNY)
    Son, James DENNY - all my lands near Mohongehala River on which
       he now dwells
    Son, Michael (or Micheal) DENNY - lands in Harford Co. after
       wife's death
    Michael's brother, Simon (DENNY ?)
    John FORWOOD || Grandson, William RAMSEY
Ex: Wife, Margret DENNY; Son, Micheal DENNY
Wt: Bennett WHEELER; Stephen HILL; Andrew WELSH

AJ-2-164 **Isaac DAWES**   5 May 1777/ 24 Mar 1789
To: Nine children (names unspec.) || Wife, Mary DAWES
Ex: Wife, Mary DAWES
Wt: Abel GREEN; Frances COLLINS; Jacob BOND

AJ-2-165 **Mary Ann DAY**   9 Aug 1793/ 26 Nov 1796
To: Son, Henry WETHERALL - Negro girl Dark
    Son, William WETHERALL - Negro boy Toby
    Daughter, Katy WETHERALL - Negro girl Sophia
    Son, James WETHERALL
    Daughters, Sarah GOLDSMITH, Mary BROWN, & Elizabeth WATTERS
Ex: Son, Henry WETHERALL
Wt: Thomas Howell BIRCKHEAD; William OSBORN; Samuel REARDON

AJ-2-166 **Margaret DENNY**   27 Jun 1790/ 16 Dec 1791
To: Daughter, Margaret WHITE || Son, Michal DENNY - Negro Maria
    Three grandchildren, the children of Rebekah BROWN & husband
       George BROWN: Elizabeth BROWN (other 2 names unspec.)
Ex: John FORWOOD; Samuel FORWOOD
Wt: George BROWN; John FORWOOD; Mary LOGUE; Sarah FORWOOD

AJ-2-167 **Richard DEAVER**   17 May 1789/ 8 Mar 1791
To: Son, James DEAVER - tract 125 a. *Chestnut Spring*, tract 74 a.
    Johns Third Addition
    James & Aquilla DEAVER, sons of James DEAVER
    Grandson, James DEAVER, son of Richard DEAVER, deceased - tract
       part of *Deavers Compulsion* including 50 a *Deavers Project*,
       20 a. *The Mount*, & 62 a. part of *Richards Retirement*
    Grandson, Richard DEAVER, son of Richard DEAVER, deceased -
       tract 85 a. *The Hawks Nest*, tract part of *Deavers Compulsion*
       including part of *Richards Retirement*
    Son, Aquilla DEAVER - tract 110 a. *Pacas Pleasure*, tract part
       of *Deavers Compulsion*
    Daughter, Sarah DEAVER - tract 61 a. *Deavers Pleasure* where she
       lives, tract part of *Deavers Compulsion*
    Daughter, Hannah DEAVER - tract *Sarah's Garden* including 80 a.
       part of *Deavers Enlargement*
    Daughter, Mary DEAVER || Wife, Sarah DEAVER
    To be rented out - tracts *Pacas Pleasure* & *Deavers Compulsion*
Ex: Wife, Sarah DEAVER
Wt: Thomas MILES; James GLADDEN; Benjamin JONES; Rachel JONES;
    Benjamin McCREERY; Mary GLADDEN

Codicil:(undated)
```
To: Son, James DEAVER
    Grandson, James DEAVER, son of James
    Daughter, Hannah DEAVER || Son, Aquilla DEAVER
    Grandchildren, sons of my son Richard DEAVER, deceased
Wt: (None listed)
```

AJ-2-171   **John DAY**   7 Dec 1790/ 19 Jan 1791
```
To: Sons, James Maxwell DAY & Gouldsmith DAY - tract 514 a.
      Maxwells Conclusion, tract 73 a. Days Double Purchase, tract
      23 a. Days Priviledge
    Also son, James Maxwell DAY - Negro man Thomas; family Bible
    Also son, Gouldsmith DAY - Negro girl Nance, the daughter of
      Claire
    Daughter, Elizabeth Maxwell DAY - Negro woman Claire & her
      future incr., except the child she now goes with
    Daughter, Martha Gouldsmith DAY - Negro woman Sarah & her
      incr., also the child that Claire now goes with
    Daughter, Mary Gouldsmith DAY - Negro girl Rachel & her incr.
    Present wife, Sarah ALLENDER, not the mother of the children
      mentioned in this will - house The Store where Michael
      CONAWAY lived & adj. tract 10 a. to SW towards Gunpowder
      River; mentions pre-marital contract with Sarah
    Daughter, Frances DAY; Son, Roderick DAY
Ex: James WETHERALL; Edward DAY, son of Edward
Wt: Robert SAUNDERS; Lambert WILMER; Thomas DORNEY; Thomas STRONG;
    Thomas WALTHAM
```

AJ-2-174   **Sarah DREW**   22 Aug 1791/ 6 Sep 1791
```
To: Granddaughter, Susan DREW; Daughter, Priscilla DREW
    Son, John NELSON - Negro fellow George
    Son, Aquilla NELSON - Negro fellow Ned
    Son, George HENDERSON - Negro boy Deck
    Two Negroes, Priss & Jacob - to be sold
Ex: Two oldest sons, John & Aquilla NELSON
Wt: Archibald BEATTY; George LITTLE
```

AJ-2-176   **Jean DESSAA**, of Baltimore Co.   31 Dec 1792/ 15 Dec 1797
           formerly of St. Lucie
```
To: Son, Jean DESSAA - property & monies held by friends in
      Havanna, on the island of St. Lucie, in France, & on the
      island of Tobago, property I may have in the hands of F.
      DELAPORTE from joint adventure to St. Lucia & another to the
      coast of Guinea
    Fournie LETANG, of St. Lucie
    Two Negro women, Cathrine & Celeste - at Fournie LETANG's on
      St. Lucie
    Non-beneficiaries: Guardian for son: Jean POUZACY, his
      godfather, a merchant at Port Lewis in the island of Tobago;
      Alternate guardian for son: F. DELAPORTE; Widow of Mastios
      DESRAMEAUX; Feberque Le FAURRE.
Ex: F. DELAPORTE
Wt: F. DELAPORTE; P. Jauna de SAUSCARIS; Auguste GREME
```

Above will translated by Francois du BLOCK, Justice of the
Peace in Baltimore City on 15 Dec 1791, verified by Auguste
GREME in Harford Co. on 1 May 1798.

AJ-2-178 **Frances DEBRULER**   Verbal: 5 Oct 1792/ 3 Nov 1792
To: Children (names unspec.) who had been helpful to me in the time
      of sickness
Ex: Jane McGAW; Mary PIKE
Wt: Jane McGAW; Mary PIKE

AJ-2-179 **Joseph DYER**, carpenter   31 Aug 1793/ 25 Sep 1793
To: Wife (name unspec.) - dwelling house built near Meeting House
      on my land & land sufficient for a garden
    Only son, Aaron DYER || Grandson, Joseph DYER
    Daughter, Phebe CARR - tract 10 a. adj. Meeting House & Rachel
      PARSON's lot
    Grandson, John Dyer CARR, son of Phebe CARR
    Daughter, Elizabeth DYER - tract 10 a. adj. Phebe's land
    Daughter, Rachel PARSONS - tract 10 a. where she now resides,
      bordering John WILSON's land, DILLON's lot, Phebe's lot &
      the Meeting House
    Grandson, Joseph Dyer PARSONS, son of Rachel PARSONS
    Two youngest daughters, Hannah & Joanna DYER
Ex: Son, Aaron DYER
Wt: John WILSON, Junior; David REESE; Samuel WILSON

                              Codicil: 12 Sep 1793/ 25 Sep 1793
To: Orphan granddaughter, Hester HENDERSON (under age 18)
Wt: John WILSON; Elizabeth WILSON; Catharine WILSON

AJ-2-181 **Claudius Francis Frederick**   8 Jan 1795/ 7 Mar 1797
          DELAPORTE, commonly called **Frederick DELAPORTE**
To: Wife, Betsy Herbert DELAPORTE - Negro woman Fany
    Brother, Francis DELAPORTE
    Sisters, Elizabeth & Joanna DELAPORTE
    Negro boy Peter, about age 9, son of Fanny - apprenticed to a
      trade & freedom at age 25
Ex: Wife, Betsy Herbert DELAPORTE
Wt: George Gouldsmith PRESBURY; Samuel VINCENT; James EDWARDS

AJ-2-184 **Anthony DREW**   10 Feb 1794/ 31 Jul 1794
To: Sons, Aquilla & Bennett DREW - tract part of *Drew's
      Inlargement*, Aquila to posses N half including dwelling,
      Bennet the S half
    Youngest son, George DREW - land if brothers have no issues;
      Negroes Ben & Poll
    Daughter, Susan DREW - Negroes Bill & Easter
    Wife, Priscilla DREW
Ex: Wife, Priscilla DREW; George CHAUNCY, Junior
Wt: James OSBORN; George CHAUNCY; John HANSON

AJ-2-186 **Sinah (or Sina) DURBIN**   _____, 1797/ 13 Oct 1797
To: Sons, Francis, Zacriall, & John CARTER
    Daughters, Rachel DICKSON, Nancy TALOR, Mary DALEY, Hanner
      CLARKE, Mary HOWARD & Drusiller FORD

Ex: Son, Frances CARTER
Wt: James HUDSON; William CHAMBERS; Thomas HILL

AJ-2-187   **Greenberry DORSEY**   29 Mar 1798/ 9 Apr 1798
To: My eleven children (names unspec.)
Ex: Frisby DORSEY; Edward DORSEY; William LESTER
Wt: William FRISBY; James McGAY; Thomas P. FRISBY; Ashberry TAYLOR

AJ-2-188   **Thomas ELY**   9 Nov 1781/ 11 Jun 1783
To: Son, Thomas ELY, Junior - tract 100 a. part of *Paradise* & part
     of *Brother's Discovery* that he lives on
    Son, Hugh ELY - tract 40 a. that he lives on & tract 10 a.
     woodland adj. John BRUCE's land, both being part of *Paradise*
     & *Brother's Discovery*
    Son, Mahlon ELY - tract 100 a., part of *Paradise* adj. Crowsdale
     WARNER's
    Son, William ELY - residue of land including dwelling house
     being part of *Paradise* & *Brother's Discovery*
    Son, Joseph ELY
    Daughters, Ruth ELY, Rachel ELY, Mary HILL, Sarah WARNER,
     Martha BALDERSTON, & Ann ELLICOTT
Ex: Sons, Hugh & William ELY
Wt: William COX; Samuel HARRIS; John BRUCE (Quakers)

AJ-2-190   **James ELLIOT**   4 Nov 1784/ 16 Nov 1784
To: Son, John ELLIOTT, now in Carolina
    Grandson, James ELLIOT || Wife, Agness ELLIOT
    Daughters, Agnes JOHNSON & Sarah ELLIOT
Ex: Wife, Agnes ELLIOT; Son-in-law, William JOHNSTON
Wt: Robert CONN; John BOND, Junr - Quaker; Thomas WILSON - Quaker

AJ-2-191   **Thomas ELLIOTT**   13 Aug 1783/ 12 Sep 1785
To: Wife, Ann ELLIOTT - plantation on which I live
    Sarah WOODMAN
    Samuel & Thomas ELLIOTT, sons of Kerenhappuch ELLIOTT
Ex: Wife, Ann ELLIOTT; Thomas ELLIOTT
Wt: James BARTON; Veazey PRICE; William WOOD

AJ-2-193   **Margaret AIKEN** (or **EAKENS**)   11 Nov 1785/ 27 Feb 1787
To: Daughters, Ellenor NORRIS & Margret SHA
    Sons, John RILEY & Solomon RELEY
    Roger McKINLA || Patrick ROCK
Ex: Son-in-law, James NORRIS
Wt: John DEMOSS, Senr.; Robert GLENN; William BEATY

AJ-2-194   **Evan EVANS**   2 May 1791/ 27 Sep 1791
To: Wife, Mary EVANS - plantation where I live in Harford Co. & my
     estate in Baltimore Co.
    Son, Griffith EVANS - land after his mother's death
    Daughters, Ann EVANS, Ruth TURK, & Elizabeth WATKINS
    Isaac WILLIAMS
Ex: Son, Griffith EVANS; John WATKINS
Wt: Daniel THOMPSON; Richard HOPE; Thomas H. AYES (or AYERS or
     HAYES)

AJ-2-196   **John EVANS**, joiner (Junior ?)   6 Oct 1791/ 27 Oct 1791
To: John BILLINGSLEA || Robert SMITH || William BILLINGSLEA
    William HALL at Swan Creek || Richard WILMOTT
Ex: James BILLINGSLEA; Robert SMITH
Wt: Godfrey WATTERS; Walter WATTERS

AJ-2-197   **William EDEN**, farmer   12 Jul 1793/ 19 Aug 1793
To: Wife, Sarah EDEN || Sons, Benjamin & Jeremiah EDEN
    Daughters, Elizabeth SMITH & Mary EDEN
Ex: Son, Benjamin EDEN; Wife, Sarah EDEN
Wt: Richard BULL; James SHIELDS; George TAYLOR

AJ-2-198   **William EVATT**   11 Nov 1793/ 20 Mar 1794
To: Wife, Margaret EVATT
    William EVATT (under age 21), called by some William SPRINGER
    Isabel WILEY, Jane WILEY, & Elizabeth WILEY
    John EVATT, Senr.; John EVATT (under age 21), son of John
    William EVATT, son of Richard
    Joseph McELRATH, son of Joseph
    Martha GLENN, wife of David GLENN, & her children
    Sarah BONER, wife of William BONER
    William BEATY, son of Archibald
    Isabel ARMSTRONG || James SHEREDINE, a bound boy
    Negro Judy - freedom 10 years from this date
    Judy's 3 children - freedom at age 30 (Bill now being 4, Dark
      2, & the youngest 2 months)
Ex: Wife, Margaret EVATT; Archibald BEATY
Wt: John ARCHER; James BELL; Robert NISBITTE (or NESBITT)

AJ-2-200   **Hugh ELY**   10 Oct 1799/ 29 Oct 1799
To: Wife, Sarah ELY - tract 50 a. including dwelling where I live,
      all left by my father
    Sisters, Ruth ELY & Rachel ELY
    Niece, Mary COOPER, daughter of Jacob COOPER, she now living
      with me
    Harriet SWEENEY, now living with me
    Four brothers, Thomas, Mahlon, William & Joseph ELY - land
      after wife's death
Ex: Wife, Sarah ELY; Joseph WARNER; Brother-in-law, Jacob
    BALDERSTON
Wt: Peter WILSON; Christopher WILSON, Quaker; Aquilla MASSEY,
    Quaker

AJ-2-202   **William FISHER**   27 Mar 1779/ 3 Jun 1779
To: Son, William FISHER - tract 102 a. where he lives, part of
      Arabia Patra, Negro man Peter, Negro girl Pegg & her incr.
    Son, James FISHER - plantation on which I dwell; Negro boy Ben,
      Negro girl Jean
    Daughter, Elizabeth JOLLEY - Negro man Daniel, Negro woman Sook
    Grandson, John FISHER (under age 21), son of my son Robert,
      deceased - Negro girl Poll
    Grandson, Robert FISHER
    Wife (name unspec.)
Ex: Sons, William & James FISHER
Wt: Robert BODKIN; Evan GRIFFITH; Daniel KENLEY

AJ-2-204   **Thomas Peregrine FRISBY**   23 Feb 1781/ 28 Apr 1781
To: Son, William Holland FRISBY - tract *Black Island*, tract
      Colletts Points, tract part of *Frisby's Conveniency* W of
      Musketo Creek, tract part of *Planter's Delight*
    Son, Thomas Peregrine FRISBY - all lands on the Bay Side except
      above part of *Coheir's Lot*, part of *Planter's Delight*, part
      of *Colletts Points*, part of *Frisby's Conveniency*
    Son, John FRISBY - lands bought of Amos CORD that I live on,
      part of *Middle Borough*, part of *Smiths Folly Resurveyed*
    Wife, Mary FRISBY
    Non-beneficiary: Francis HOLLAND: guardian to children if Mary
      dies
Ex: Wife, Mary FRISBY; Relation, Francis HOLLAND
Wt: William WRAIN; Amoss CORD; Milcah MATHEWS

AJ-2-206   **Manassah FINNEY**   8 Feb 1788/ 25 Mar 1788
To: Son, John FINNEY's 2 sons & 2 daughters (names unspec.)
    Daughter, Hannah LOWREY, wife of John LOWREY - use of 10 a.
      tract where she & husband dwell for 6 years
    Son-in-law, John LOWREY || Granddaughter, Jean COVINTREE
    Three daughters, Sarah WILSON, Isabell SCOTT, & Martha BARNETT
    Son-in-law, James BARNETT
    To be sold - all lands
    Guardians: John BARCLAY, James CLARK
Ex: Son-in-law, James BARNETT
Wt: James DAVISON; Joseph BARNETT; John BARCLAY

AJ-2-208   **Baltis FYE**, farmer   13 Jul 1789/ 17 Oct 1789
To: Wife, Mary FYE
Ex: John KIMBELL
Wt: John HALL; Utey COMBESS (or Uty COMBEST)

John KIMBELL resigned in form his right of executorship.
The widow gave up her right to the administration of the
estate.

AJ-2-209   **John FITZGERALD**   Verbal: 9 Apr 1791/ 29 Apr 1791
To: Thomas HARGROVE
Ex: (None named)
Wt: Bridgett HASSETT; John McMULLEN

AJ-2-210   **Samuel FOSTER**   16 Apr 1789/ 1 Oct 1793
To: Sons, Samuel & Benjamin FOSTER || Daughter, Marget WARD
    Sons, Henry, William, Moses, Aaron, & John FOSTER
    Every one of my grandchildren (names unspec.)
    Wife, Margaret FOSTER
Ex: Wife, Margaret FOSTER; Son, Aaron FOSTER
Wt: Richard JEWELLS; Philip CREAL

AJ-2-211   **Mary FORD**   22 Jan 1794/ 8 Feb 1794
To: Two children, Aquila FORD & Clemency FORD || Richard COLEGATE
    Bernard PRESTON || Heirs of Martin PRESTON, deceased
    To be sold - brick house in Abingdon
Ex: Brother, Benjamin HOWARD
Wt: Robert SAUNDERS; Nancy NIGHT (or KNIGHT); Elizabeth SAUNDERS

AJ-2-212   **Margaret FOSTER**   Verbal: 23-24 Feb 1794/ 11 Mar 1794
To: Son, Aaron FOSTER   (Died Feb 24 at 5 pm)
Ex: (None named)
Wt: James ACHIN; Margarett DIXON; Daughter-in-law, Catharine
       FOSTER

AJ-2-213   **William GRAFTON**,   19 Aug 1769/ 11 Sep 1769
       of Baltimore Co.
To: Eight children, Cassandra, William, Margaret, Samuel, Daniel,
       Prissilla, Aquilla, & Nathaniel GRAFTON
    Wife, Sarah GRAFTON - tract *Graftons Entrance* inc. plantation
       where I dwell; Negro man Tom, molatto woman Temperance, &
       molatto woman Catharine
    Son, Nathan GRAFTON - land after wife's death
Ex: Wife, Sarah GRAFTON
Wt: Jacob BOND - Quaker; David ARMSTRONG

AJ-2-215   **James GALLION**, planter   2 Sep 1773/ 12 Apr 1774
       of Baltimore Co.
To: Wife, Pheeby GALLION - use of plantation rented of James
       PHILLIPS
    Son, Nathan GALLION - above plantation after mother's death
    Daughter, Rachel GALLION - Negro boy Daniel
    Daughter, Martha GALLION - Negro girl Nan & future incr.
    Daughter, Mary GILBERT - Negro girl Hager & future incr.
    Sons, John, Jacob, James & Samuel GALLION, already settled &
       doing for themselves
    Son Jacob GALLION's 2 children (names unspec.)
Ex: Wife, Pheeby GALLION
Wt: John RUFF; Robert McGAY; John GALLION

                              Codicil: 2 Sep 1773/ 12 Apr 1774
To: Son, John GALLION - Negro wench Dinah & future incr.
    Son, James GALLION - Negro boy Joe
    Son, Samuel GALLION - Negro man Robin
    Son, Nathan - Negro man big Jonn
    Daughter, Rachel GALLION - Negro boy Bobb
    Daughter, Mary GILBERT - Negro man Jupeter
    Daughter, Martha GALLION - Negro boy little Jame
    Grandchildren, son & daughter of son Jacob, deceased (names
       unspec.) - Negro boy Sip
Wt: John RUFF; Robert McGAY; John GALLION

                              Codicil: 7 Nov 1773/ 12 Apr 1774
To: Sons, Nathan & Samuel GALLION
    Daughters, Marth GALLION & Rachel GALLION
    Grandchildren, children of son Jacob, deceased (names unspec.)
Wt: Amos GARRETT

AJ-2-219   **Nathaniel GILES**   8 May 1775/ 5 Jun 1775
To: Tabitha RICHARDSON || Sarah COALE || Sister, Sarah RIGBIE
    Five daughters, Hannah, Sarah, Elizabeth, Caroline, & Charlotte
Ex: Brothers, William HAMMOND & Nathan RIGBIE; Thomas ANDREWS
Wt: Larkin HAMMOND; Daniel SHEREDINE; Cassandra SHEREDINE

Manumission of Slaves: Codicil: 10 May 1775/ 5 Jun 1775
To: Negroes Cato, Nero, Ceesar, Scipia, Polidare, & Lancaster Tom
    - freedom as of Jan 1, 1779
    Negroes Pompey & Cissero - freedom after Jan 1, 1781
    Youngest Negro Tom - freedom after Jan 1, 1786
Wt: Mary COX; Larkin HAMMOND; Daniel SHEREDINE

AJ-2-220   **John GALLION**, farmer   17 Feb 1775/ 22 May 1775
           son of James
To: Negro wench (name unspec.) - to be sold
    Wife, Elizabeth GALLION
    Seven children, Martha, Mary, Rachel, James, Joannah,
       Elizabeth, & William GALLION
    Servant man Michael TRUELOVE - freedom
Ex: Wife, Elizabeth GALLION
Wt: Martha GALLION; Josias William DALLAM; Amos GARRETT

AJ-2-222   **Henry GARLAND**   21 Nov 1774/ 26 Sep 1777
           of St. George's Parish, Harford Co.
To: Cousins, Anne & Randal, children of Josias HITCHCOCK - young
       Negro Jacob
    Henry HITCHCOCK || Nephew, Francis GARLAND || Thomas FISHER
    All my cousins (names unspec.) except William COLE
Ex: Josias HITCHCOCK
Wt: John COTTER; John WHITACRE; Mary JOHNSON

AJ-2-223   **Richard GARRETTSON**   4 Aug 1778/ 26 Aug 1778
To: Son, Freeborn GARRETTSON - tract adj. & SE of *Eden's
       Addition*; Negro woman Moll, girl Fan, & girl Rachel
    Son, Aquilla GARRETTSON - all rem. part of my land; Negro boy
       Cuff, girl Grace, & girl Hannah
    Daughter, Elizabeth GARRETTSON - Negro girl Poll, Negro woman
       Cumbo
    Non-beneficiaries: Elizabeth's aunt, Sophia GARRETTSON
Ex: Sons, Freeborn & Aquilla GARRETTSON
Wt: Greenberry DORSEY; Norris LESTER; John CASELDINE; Patrick
       McCLAIN

AJ-2-225   **Mary GRIFFITH**   6 Mar 1776/ 7 Sep 1776
To: Sons, Luke GRIFFITH & Samuel GRIFFITH
    Granddaughter, Elizabeth GRIFFITH, daughter of Luke GRIFFITH
       & Catharine his wife
    Granddaughter, Elizabeth TREDWAY (under age 16), daughter of
       John TREDWAY & Sarah his wife
    Daughter, Mary WARD, wife of Edward WARD
    Daughter, Avarilla FREEMAN, wife of Abraham FREEMAN
    Four granddaughters, Mary, Avarilla, Elizabeth & Sarah HANSON,
       daughters of Benjamin HANSON & Elizabeth his wife
Ex: Son, Luke GRIFFITH
Wt: Levin MATHEWS; Samuel DARLEY; Rachel HITCHCOCK

AJ-2-227   **John GRIFFITH**   14 Sep 1779/ 17 Jan 1780
To: Wife, Avarilla GRIFFITH
    Two oldest sons, James & William GRIFFITH - 2 first children
       of Negro wench Daphne as they arrive at age 4

```
        Also son, James GRIFFITH - plantation 60 a. Gravelly Bottom &
           Woods Close on which I dwell
        Son, John GRIFFITH - one young Negro (name unspec.)
        Also sons, William & John GRIFFITH - tract 100 a. Perrimans
           Revise
        Four daughters, Hannah CRAWFORD, Elizabeth, Frances, & Mary
           GRIFFITH - 1 young Negro each (names unspec.)
        All other Negroes - to be sold after wife's decease
    Ex: Father-in-law, James PRITCHARD, Senr.; Wife, Avarilla GRIFFITH
    Wt: Henry STUMP; Obadiah PRICHARD; William COWAN
```

AJ-2-230   **Susanna GARRETTSON**   9 Jan 1780/ 15 Mar 1780
```
    To: Son, Garrett GARRETTSON - Negro boy Peter
        Daughter, Elizabeth GARRETTSON - Negro boy James
        Daughter, Sarah GARRETTSON - Negro boy Jupiter
        Sons, William, Thomas, & John BROWN
        Daughter, Elizabeth STEWART, wife of James STEWART
        Daughter, Susannah OSBORN, wife of Cyrus OSBORN
    Ex: Son, John BROWN
    Wt: Frances GARRETTSON; Archibald BEATTY; Samuel GRIFFITH
```

AJ-2-231   **John GUYTON**   17 Nov 1782/ 25 Mar 1783
```
    To: Grandson, Thomas Mitchell GUYTON
        Daughters, Sarah GUYTON & Mary UNDERHILL
        Seven sons, Samuel, Joseph, Nathaniel, Isaac, Jacob, John, &
           Joshua GUYTON
        Wife, Mary GUITON (or GUYTON)
    Ex: Son, Abraham GUITON; Wife, Mary GUITON (or GUYTON)
    Wt: John GRAY; John McDONALD; William PATTERSON
```

AJ-2-232   **Frances GARLAND**   26 Mar 1781/ 31 Aug 1781
```
    To: Niece, Ann WHITAKER, daughter of sister Susannah
        Niece, Catherine GARLAND, daughter of brother James
        Trustee: Jacob FORWOOD, for sister Catherine GARLAND
    Ex: Jacob FORWOOD
    Wt: John COSLEY; John CONDRIN
```

AJ-2-233   **William GALE** (or **GAILE**)   29 Mar 1781/ 15 Nov 1781
```
    To: Four eldest children, James, William, Benjamin & Reason GALE
        Daughter, Mary GALE
    Ex: Thomas BROWNING
    Wt: Isaac WEBSTER; Paul SHIELDS; Elizabeth Ann BARRY
```

AJ-2-234   **Michael GILBERT, Senr.**   6 Nov 1779/ 17 Feb 1784
```
    To: Wife, Mary GILBERT
        Son, Micah GILBERT - tract 100 a. where he now lives
        Son, M. Taylor GILBERT - tract 100 a.
        Son, Parker GILBERT - tract 100 a. where he now lives
        Son, Charles GILBERT - tract 100 a. where he now lives
        Son, Phillip GILBERT - tract 50 a. east of Micah
        Son, Samuel GILBERT - tract 30 a. between Parker & Charles
        Grandson, Garvis GILBERT, son of Garvis - tract 100 a. between
           Parker & Charles
        Son, Michael GILBERT - houses, orchard, meadows & rem. of my
           land
```

Ex: Wife, Mary GILBERT
Wt: Samuel PRITCHARD; Benjamin PRITCHARD

AJ-2-236 **Samuel GRAY**   Verbal: 25 Jul 1789/ 28 Jul 1789
To: James AMOS, son of Joshua AMOS
Ex: (None named)
Wt: Ellenor JORDAN; James SHARP; William COOPER

AJ-2-237 **Jacob GILES**   17 Jan 1784/ 11 Feb 1784
To: Two granddaughters (names unspec.), co-heiresses of son
    Nathaniel GILES, deceased - tract 712 a. *Land of Promise*;
    all slaves from their father's estate to be free upon coming
    of age
  Son, James GILES - 2 tracts 500 a. *Benjamin's Choice* & *James
    Park*, tract *Cranberry Meadows*; land, part of *Combine's
    Chance* pur. of Thomas TAYLOR
  Granddaughter, Elizabeth GILES, daughter of Jacob GILES
  Mentioned: Co-partnership with William SMITH, Jr; rents due
    from Cumberland Forge
  Mentioned: deed of conveyence to son, Jacob GILES, deceased -
    tracts part of *Brother's Lott*, part of *Rick Bottom
    Corrected*, *MacCarteys Neighbors*, *Giles Angles*, & *Addition to
    Brothers Lott*
  Son, Thomas GILES - tract 500 a. E part of *Brother's Lott* adj.
    Robert STOKES land, tract 156 a. E part of 2 tracts *Rick
    Bottom Corrected* & *Levels Addition*, plantation house *Mount
    Felix Seat* & all other houses
  Son, Aquilla GILES - lands on N side of Deer Creek viz. 500 a.
    Ellburton, 200 a. *Rigbies Hope*, 30 a. part of *Rigbies Hope*
    & part of 100 a. condemned for Cumberland Forge, 45 1/2 a.
    Parkers Chance bought from William HUSBANDS, 33 a. *Giles
    Addition*, a moiety or undivided half part of tract 100 a.
    Combs Adventure in Baltimore Co. on S side of Patapsco
    River, tract 48 1/2 a. part of *Saint Martins Ludgate*, tract
    108 1/2 a. W part of *Rick Bottom Corrected* bought from my
    son Jacob
  Mentioned: deed of conveyence to son Edward GILES, deceased -
    tracts *Rumsey Marsh*, *Atkinsons Purchase*, island in Rumsey
    Creek called *Minorea*, *Hogs Neck*, *Shepherd's Choice*,
    Shepherds Adventure, & part of *Nats Island*
  Grandson, William Axtell GILES, eldest son of Aquilla GILES
  Grandson, Winston SMITH, youngest son of daughter Elizabeth
    (deceased), late wife of William SMITH - tract *Mountserada*
    on Susquehanna River pur. of Henry Ward PEARCE, tract 8 1/2
    a. *Montserada Addition* adj. above *Mountserada*
  Grandson, Jacob Giles SMITH, eldest son of daughter Elizabeth
    (deceased), late wife of William SMITH
  Son-in-law, William SMITH
  Granddaughter, Joanna Giles WATERS - Negro boy Tom, now 6 years
    old, until age 30; Negro girl Lydia now 5, until age 25
  Wife, Joanna GILES - Negro boy George, Negro woman Suck
  Step-daughter, Susanna SCOTT, now a widow
  Nathaniel RIGBIE, husband to my deceased daughter Sarah RIGBIE
  Nathan SHEREDINE, son of Cassandra SHEREDINE, deceased
  Hannah JOHNS, wife of Skipwith JOHNS

Sons, Thomas GILES, Aquilla GILES & friend Phillip COALE -
  Negroes Sam, Morea, Poll, Grace, & Tom (after age 30) &
  Lydia (after age 25)
  Trustees: Dr. John ARCHER & Samuel HUGHES, Esq
Ex: Sons, Thomas & Aquilla GILES; Phillip COALE
Wt: Thomas BOYLE; William EVATT; John WILLIAMS

AJ-2-247   **Amos GARRETT**   28 Mar 1786/ 2 Feb 1789
To: Elizabeth CORD or her second son, Jacob CORD
  Granddaughter, Harriot PENROSE, daughter of daughter Cassandra
    PENROSE
  Granddaughter, Frances PENROSE || Daughter, Frances GARRETT
  Daughter, Milcah HALL, wife of Benedict
  Child that Milcah HALL is now pregnant with, if it should be
    a boy & named Sydney
  Grandson, Henry HALL (under age 21)
  Daughters of Milcah & Benedict HALL (names unspec.)
Ex: Benedict Edward HALL
Wt: Greenberry DORSEY; Thomas ASHLEY; William HALL; Michael
  PINNITON

AJ-2-249   **Garrett GARRETTSON**, mariner   8 Sep 1791/ 5 Feb 1794
To: Sister, Susanna OSBORN, wife of Cyrus OSBORN, family now in
  Great Britain - land pur. of William SMITH called *Cramberry*
  being part of *Benjamins Choice* & part of *James Park*
  Sister, Elizabeth CHANCEY - plantation inherited from father
  Garrett GARRETTSON & all lands adj. bought of William SMITH
  excepting above
Ex: Brother-in-law, John CHANCEY
Wt: Aquilla HALL; Josias Carvil HALL; Nathaniel RAMSEY

AJ-2-251   **Priscilla GOVER**   31 Jan 1790/ 6 Sep 1790
To: Nephews, Benjamin Kidd WILSON & Henry WILSON, sons of Benjamin
  Kidd WILSON
  Samuel, Elizabeth, Gerard, Robert, Philip, Mary, & Priscilla
  GOVER, children of Philip GOVER, deceased
Ex: Samuel GOVER; Robert GOVER
Wt: Mary JOHNS; Elizabeth PUSEY; Ephraim Gittings GOVER

AJ-2-252   **Clement GREEN**, of Baltimore Co. 17 Oct 1795/ 8 Nov 1796
To: Wife, Hannah GREEN - tract part of *Brook Cross* then to nephew
  Clement GREEN; Negroes Major, Mary (alias Pug - Major's
  wife), James, Kate, Bet, Dole, Ester, & Jean
  Nephew, Clement GREEN, 3rd son of brother Benjamin GREEN of
  Harford Co.
  Niece, Henrietta GREEN, daughter of brother Benjamin GREEN -
  Negro man Abraham
  Negro Mary (alias Pug), her daughter Kate, & granddaughter Jean
  - freedom after wife's decease
  Clement BUSSEY, son of Bennet BUSSEY of Harford Co.
  John MacNABB, second son of my friend John MacNABB
Ex: Wife, Hannah GREEN; Nephew, Benjamin GREEN, son of Benjamin
Wt: John MacNABB; Robert LOVE; William LOVE

AJ-2-254   **Ann GIBSON**   19 Jul 1794/ 12 Aug 1794
To: Son, William GIBSON || Daughter, Sarah RAMPLY, wife of James
    Granddaughter, Ann BEATY || Grandson, Thomas Johnson RAMPLY
    Daughter, Elizabeth McCORMICK, wife of George
    Temperance CORBIN, an orphan child living with me
Ex: Son, William GIBSON
Wt: Ezekiel JONES; John COX - Quaker

AJ-2-256   **Charles GILBERT**,   Verbal: __ Jul 1794/ 31 Jul 31, 1794
            son of Taylor GILBERT
To: Wife, Mary Gilbert GILBERT
Ex: (None named)
Wt: William PRESBURY; Elizabeth GILBERT; Martha GILBERT

AJ-2-257   **Joseph GORRELL**   14 Apr 1792/ 3 Jun 1793
To: Wife, Mary GORRELL - tract part of *Smiths Mistake*, then to son
    Lawson
    Son, Lawson GORRELL || Sisters, Hannah & Easter GORRELL
    Daughter, Elizabeth HAMTON
Ex: Wife, Mary GORRELL; John COOLEY
Wt: John HARDY; Joseph EWING; John EWING

AJ-2-258   **Samuel GRIFFITH**   12 Jan 1794/ 4 Jun 1794
To: Heirs of brother Luke GRIFFITH (names unspec.) - tract 100 a.
    pur. of Col. Thomas WHITE lying between William's Swamp &
    Long Bridge
    Son, Samuel Gouldsmith GRIFFITH (under age 21) - lands in
    Rumney Neck; Negroes Paraway & her incr., little Bill,
    Mariah, & Jack, son of Abigail
    Daughters, Frances & Sarah GRIFFITH & daughter, Martha SMITH,
    wife of Col. Alexander Lawson SMITH - tract *Tapley Neck*
    lying in Gunpowder Neck from brother Samuel
    Sons, John Hall GRIFFITH, Edward, Luke, & Alexander GRIFFITH
    Wife, Martha GRIFFITH - use of farm on Swan Creek during
    widowhood, then sold
    Sister-in-law, Frances GARRETTSON
Ex: Col. Alexander L. SMITH; Dr. Elijah DAVIS; Dr. Samuel
    GRIFFITH; Sister-in-law, Frances GARRETTSON
Wt: Frisby DORSEY; Lewis GRIFFITH; Thomas SHAY; Robert JONES

AJ-2-261   **Henry GREEN**   10 Apr 1795/ 16 May 1797
To: Daughter, Ann BUSSEY, wife of Bennett BUSSEY - plantation on
    which I dwell & all adj. lands
    Granddaughter, Mary COOPER, wife of Henry COOPER, Jr - Negro
    girl Betty
    Granddaughter, Elizabeth GREEN - Negro boy Jack
    Granddaughter, Martha GREEN - Negro girl Sall
    Granddaughter Sarah GREEN - Negro boy Josias
    Granddaughter, Susannah GREEN - Negro girl Jean
    Five grandchildren - all land bought of Benjamin BUTTERWORTH
Ex: Bennett BUSSEY; Henry COOPER, Junr.
Wt: David COOK; James DENNING; John LOVE

AJ-2-263   **Charles GILBERT**, aged 73 years 26 Nov 1797/ 1 Oct 1798
To: Wife, Elizabeth GILBERT - half of lands on Swan Creek on which

I dwell; Negro girl Susanah
Grandson, Charles GILBERT (under age 21), son of son Michael GILBERT - tracts *Clark's Tobacco, Union, Obediah's Venture, The Improved Venture, Gilberts Pipe, Jacks Purchase, Double Loan*, all on head of Swan Creek
Grandson, William Presbury GILBERT, son of son Michael GILBERT - tract 220 a. in the forest named *West Wood*
Also to grandsons, Charles GILBERT & William Presbury GILBERT - tract in Gunpowder Neck pur. of Mrs. Avarilla PATTERSON
Clemency & Elizabeth GILBERT, children of son Michael GILBERT
Daughter-in-law, Elizabeth COLE & my 2 grandchildren (names unspec.) that she has living with her
Daughter, Mary HORNER
Daughter, Martha GILBERT - Negro woman Lidde & her son Peter aged about 4 years
Daughter, Elizabeth MORGAN - Negro woman Ester & her daughter Betsy aged about 4 years
Ex: Wife, Elizabeth GILBERT; George PATTERSON; Thomas HALL
Wt: Richard WEBSTER; Benjamin HERBERT; John GILMORE; Chrispin CUNNINGHAM; Benjamin McFADIN

AJ-2-265 **Martin Taylor GILBERT** 13 Aug 1797/ 16 Oct 1797
To: Son, Martin Taylor GILBERT - all lands I now possess
   Wife, Martha GILBERT
   Children, Elizabeth WILSON, Sarah, Ann, Martha, & Julia GILBERT
Ex: Wife, Martha GILBERT; Son, Martin Taylor GILBERT
Wt: Charles GILBERT; Philip GILBERT; Joseph EWING; James Cole GILBERT

AJ-2-266 **Elizabeth GALLION** 28 Apr 1797/ 16 Dec 1799
To: Daughters, Rachel, & Elizabeth GALLION - Negro boy Sam
   Daughter, Hanna GALLION, who is in Carolina
Ex: John HOWARD
Wt: Thomas CHRISHOLM; Leonard HOWARD

AJ-2-267 **William GROVES** Verbal: (undated)/ 10 Mar 1800
To: Four youngest children, Abraham, Isaac, Sarah, & Asael GROVES
Ex: (None named)
Wt: John Hammond DORSEY; Samuel STEWART

AJ-2-268 **John HALL**, of Baltimore Co. 20 Sep 1770/ 11 May 1774
To: Eldest son now living, Benedict Edward HALL - tracts on or near Muscator Creek & Romney Creek, *Halls Purchase, Beaver Neck, Young Man's Addition, Hall & Bones Discovery, Sheriffs Hall, Dismall Swamp, Middle Borough, & Smiths Folley Resurveyed*
   Son, Josias Carvill HALL - tracts on or near head of Swan Creek, *Halls Park, Halls Chance Addition*, the Mill on Swan Creek Run, part of *Paradise* bought of Col. Thomas WHITE
   Daughter, Martha GILES - tracts *Taylors Good Hass (or Half ?), Timber Neck, Green Spring Forrest*
   Son-in-law, Benjamin RUMSEY; Daughter, Mary RUMSEY
   Wife, Hannah HALL - plantation on which I dwell
Non-beneficiary: Son, John HALL, deceased
Ex: Wife, Hannah HALL; Son, Benedict Edward HALL; Son, Josias Carville HALL; Daughters, Martha GILES & Mary RUMSEY

Wt: James MATHEWS; William HALL; Rebecca MATHEWS; Sophia HALL;
    Samuel GALLION

AJ-2-271 **William HUGHES,**   14 Feb 1765/ 26 Mar 1776
          of Baltimore Co.
To: Wife, Amy HUGHES - all my lands
    Son, William HUGHES, & his son if alive (name unspec.)
    Son, Rowland HUGHES' children ¦¦ Son John HUGHES
    Lies CAYNS' children (names unspec.) lawfully of him & his wife
        deceased
    David KNIGHT's children (names unspec.)
Ex: Wife, Amey HUGHES; Son, Rowland HUGHES
Wt: Moses CAMPBELL; Arthur INGRAM; James BONAR; Michael GILBERT;
    Sarah DEAVER
                                              Codicil: 5 Apr 1774
To: Roland HUGHES himself & his son William to be

AJ-2-273 **James HARRIS**   17 Jan 1777/ 17 Oct 1777
To: Mother, Elizabeth HARRIS
    Sisters, Jean, Sarah, & Dorthea HARRIS
    Sister, Susannah McCLINTOCK, wife of Mathew
    Sister's children, Jean & Samuel FULTON
Ex: Richard WILMOTT; John ARCHER
Wt: James ALLISON; John JAMISON; James MAY

AJ-2-274 **Aquila HALL,** of Baltimore Co. 15 Aug 1769/ 10 Apr 1779
To: Son, Thomas HALL - lot & storehouse in Bush Town; Negro men
        Cudgoe & Harry, Negro woman Moll
    Son, James White HALL - land in forest on Swan Creek Run &
        Coxes Mill, *Aquilas Inheritance*, *Aquilas Begining*, *Wilburns
        Adventure*, & part of *New Westwood*, all contiguous
    Son, William HALL - grist mill & saw mill & all adj. lands on
        Nams Run 1/2 mile above Bush Town
    Son, John HALL - land in the swamps; land added in *Halls
        Meadows* by a resurvey on *Murpheys Hazard*; land pur. of
        Timothy MURPHY, Jonas GARRETT, Jacob COMBEST, & the KIMBALS
    Son, Edward HALL - Negro boys Isaac & Gustus, Negro boy Sam
        (brother to Gustus), Negro girl Perina, Negro girl Dinah
        (born of Judah)
    Daughter, Charlotte HALL - Negro girl Rachiel (born of Judah),
        Negro girl Dinah (had of Daniel MAGEE), Negro girl Jenny,
        Negro boy Emanuel
    Daughter, Mary HALL - Negro girls Easter, Lucy, & Moll, Negro
        boy Jacob
    Daughter, Sophia HALL - Negro girl Margaret (daughter of
        Hager), Negro girls Neamy & Judah, Negro boy Sam (born of
        Hannah)
    Daughter, Martha HALL - Negro boy Medarah (Micah ?) & Negro
        girl Jeney (son & daughter of Hannah), Negro girl Hannah
        (daughter of Rachiel), Negro girl Hager (daughter of Pegg)
    Wife, Sophia HALL - Negro women Judah & Hannah, Negro girls
        Hager, Negro men Peter & Leander, Negro boys Jo & Ned
Ex: Wife, Sophia HALL
Wt: Isaac WEBSTER; Thomas Peregrine FRISBY; William HALL; John Lee
    WEBSTER (Quakers)

AJ-2-276   **John HALL**, gentleman   21 Jan 1779/ 10 Sep 1779
            of Cranberry
To: Eldest son, Edward HALL - tract part of *Cranbury Hall* not
    hereinafter devised; tract 10 a. part of *Halls Chance* pur.
    of Col. John HALL; mill with 20 a. of land; my silver
    cutlass; 3 Negroes, Sam or Sampson, Kate & Negro man
    Sharper, a blacksmith
    Second son, John Beedle HALL - tract part of *Cranbury Hall* on
    N & NW of the Great Road; my small sword; three Negroes,
    Sue, Bacchus, & Cuff
    Third son, Josias HALL - tract *Mount Real*, part of *Halls Plains*
    not devised by my grandfather to his daughter Sophia, lot
    in Charles Town; 3 Negroes, Cupid, Diamond, & Hannah
    Daughter, Avarilla HALL (under age 16) - Negro boy Ben &
    mulatto girl Cass (girl to be freed at age 31)
    Daughter, Priscilla HALL (under age 16) - Negro girl Dinah,
    mulatto boy Manuel (boy to be freed at age 31)
    Daughter, Mary HALL (under age 16) - Negro girl Phillis,
    mulatto girl Sarah (to be free at 31)
    Daughter, Elizabeth HALL (under age 16) - Negro girl Linda &
    mulatto girl Jane (to be free at 31)
    Wife, Barthia HALL - Negroes Primus, Stepney, Perry, Phill,
    Tom, Mingo, Judah, Beck, Milcah, & yellow Kate
    Eldest daughter, Martha PRESBURY, now living with me
    Non-beneficiary: Grandfather, John HALL; Sophia WHITE, daughter
    of grandfather John HALL
Ex: Wife, Bathia HALL; Sons, Edward, John Beedle, & Josias HALL
Wt: M. GILBERT, Junr.; William FELL; Garret GARRETTSON; James
    MATHEWS

13 Oct 1779 - Wife quit her claim.

AJ-2-280   **Sophia HALL**   1 Dec 1779/ 8 Feb 1785
To: Sons, William & Edward HALL - tracts 373 1/2 a. *Constantinople*,
    Antrim, *Lacedeman*, *Kilkenny*, *Londonderry*, & *Little Hopewell*
    Eldest son, Thomas HALL - tracts *Sophias Dairy* & the *Diary
    Improved*
    Son, Benedict HALL - tract 8 a. *Little Worth* & tract 282 a.
    Montserada; land pur. of Samuel CHASE in Frederick Co. &
    land pur. of George DAUGHERTY in Harford Co.
    Son, John HALL - tracts *Simmons Neglect* & the *Addition to
    Simmons Neglect*
    Daughters, Charlotte, Mary, Sophia, & Martha HALL - tracts 2205
    a. *Abbots Forrest*, *Hawthawas Hazard*, *James Addition*, &
    Monreal or Montreal
    Son, James HALL
Ex: Sons, Thomas, James, & William HALL
Wt: Benedict Edward HALL; Charles GILMORE; Thomas ANDREWS

AJ-2-282   **James HUTCHISON**   2 Jun 1780/ 1 Jul 1780
To: Wife, Jennet HUTCHISON
    Children, Mary, Agness, Jean, Elizabeth, Margaret, & Ann
    HUTCHISON (all under age 18)
Ex: Wife, Jennet HUTCHISON; James CLARK
Wt: John McFADIN; John BARCLAY; Robert BRADLEY

AJ-2-283 **Richard HILL**   2 Apr 1780/ 22 Aug 1780
To: Sons, John Green HILL & Richard HILL - all my lands
    Daughter, Martha HILL ¦¦ Son-in-law, Samuel GANT
Ex: Samuel G. OSBORN
Wt: John DAY, Junr.; Thomas STRONG; Benjamin MEADS; Richard HILL;
    Lambert WILMER

AJ-2-285 **Elizabeth HENDERSON**   27 Nov 1781/ 7 Feb 1782
To: Son, Nathaniel HENDERSON - tract 10 a. I now live on bought of
    Col. Thomas WHITE
Ex: (None named)
Wt: John PARIMAN; James GRAY; George PATTERSON

AJ-2-286 **Hannah HALL**   11 Nov 1781/ 9 Feb 1782
          widow of Col. John HALL
To: Son, Benedict Edward HALL - Negro wench Diner or Dinah, her
    daughter Poll, her daughter Pris younger than Poll, & their
    future issues
    Son, Josias Carvill HALL - Negroes Hannah, Gustus or Augustus,
    Ursulah or Sulah, James or Jem, Jane or Jen, Mirtilla &
    Jack, & all their future incr., & all other Negroes not
    mentioned elsewhere in this will
    Daughter, Martha RUMSEY
    Daughter, Mary RUMSEY - Negro woman Dorcas or Darkey, Negro
    girl Lydia or Liddy, & all their future incr.
    Granddaughter, Charlotte White HALL, daughter of son Benedict
    Edward HALL & Milcah his wife - Negro girl Rachell, daughter
    of Dinah & her issue
    Grandson, John Carvill HALL, son of son Josias Carvill HALL &
    wife Jane - Negro boy James or Jem, son of Jem or James
    Granddaughter, Henrietta RUMSEY, daughter of John RUMSEY & my
    daughter Martha - Negro woman Patience & her future incr.
    Granddaughter, Mary RUMSEY, second daughter of John RUMSEY &
    daughter Martha - Negro boy Charles
    Granddaughter, Charlotte RUMSEY, 3rd daughter of John RUMSEY
    & my daughter Martha - Negro girl Elizabeth, Betty, Bett or
    Bess & her future incr.
    Granddaughter, Hannah RUMSEY, daughter of John RUMSEY & my
    daughter Martha - Negroes Violette or Vi, Fanny, & Sohia,
    Nesbitt, daughter of Dorcas, & their future incr.
    Grandson, Benjamin RUMSEY, Jr, son of Benjamin RUMSEY & my
    daughter Mary his wife - Negro lad or boy called Jo
    Grandson, John RUMSEY, son of Benjamin RUMSEY & my daughter
    Mary - Negro boy Bill
Ex: Son, Josias Carvill HALL
Wt: Frances HOLLAND; Thomas DORSEY

AJ-2-288 **Cordelia HALL**   6 Jul 1782/ 21 Sep 1782
To: Sons, Francis & Aquilla HALL
    Daughters, Frances HOWARD & Cordelia (TOLLEY ?)
    Daughter, Sarah (nee HALL)
    Son, William HALL - Negro boy Bill
    Negro women little Dinah & Mariah, Negro men Aby & Jemmy - set
    free
    Son, Parker HALL - Negroes George, Jantee, Isaac, Ben, &

       Abigail
       Grandson, James TOLLEY - Negro girls Hager & Doll & their incr.
       Grandchildren (names unspec.), children of daughter Cordelia
       Grandson, Edward HALL - Negroes Jem, Gwin, Joe, & Milley
       Grandchildren (names unspec.), children of daughter Sarah
       Granddaughter, Martha TOLLEY - Negro girl Rachael & her incr.
       Granddaughter, Hetty HALL - Negroes Jacque & Hannah & her incr.
       Granddaughter, Elizabeth HOLLAND
       Granddaughter, Cordelia HALL
Ex: Son, William HALL
Wt: Michael GILBERT, Junr.; Benedict Edward HALL

AJ-2-290   **Aaron HILL**   15 Nov 1782/ 13 Feb 1783
To: Wife, Sarah HILL ¦¦ Sons, Moses & Aaron HILL
Ex: Wife, Sarah HILL
Wt: Samuel RICKETTS; Edward RICKETTS; John ROBERTS

AJ-2-291   **William HILL**   12 Mar 1777/ 15 Apr 1783
To: Sisters, Elizabeth & Mary (nee HILL)
    Nephews, William McGOVREN - tract 191 a. plantation on which
       I dwell part of *Bonds Gratuety*
Ex: Sisters, Elizabeth & Mary (nee HILL)
Wt: David TATE; James VERNAY; Samuel ASHMEAD

AJ-2-292   **John HAWKINS**   18 Aug 1783/ 23 Oct 1783
To: Son, Richard HAWKINS
    Son, Samuel HAWKINS - tract plantation on which I dwell part
       of *Newstead*, adj. land Thomas SMITH's *Aqua Demnum* leased
       from Martha SMITH; Negro boy Jerry age 17, Negro girl Sarah
       age 15, Negro boy Pompey age 13, all to be free at age 30
    Three aged Negroes, Cuff, Jimeney, & Mary - at liberty to go
       or stay with Samuel, as they choose
    Grandchildren, Mary & Hosea JOHNS
Ex: Joseph MILLER
Wt: Richard W. DOWNING; Capt. John SMITH; Thomas WALLIS

AJ-2-294   **James HAYHURST**   7 Dec 1782/ 20 Sep 1783
To: Wife, Ann HAYHURST
    Eldest son, James HAYHURST - all my lands except 100 a.
    Second eldest son, David HAYHURST - tract 100 a. to include 30
       a. of woodland adj. Thomas MANFORDS land & 70 a. with the
       mansion house & orchard
    Eldest daughter, Elizabeth HAYHURST ¦¦ 2nd daughter, Ruth
       HAYHURST
    Daughters, Hannah & Sarah HAYHURST (both under age 18)
Ex: Wife, Ann HAYHURST; Eldest son, James HAYHURST
Wt: William AMOS; John SMITH; John WILSON; Moses DILLON

                              Codicil: 27 Jul 1783/ 20 Sep 1783
To: Daughter, Elizabeth, wife of Thomas LACEY
    Son, David HAYHURST (under age 21)
Wt: William BULL; Moses DILLON; Joseph TOWNSEND

AJ-2-296   **Barthia HALL**   9 Jan 1784/ 20 Feb 1784
To: Son, Edward HALL - mulatto slave Jacob

                                37

    Son, John Beedle HALL
    Son, Josias HALL - Negro girl Sall
    Daughter, Martha GRIFFITH, wife of Samuel GRIFFITH
    Daughter, Avarilla PATTERSON, wife of John PATTERSON
    Daughter, Priscilla CHRISTIE, wife of Gabriel CHRISTIE
    Daughter, Mary HALL - Negro Perry & Tom, & servitude or time
        of mulatto woman Kate
Ex: Sons, Edward & Josias HALL
Wt: James GILES; Henry COTTINGHAM; John ARCHER

AJ-2-298   **Joseph HOPKINS**   21 Apr 1783/ 30 Oct 1784
To: Daughter, Margaret HARRIS - plantation she now lives on & land
    to W of road thru plantation for her life, then to son
    Joseph
    Son, Joseph HOPKINS - all rem. land being part of *Phillips
        Purchase*; young Negroes named David, George, Sharper, &
        Dafney
    Daughters, Sarah COALE & Mary WORTHINGTON
Ex: Son, Joseph HOPKINS
Wt: John WORTHINGTON; Samuel GOVER; Robert GOVER

AJ-2-300   **Samuel HENRY**   20 Sep 1784/10 Apr 1786
To: Wife, Mary HENRY || Sons, John & Isaack HENRY
    Daughter, Elisabeth (nee HENRY) & her son John
    Non-beneficiary: John LATHAM; Walter ROBINSON
Ex: Son, Isaack HENRY
Wt: (sent for, but he died before they arrived)

12 Apr 1785 - Widow made over all claim to husband's estate to son
            Isaac HENRY.

AJ-2-301   **William HOLLIS**   5 Feb 1782/ 23 Mar 1786
To: Son, William HOLLIS - tract part of *Swampipoint*, tract part of
    Elling, tract *North Union*, tract part of *Islington*; Negro
    man Bendow, Negro boy Triless, Negro man Jack
    Son, Clark HOLLIS - tract part of *Swampipoint*, tract part of
    Eling, tract part of *Howels Nest* also called *Owlets Nest*,
    tract part of *Planters Neglect*; Negro woman Julia, Negro
    girl Grace, Negro boy Phillip
    Daughter, Frances COPELAND - Negro girl Patience, Negro man
    Toney
Ex: (None named)
Wt: William SAVORY; Samuel RICKETTS; Anthony DREW

23 Mar 1786 - Widow, Elizabeth HOLLIS, refused to abide by the will
            & made choice of her dower or third part of estate.

AJ-2-303   **Thomas HORNEY**, of Kent Co.   26 Dec 1785/ 15 Mar 1787
To: John CASSELDINE, Jr., son of John & Mary CASSELDINE of Harford
    Co.
Ex: John CASSELDINE, Sr.
Wt: John RYAN; William ALLEN; Hezekiah WHITAKER; Charles PINNEY

AJ-2-305   **William HOPKINS**   24 Mar 1788/ 11 Jun 1789
To: Son, Samuel HOPKINS - Negro boy named Ned

Sons, Gerrard, William, & Charles HOPKINS
Daughters, Elizabeth HUSBANDS, Susanna MASON, & Hannah Moor
  SNOWDONS (or SNOWDON)
Daughter-in-law, Frances HOPKINS, a widow - tract 4 1/2 a.
  where she now lives, then to son Charles
Wife, Rachel HOPKINS
Ex: Wife, Rachel HOPKINS
Wt: Joseph MILLER; John WILSON; John DALLAM

AJ-2-306   **Edward HALL**   30 Apr 1788/ 16 Aug 1788
To: Brother, John Beedle HALL - tract part of *Cranberry Hall*, tract
    10 a. *Halls Chance*, Mill & 20 a. land condemned to it; my
    silver cutlass; Negroes Jacob, Sampson, Corbin, Kate, Silvy,
    Nace, & Minty
  Brother, Josias HALL - my small sword; Negroes Sharper, Wilks,
    Nell, Belinda, Liberty, Cupid, Bellily, & Gill
  Sisters, Martha GRIFFITH, Avarilla PATTERSON, Priscilla
    CHRISTIE, Mary HALL, & Elizabeth HALL
  Non-beneficiary: father, John HALL of Cranberry
Ex: Brother, Josias HALL
Wt: Benedict Edward HALL; Elijah DAVIS; Jacob FORWOOD

AJ-2-309   **Charles HUGHES**   14 Jan 1789/ 3 Feb 1789
To: Sons, Thomas, John, Timothy, Samuel, Joseph, & George HUGHES
  Daughters, Mary, Elizabeth, Sarah, Jean, Margaret, Ann,
    Susannah, & Martha HUGHES
Ex: Thomas HOPE; James CLENDENON (or CLENDINEN)
Wt: Samuel HUGHES; Joseph HUGHES; Aram HUGHES

AJ-2-311   **Amos HOLLIS**   11 Apr 1789/ 9 May 1789
To: Son, Amos HOLLIS - tract *Hollis Refuse* except what George
    CHAUNCEY holds, tract 25 a. part of *Holly Hill*
  Son, Benjamin HOLLIS - tract part of *South Union* unsold which
    William ROBINSON lives on
  Wife (name unspec.)
  Avarilla, William James, Catharine, & Clark HOLLIS
Ex: (None named)
Wt: George CHAUNCY; William HOLLIS; William Budd GOULD

AJ-2-312   **John HAY**   23 Sep 1789/ 8 Oct 1789
    late of the Island of Tobago but now of Harford Co.
To: Robert OLIVER of Baltimore Town
  Guardians for my 2 children (names unspec.): Robert MILLER &
    Charles CRAIG of Tobago
  Henry ROBINSON, ship's carpenter || Mr. BIGGERS in Baltimore
  James OSBORN
  Capt. Nehemiah SANGSTER - residue of property in America
Ex: Capt. Nehemiah SANGSTER
Wt: John RYAN; William HOLLIS

AJ-2-313   **Gerrard HOPKINS**   14 Feb 1791/ 9 Dec 1799
To: Wife, Sarah HOPKINS || My children (names unspec.)
  Negro Jane & 3 young children, Mary, John, & Samuel - freedom
  Negro man Isaac - freedom from this date
  Negro man William - freedom 6 months from this date

        Negroes Susannah (age 16), Linta (age 14), Hannah (age 7) -
          free at 18
Ex: Wife, Sarah HOPKINS
Wt: William COALE; John WILSON; Samuel HOPKINS

AJ-2-314   **Asel HITCHCOCK**   5 Dec 1791/ 3 Jan 1792
To: Wife, Sarah HITCHCOCK
    Sons, William, Asel, Josias & John HITCHCOCK
    Son, Isaac HITCHCOCK - Negro boy Ned
    Daughter, Nancy HITCHCOCK
    Daughter, Mary (nee HITCHCOCK) & her children (names unspec.)
    Son Josias HITCHCOCK's children (names unspec.) - tract 10 a.
      with house & shop where he lives
    Son John HITCHCOCK's children (names unspec.) - Negro boy York
Ex: Wife, Sarah HITCHCOCK; Son, Asel HITCHCOCK
Wt: Jesse JARRETT; William NORRIS, Junr.; Patrick DORAN

AJ-2-316   **John HANSON**, farmer   21 Sep 1790/ 16 Feb 1793
           of Bush River Neck
To: Son, John HANSON - tract *Narrow Neck* where I now live, land
      adj. same, tract 50 a. part of what I bought of John
      RODGERS; Negroes Hannah, Seasor, Ned, & Priss
    Grandson, Thomas COALE ¦¦ Grandson, John THOMPSON (minor)
    Grandsons, John & Benjamin HANSON, by my son Hollis (deceased
      ?) - all rem. land bought of John RODGERS, tract bought of
      William SMITH adj. James DREW
    Daughter-in-law (name unspec.), mother of John & Benjamin
    Three daughters, Sarah, Sophia, & Semelia (nee HANSON)
    To be sold - land in & about Rich Neck
Ex: Son, John HANSON
Wt: Henry WARFIELD; Amos HOLLIS; William HOLLIS; Jonathan SUTTON

AJ-2-318   **Joseph HOPKINS**   27 Dec 1794/ 24 Nov 1795
To: Wife, Elizabeth HOPKINS - tract 200 a. with dwelling house,
      outhouses & orchards, then to son John; young Negroes Sarah,
      George, Sharp, Murriah, Pompy, Cato, John, Hannah, &
      Gaberial - males to be free at age 21 & females at the age
      of 18
    Sons, John & Joseph HOPKINS
    Daughters, Ann & Elizabeth HOPKINS
    Sons, Samuel & Epheram HOPKINS - rem. of land
    Non-beneficiary: Isaac MASSEY - to assist in settlement
Ex: Wife, Elizabeth HOPKINS; Son, John HOPKINS
Wt: James JOHNSON; Joseph HARRIS; Isaac MASSEY

19 Dec 1795 - Elizabeth HOPKINS renounced will of her husband
              Joseph HOPKINS & claims in lieu her third as directed
              by law.
Wt: Ephraim Gittings GOVER; Isaac MASSEY

AJ-2-321   **Rachel HOPKINS**   (Undated)/ 17 July 1795
To: Son, Gerrard HOPKINS - tract of land
    Daughter, Susannah MASON - Negro boy William HOWE, to be free
      when he comes of age
    Daughter, Hannah WATERS - Negro girl Harriot, to be free when

```
          she comes of age
  Daughter, Elizabeth HUSBAND - Negro girl Margerret, to be free
     when she comes of age
  Son, Samuel HOPKINS - tract of land; Negro girl Cassandra, to
     be free when she comes of age
  Son, Charles HOPKINS - tract of land
  Son, William HOPKINS - tract of land I reserved for my own use;
     Negro boy Stephen, to be free when he comes of age
  Grandchildren, Joel HOPKINS & Elizabeth HOPKINS, son &
     daughter of Fanny HOPKINS
  Negro boy George, Negro girl Suck, Negro girl Nell - to be free
  Non-beneficiaries: David CLARK, Joseph MILLER, Peter WILSON &
     Edward JOLLEY
  (Written by: William BAGLEY & read to Rachel HOPKINS.)
Ex: Samuel HOPKINS
Wt: William BAGLEY

17 July 1795 - Verified by Samuel HOPKINS

AJ-2-324    Francis HOLLAND              25 May 1795/ 9 Sep 1795
To: Negroes, age 25 or more - freedom 1 year after my decease
    Negroes under 25 - freedom at age 25
    Naomy (or Neomi) MATHEWS
    Youngest children (names unspec.), minors
Ex: Josias Carvill HALL; Aquilla HALL, my brother (?)
Wt: Roger MATHEWS; Carvel MATHEWS; William FRISBY

                                          Codicil:(Undated)

    Ages of my Negroes in January 1792:
    Tom: 51        Nan: 46        Jacob: 41      Prinor: 25
    Toney: 41      Dinah: 21      Dave: 36       Sal GWINN: 18
    Santy: 17      Sal BROWN: 18  James GWINN: 14 Rachael: 17
    James RACO: 12 Lyd: 13        Manuel: 11     Bet: 9
    Isaac: 7       Cass: 4

AJ-2-325    Jean HORNER                  6 Sep 1798/ 18 Oct 1798
To: Sons, William & Mathew WIGFIELD
    Daughter, Rachel HORNER - Negro man James, free after 3 years
    Granddaughter, Mary WATTERS ¦¦ Sons, Nathan & Nicholas HORNER
Ex: (None named)
Wt: William BAKER; Stephen WATTERS

AJ-2-327    John HANSON                  28 Feb 1799/ 6 Apr 1799
To: Nephew, Thomas COLE, now a minor under my care - lands willed
       to me by my father John HANSON
    Nephews, Jonas COURTNEY, John HANSON, son of Hollis HANSON &
       John Hanson OSBORN
    Nephew, Benjamin HANSON, son of Hollis - house & lot bought of
       Benjamin Osborn HOLLIS
    William OSBORN of James ¦¦ Hanson COURTNEY of Thomas
    Semelia LANCASTER, a minor under my care - Negro girl Fan
    John DONOVAN, who now lives with me
    Sister, Semelia, wife of James OSBORN, her present husband -
       land on E side of Rumney Creek bought of Jacob FORWARD Esq.;
    Negroes bought of James OSBORN
```

```
         James OSBORN, son of James || Benjamin OSBORN, Junr.
         Children of my 3 sisters, Samelia LANCASTER, Sarah & Elizabeth
Ex: Nephew, Jonas COURTNEY
Wt: George CHAUNCEY; Amos HOLLIS; William POWELL
```

                                    Codicil: 1 Mar 1799/ 6 Apr 1799
To: Negroes bought of James OSBORN - to return to him should he
      survive his present enthralments
Wt: James COLE; Alexander FLANAGAN

AJ-2-331   **John HUGHSTON**   3 Oct 1784/ 23 Oct 1784
To: Mother, Jane HUGHSTON - lot 14 in town of Joppa
    Son, Thomas Waltham HUGHSTON || Daughter, Elizabeth HUGHSTON
    Children of my sister, Rebecca CAMPBELL in North Carrolina
    Negroes (names unspec.) - to be equally divided between my
      2 children
Ex: Robert DUTTON
Wt: Jacob BOND; Nathaniel STRONG; John DUTTON

AJ-2-333   **John JOHNSON**   15 Aug 1774/ 24 Oct 1774
To: Wife, Ann JOHNSON - tract *Johnson's Choice*, tract 50 a. *Margins
      Grove*, leased tract 23 1/2 a. *Walkers Desire*
    Son, Barnet JOHNSON
    Daughter, Sarah JOHNSON (under age 16)
    Son, James JOHNSON - tract on S side of Deer Creek
    Sons, John & Josiah JOHNSON - rem. lands N side of Deer Creek
      bargained for with Richard DEAVER
Ex: Wife, Ann JOHNSON
Wt: Thomas JOHNSON; James BRICE; William McDOUGH; Mary RENSHAW

AJ-2-335   **William JAMISON**   23 Jun 1767/ 12 Apr 1774
            ship carpenter of Baltimore Co.
To: Samuel & Elizabeth ROBERTS, youngest children of Peter ROBERTS
      & Arramenta his wife, late of Baltimore Co, deceased
    Negro Roger - freedom
Ex: William PRESBURY, brick layer
Wt: Thomas PRESBURY; William ROBINSON; Richard BENNETT

AJ-2-336   **Alice JOHNSON**   30 May 1774/ 16 Feb 1775
To: Daughter, Mary RENSHAW
    Two grandsons, Samuel & Joshua JOHNSON, surviving sons of my
      son William JOHNSON - tract 200 a. part of *Bond's Lot* willed
      by my father William BONDS (or BOND)
    Daughter-in-law, Rachel JOHNSON, widow of son William JOHNSON
    Granddaughter, Christian NORRISS
    Granddaughter, Sarah JOHNSON, daughter of son Thomas JOHNSON
    Three grandsons, Barnett, Thomas, & Robert JOHNSON, issues of
      son Barnett
    Granddaughters, Alice, Rachel, Hannah, & Mary JOHNSON, issues
      of son William
    Son William JOHNSON's 6 children (additional names unspec.)
    Sons, Thomas & John JOHNSON
Ex: (None named)
Wt: John LOVE; Edmund BULL; Job KEY; John WOODWARD

AJ-2-338   **Martha JEFFERY**   26 Jul 1776/ 12 Sep 1776
             widow of Thomas JEFFERY
To: Son, Samuel JEFFERY || Daughter, Jean THOMSON
     Sons, Hugh, Thomas, Alexander, & Robert JEFFERY
Ex: Robert BLACKBURN & Hugh JEFFREY
Wt: John McADOW; John LYNCH; Thomas ROWNTREE

AJ-2-340   **Abraham JARRETT**   (Undated)/ 4 Mar 1776
To: Eldest son, Jesse JARRETT - tract part of *Isles of Caperea*, 2
     adj. tracts *Jarrett's Fatigue* & *Elliots Refuse*
     Second son, Abraham JARRETT - tract 610 a. *Wild Cat Denu (Den
     ?)*, small tract *Johnson's Enlargement*, leasehold tracts
     Whitemarsh, *Ellinor's Choice*, *Wells Denu*, *Durbin's
     Beginning*, & *The String of Good Luck*
     Third son, Bennett JARRETT - tract *Buchanans Deer Park*, all my
     land on the provincial line & W end of *Wild Cat Denu*, tract
     70 a. in York Co. pur. of George BUCHANAN, tract 13 a. *Trap
     in York Co*, 2 tracts *Whitacres Delay* & *Daniels Land*, tract
     Blacksmiths Lot
     Fourth son, Eli JARRETT - leasehold tracts *John's Forest*,
     Road's Necessity & 2 adj. tracts purchased of his Lordship
     Commissioners, tract part of *Guyton's Addition*, tract near
     Blue Rocks, tract *Jacobs Delight*, land near Gunpowder Falls
     Youngest son, Elisha JARRETT - tract 138 a. on provincial line
     in York Co. purchased of Ephraim JOHNSON, leasehold tract
     Jacobs Mount & adj. tract, tract 60 a. *Deavers Goodwill*,
     tract 78 a. *Tarry's Choice*, & adj. tract purchased of his
     Lordship Commissioners, tract *Gordon's Meadows*, tract
     Parson's Lot & adj. tract 230 a.
     Daughters, Ellinor JARRETT - tracts *Branters Ridge* & *Sons
     Addition*, tract *Roches Choice*
     Daughter, Mary JARRETT - tract 186 a. *Fates Neighbor*, lot in
     Baltimore Town
     Five sons - 2 tracts 50 a. *Pearsons Outlet* & *Weatheralls Last
     Addition*, tract *Pattersons Regulation*, tract *Jarretsburg*,
     part of 2 tracts *Pattersons Chance* & *Standiford Meadows*,
     tract *Talbots Addition*
     Abraham WILLIAMS - tract 58 a. *Potees Industry*
     To be sold: tract 20 a. part of *Brookers Cross* with mill, tract
     54 a. *George & Josephs Farm*, tract 100 a. *Marys Delight*,
     tract 136 a. *Tricks & Things*, tract 3 1/4 a. *Bryerlys
     Refuse*, tract 27 a. *Abrahams Spot*, my part of the deserted
     lot & *Ellinors Choice*, tract 170 a. *Stoney Batter*, tract 36
     a. *Jarretts Discovery*, tract *Noth Wales*, tract 150 a. *Three
     Sisters*, tract 80 1/2 a. *Mow Meadow*, all other lands not
     specifically mentioned
     Trustees: Jesse BUSSEY, Dixon STANSBURY, Robert AMOS
Ex: Wife, Martha JARRETT; Son, Jesse JARRETT
Wt: Thomas BOND; Edmund STANSBURY; James BARTON; Thomas JAMES;
     Edward ROBINSON
AJ-2-344   **Richard JAMES**   27 Sep 1777/ 3 Nov 1777
To: Son, Sedgwick JAMES - estate in Sussex Co, Penn.
     My other children, Rachel, Mary, Sarah, Ester, Richard, Latis,
     Elizabeth, & John JAMES (all under age 21)
     Guardian: James BARNETT

Ex: Son, Sedgwick JAMES
Wt: Robert BRADLEY; James BARNET; John JACKSON

                                      Codicil: (undated)/ 3 Nov 1777
To: Children, Rachel LYNCH, Mary, Sarah, Ester, Richard, Latis,
    Elizabeth, & John JAMES

AJ-2-346   **Joseph JONES**   25 Nov 1777/ 26 Aug 1778
To: John & Hannah FORWOOD, husband & wife
    Grandson, Reubin JONES - dwelling plantation 58 a. part of
      Arabia Petra
    Daughter, Rachel JONES
Ex: John FORWOOD & Nathan RIGBIE
Wt: Joseph HOPKINS, Senr. - Quaker; William COX, Quaker; Joseph
    HOPKINS, Junr. - Quaker

                            Verbal codicil: (undated)/ 24 Jul 1780
To: Son, Obier JONES - gets nothing
Wt: Elizabeth SLACK; Mary IRONS

AJ-2-348   **Richard JOHNS**   9 Dec 1776/ 1 Dec 1780
To: Brother, Nathan JOHNS - half of my land with dwelling house;
    Negro Sarah
    Younger brother, Henry JOHNS - W most half of my land; Negroes
      Robert & Meriah his wife
    Kinsmen, James & Nathan RIGBIE - Negro man Thomas, Negro woman
      Affey, Negro men William, Mingoe, George, Tower, &
      Pollidore, Negro woman Polley & her son Jack & any future
      issue, Negro woman Dinah & her children Billie & Jack & any
      future issue
    Negroes Thomas, Affey, & William
Ex: Brothers, Nathan & Henry JOHNS
Wt: Thomas BOYLE; Bennett BARNES; William EVATT; Christopher PAGE

AJ-2-350   **John JOLLEY**, blacksmith   20 Jun 1781/ 6 Aug 1781
To: Wife, Elizabeth JOLLEY - 1/3 of my mansion plantation; Negroes
    Daniel, Will, Suck, & Judath & their issue
    Son, Edward JOLLEY - 2 tracts where John PENIX lives, my part
      of the Mills bought of David SWEENEY; Negro boy Joe, Negro
      Dampiere to be set free 18 months after my decease
    Son, William JOLLEY (under age 21) - tract 150 a. with mansion
      house, orchard & barn after his mother's death
    Son, John JOLLEY (under age 21) - tract 150 a.
    Daughter, Nancy JOLLEY (under age 16) - Negro girl Lint
    Daughter, Cassandra JOLLEY (under age 16) - Negro girl Hanna
    Daughter, Betsey JOLLEY (under age 16) - Negro girl Poll
    Daughter, Isabela JOLLEY (under age 16) - Negro girl Jane
    Daughter, Sally JOLLEY (under age 16) - Negro girl Beck
Ex: Wife, Elizabeth JOLLEY; Son, Edward JOLLEY
Wt: David SWEENEY, Junr.; Henry WATTERS; Christopher HALL

AJ-2-352   **Joseph JOHNSON**   3 Apr 1781/ 23 Aug 1781
To: Youngest son, Isaac JOHNSON - half of tract 90 a. *Mountain* on
    N side of Deer Creek between *Simmonses Choice* & said creek
    Daughter, Martha JOHNSON - other half of above land

```
        Eldest son, Thomas JOHNSON
        Daughters, Mary, Elizabeth, Ann, & Martha JOHNSON
    Ex: Son, Isaac JOHNSON; Daughter, Martha JOHNSON; William MORGAN
    Wt: Joseph WILSON, Junr.; William MORGAN; Christopher BENCHOOF;
        James CRAWFORD
```

AJ-2-354   **Walter JAMES**   19 Jul 1779/ 3 May 1782
```
    To: Wife, Cordelia JAMES
        Nephew, Nathaniell JAMES, son of Henry JAMES
        Nephew, Walter CROOK, son of Joseph CROOK
    Ex: Wife, Cordelia JAMES
    Wt: John DAY, son of Edward; Samual RICKETTS; Lambert WILMORE
```

AJ-2-356   **Robert JEFFRYS**   12 Apr 1782/ 16 May 1782
```
    To: Wife, Elizabeth JEFFRYS, & her daughter, Elizabeth COWEN -
            tract where I now live
        My boy, Daniel HARE
    Ex: Wife, Elizabeth JEFFRYS
    Wt: William LUCKIE; William WILSON, Quaker; John STEPHENSON
```

AJ-2-357   **John Clark JENKENS** (or **JINKINS**) 11 Aug 1784/ 4 Dec 1784
```
    To: Henry WATERS - all my Negroes (names unspec.)
        Mother, Mary PEACOCK, wife of John PEACOCK
        Two sisters, Mary & Cassandra PEACOCK (both under age 21)
        Stepfather, John PEACOCK  ||  Freeborn BROWN
        Uncle, Francis JINKINS  ||  Uncle, Samuel JINKINS
        To be sold: tract Free Land's Mount on N side Deer Creek
    Ex: Henry WATTERS; William ALLINDER
    Wt: Joseph ROGERS; John McLAUGHLIN; Josiah LEE
```

AJ-2-359   **Archibald JOHNSON**   18 Jun 1784/ 23 Jun 1785
```
    To: Sons, John, Joseph, & Archibald JOHNSON
        Daughters, Mary BECK & Ann JOHNSON
        Sons, Adam & Thomas JOHNSON
        Non-beneficiary: Norris LESTER
    Ex: (None named)
    Wt: John RUFF; Francis Lovill (Lovitt ?) PITT; George DREW
```

AJ-2-360   **John JAMES**, yeoman   25 Jan 1788/ 31 Jan 1792
```
    To: Sister, Mary THOMAS
        Nephew, Jesse LEWIS - all land I now hold
    Ex: Nephew, Jesse LEWIS
    Wt: Robert MORGAN; William PRIGG; Edward PRIGG
```

AJ-2-362   **Mary JOHNSTON**   13 Mar 1793/ 16 Apr 1793
```
    To: Elizabeth WHITAKER, daughter of John S. WHITAKER
        Rachel WHITAKER, daughter of John S. WHITAKER
        Sister, Rachel WHITAKER, wife of John S. WHITAKER
    Ex: John S. WHITAKER
    Wt: Susanna NORRIS; Elizabeth GAWTHROUP; John NORRIS
```

AJ-2-363   **Benjamin JONES**   8 Oct 1794/ 21 Nov 1794
```
    To: Wife, Sarah JONES - 1/3 of all lands with house & apple orchard
        Son, Stephen JONES
        Sons, Benjamin, & Charles JONES - rem. of lands, half to each
```

Daughters, Sarrah WRIGHT, Rachel JONES, Francis JONES,
  Elizabeth BRINLEY, & Rebeckah JONES
Ex: Sons, Benjamin & Charles JONES
Wt: Aquila JONES; Matthew MORRISSON; William MONTGOMERY

AJ-2-364 **Eli JARRETT**   1 Dec 1793/ 11 Feb 1794
To: Brother Jesse JARRETT's children (names unspec.)
    Sister Eleanor THOMAS's children (names unspec.)
    Sister Polly LEWIS' children (names unspec.)
    Brother Bennett JARRETT's daughter, Emeline JARRETT - all my
      lands lying about the Upper Cross Road
    Brothers, Jesse, Abraham, Bennett, & Elsha JARRETT
    Sisters, Eleanor THOMAS, & Mary LEWIS
Ex: Brothers, Abraham & Bennett JARRETT
Wt: James BARTON; Thomas COX; Edward B. BUSSEY

AJ-2-366 **Moses JOHNSON**   6 Jul 1796/ 13 Dec 1796
To: Wife, Priscilla JOHNSON ¦¦ John & Ann PARKER, my daughter
    Children, Tabitha, Thomas, William, Priscilla, & Moses JOHNSON,
      Junr.
    Son-in-law, Samuel FRAZIER, & my daughter, his wife, Penelone
Ex: Wife, Priscilla JOHNSON; Son, Thomas JOHNSON
Wt: David JOHNSON; Melchesedec JOHNSON; John TILBROOK

AJ-2-368 **Stephen JAY**   28 Mar 1796/ 10 May 1796
To: Son, Thomas JAY - tract 50 a. part of the estate I live on at
      mouth of Spring Branch near Negro Joe's cabin running E
    Children, Elizabeth, Joseph, & Martha JAY - rem. of said tract
    Daughter, Hannah THOMPSON ¦¦ Son, Samuel JAY
    Negroes, Ceaser & Ben - freedom one month after my decease
    Negroes, Elisha & Paris - freedom at age 21
    Negro, Harriott - freedom at age 18
Ex: Son, Samuel JAY
Wt: John DALLAM; Joseph MILLER; Peter WILSON

AJ-2-369 **James KIMBLE**   5 Dec 1779/ 19 Feb 1780
To: Francis KIMBLE - tract 255 a. *Purgetary*; Negro Fill, Negro Jane
      & all her children, Negro Cas (a child of Negro Judgeth),
      Negro Darke (a child of Negro Judgath)
    Sarah KIMBLE, daughter of Francis KIMBLE - tract *Kimbles Debble
      Purchis* bought of Stephen KIMBLE, tract *No Name*, tract part
      of *Kimble Addition*; Negro Will (a child of Negro Judgath),
      Negro Marget (child of Negro Judgath), Negro Peton, the
      child that Negro Judgath is now with, Negro Moll (child of
      Negro Judgath), all the children that Negro Hagor may have,
      & the child that Negro Hagor has now asucking; Sebaboye
Ex: Francis KIMBLE; John Lee WEBSTER
Wt: Greenberry DORSEY; Freeborn GARRETTSON; Norris LESTER

AJ-2-371 **Stephen KIMBLE**   28 Jul 1780/ 17 Jun 1784
To: My sons & my daughters (names unspec.)
Ex: (None named)
Wt: Robert TAYLOR; Giles KIMBLE; Amasa TAYLOR; Asa TAYLOR

1784 - Verified by Margaret KIMBLE

AJ-2-371   **John KIDD**   10 Jul 1779/ 20 Jul 1782
To: Sons, James & Hennery KIDD - all my lands & tenements
    Sons, William, John, & Joshua KIDD ¦¦ Daughter, Rebekah KIDD
    Daughter, Elizabeth, wife to John WEIR
Ex: Sons, James & Hennery KIDD
Wt: Hugh WILSON; Joseph McCLASKEY; John CHANCE

AJ-2-373   **Robert KENNEDY** (or **KENADY**)   28 Feb 1780/ 8 Sep 1783
To: Son, William KENNEDY; Wife, Hannah KENNEDY
    Eldest daughter, Elizabeth JONES
    Second daughter, Margaret McCOMAS
    Three youngest daughters, Ann, Hannah, & Mary KENNEDY
Ex: Wife, Hannah KENNEDY
Wt: Alexander RIGDON; William CUNNUM (or CANNON); William CASH

8 Sep 1783 - Widow quit her claim & elected her dower or 1/3.

AJ-2-374   **Nicholas KRUSON** (or **KROSON**)   7 May 1785/ 12 Dec 1776
To: Son, Richard KENNEDY - tract 200 a. bought of Richard KEEN on
    S side of Deer Creek, tract 50 a. *Cedar Swamp* in West Jersey
    Son, John KENNEDY - all rem. land I live on, approx. 240 a.
    Granddaughter, Mary KRUSON, daughter of son Garrett KRUSON,
        deceased
    Grandson, John KRUSON, son of son Garrett KRUSON, deceased -
        tract 150 a. on N side of Deer Creek pur. of Joseph RENSHAW
Ex: Mayor Samuel SMITH; Granddaughter, Mary KRUSON
Wt: George VANDERGRIFTE; William MARTIN; Daniel KENLY

AJ-2-376   **Thomas KELL**, mariner   5 Apr 1786/ 9 Nov 1790
To: Wife, Alisanna KELL
    Nine children, Pamela, John, Thomas, Isaac, William, Nathan,
        Alisanna, Elizabeth, & Anna KELL & child my wife is now
        pregnant with
Ex: Wife, Alisanna KELL; Sons, John & Thomas KELL
Wt: Richard JOHNS; Margaret CONN; Susanna JOHNS; Grace BRABZON

AJ-2-378   **Samuel LOCKHARD**   30 Oct 1770/ 17 Apr 1791
    of Baltimore Co.
To: Daughter, Sarah LOCKHARD - tract 100 a. part of *Abraham's
    Inheritance* bought of Abe RENSHAW on the draught of Broad
    Creek in Baltimore Co. adj. Richard JAMES & Robert LYONS
    Five grandchildren, Samuel, Martha, Jane, William, & John
        CROSEN
    Daughter, Elizabeth (CROSEN ?) (nee LOCKHARD) - tract 100 a.
        part of above
    Brother's son, Samuel LOCKHARD ¦¦ Wife, Martha LOCKHARD
Ex: Brother, Frances LOCKHARD
Wt: Nicholas ORRICK; Francis LOCKHARD; William WEIR

AJ-2-379   **Alexander KELLY**   28 Jan 1794/ 6 Nov 1794
To: Daughter, Martha GORRELL - plantation 50 a. part of *Knight's
    Increase* on the draft of Deer Creek
    Son-in-law, James GORRELL ¦¦ Son, Robert KELLY
    Daughters, Jane HALL, Elizabeth GORRELL, Ann GORRELL, & Rachel
        Hambleton SMITH

Non-beneficiary: son, Andrew KELLT, deceased
Ex: James GORRELL; Martha GORRELL
Wt: William COX; William HANNA; Abraham TAYLOR

AJ-2-381   **Rachel KITELY**   1 Jul 1799/ 21 Dec 1799
To: Negroes Bob, Darkey, Philis, Isaac, Freeborn, Jack, Hannah,
      Sam, & Jim - free at my decease
    Niece, Rachel MURPHY
    Negro girl Louisa - free at my decease
Ex: Henry MURPHY
Wt: Daniel GILDEA (or GILDER); Christian WASKEY

AJ-2-382   **John LUSBY**   25 Mar 1775/ 22 May 1775
To: Four sisters, Elizabeth, Susanna, Milcah, & Sarah (nee LUSBY)
      - Negro Limry, the blacksmith
    My sister's son, James PRESTON
Ex: (None named)
Wt: Clothworthy CUNNINGHAM; George BELL

22 May 1775 - Four sisters requested for Amos GARRETT to be
      appointed administrator of John LUSBY's will as they
      were unqualified.

AJ-2-384   **James LEE, Sen.**, of Deer Creek 26 Aug 1776/ 1 Dec 1778
To: Son, James LEE, (Jun) - tract 214 a. part of *Isaac's
      Inheritance* now called *Isaac's Double Purchase*
    Son, Samuel LEE - tract 200 a. part of *Isaac's Inheritance*
    Son, Josiah LEE - tract 259 a. *Planters Paradise* with addition
      of 10 a. part of *Freelands Mount*, alias *Mountain* pur. of
      Thomas JOHNSON, tract 200 a. part of *Simmonds Choice* I live
      on, with adj. 50 a. *Dooleys Mistake*
    Grandson, James LEE, son of Samuel LEE - tract 10 a. part of
      Simmonds Choice & *Dooleys Mistake*; Negro boy Sam
    Granddaughter, Mary LEE, daughter of Samuel LEE
    Daughter, Cassandra, wife of William MORGAN - 4 Negroes, Nan,
      Kater, Hannah, & Jerry
    Daughter, Mary WILSON, wife of Samuel WILSON - 3 Negroes, Cloe,
      Dinah, & Natt
    Granddaughter, Elizabeth VANCLEAF - Negro girl Jenny
    Granddaughter, Mary VANCLEAVE - Negroe girl Bett
    Grandson, William WEBB, son of William WEBB - Negro boy Tower
    Granddaughter, Margeret Lee WEBB - Negro girl Sophia
    Granddaughter, Constance Priscilla WEBB - Negro girl Moll
    Wife, Elizabeth LEE - Negro man Duke for 4 years & then to be
      set free; Negro woman Hagar & Negro man Forest, his wife
      Dutchess, Negro man Nan, house wenches Lamer, Mariah, &
      Rachael
Ex: Wife, Elizabeth LEE; Brother-in-law, William WILSON
Wt: John WILSON, Quaker; William WELLS; James PACA

AJ-2-388   **John LYNCH**   2 Apr 1777/ 1 Jul 1777
To: Wife, Mary LYNCH; Sons, Anthony, & John LYNCH
Ex: Wife, Mary LYNCH
Wt: John McADOW; Richard WILMOTT; Alexander CRAWFORD

AJ-2-389   **Jonathan LYON**   20 May 1784/ 8 Jun 1784
To: Sons, John, Jonathan, Elijah, & Leonard LYON
    Daughter Casandra LYON - Negro girl Dinah & her incr.
    Daughters, Martha, Sarah, Nancy, Easter, & Mary LYON - Negroes
       Nell, Lanney, Jacob, Ned, & Jim
    William ERWIN
    Daughter, Susannah BRIARLY, wife of George BRIARLY
    Negro Sam - choice of masters among eleven children
Ex: Josiah HITCHCOCK; John LYON
Wt: Josiah HITCHCOCK; Sarah STEWART; Dedlia (or Cordelia)
    HITCHCOCK; Ann CONDRON

AJ-2-391   **Thomas LINGAN**   16 Feb 1781/ 22 May 1781
To: Son, Thomas LINGAN - Negro woman Pegg
    Son, James McCubbin LINGAN - Negro man Nessey
    Son, Nicholas LINGAN - Negro man Andrew
    Three sons - tracts of fathers land in Calvert Co. *Batchelars
       Quarter* & *Lingans Adventure* now in possesion of the
       WILLIAMSONs, all land in Baltimore Co. that I may have claim
    Daughters, Mary PRESBURY, Susanna LINGAN, Ann McCUBBIN,
       Elizabeth LINGAN, & Martha LINGAN
Ex: Son, James McCubbin LINGAN
Wt: Benjamin BOYCE; John BOYCE; Alexander COWAN

AJ-2-393   **Elizabeth LUSBY**   Verbal: 6 Nov 1781/ 10 Nov 1781
To: Susannah THOMPSON || James PRESTON
    Daughter, Susannah (nee LUSBY) - Negro Tom
    Daughter, Sarah (nee LUSBY)
    Four daughters, (other two names unspec.)
    Negroes, Jack & Hector - free
Ex: (None named)
Wt: Elizabeth SAUNDERS; Hannah KITELY

AJ-2-394   **Elizabeth LYTTLE (or LIGHTL)**   __ Nov 1784/ 9 Dec 1784
To: Son, Daniel RUFF - tract *Second Adventure* on N side of Deer
       Creek; Negro lad Sam for 12 years & then set free; Negro
       woman Hager for 8 years & then set free
    Son, John RUFF - tract *Second Long*, alias *Oblong* on N side of
       Deer Creek; Negro Easter (or Ester) for 8 years & then set
       free
    Son, James LYTTLE - 2 Negroes, Lemon & Harry
    Son, Nathan LYTTLE - Negro child Mettway
    Son, Jacob LYTTLE - Negro boy George
    Negro Jerry to be hired out for 8 years & then set free
    Daughter, Hannah LYTTLE - Negro girl Han, & Negro boy Tom
    Daughter, Ann LYTTLE
Ex: Son, Jacob LYTTLE
Wt: Josiah SMITH; Peregrine BROWN; Richard MONK

AJ-2-396   **James LEE**   4 Apr 1786/ 31 May 1786
To: Wife, Milca LEE, who may be with child
    My sisters (names unspec.) || My children (names unspec.)
Ex: Wife, Milca LEE; Parker Hall LEE; Roger MATHEWS
Wt: Augustin BAYLES; Corbin LEE; Bennet MATHEWS of John; Jacob
    FORWOOD

13 Jun 1786 - Roger MATHEWS & Parker Hall LEE renounced
           executorship.

AJ-2-397   **Elizabeth LEGO**, widow of Joppa   1 Sep 1786/ 6 Mar 1787
To: Eldest daughter, Alice LEGO ¦¦ Daughter, Mary LEGO
    Sister, Ann JERVIS ¦¦ Col. Richard GRAVES
Ex: Samuel Groom OSBORN, Esq.
Wt: Lucina ALLINDER; John HAY; Benjamin FRENCH

6 Mar 1787 - Samuel Groom OSBORN renounced executorship.

AJ-2-399   **John LATIMORE** (or **LETIMORE**)   10 Jan 1777/ 10 May 1790
To: Sister, Mary DEYERMID & her daughter Catharine
Ex: Thomas BLEANY
Wt: Thomas BLEANY; John DARMOT (or DEARMOTT)

AJ-2-400   **Samuel LEE**   7 Jan 1790/ 4 Dec 1798
To: Wife, Mary LEE ¦¦ Sons, John, Thomas, & Samuel LEE
    Daughters, Sarah SCOTT, Mary & Rachel LEE
Ex: Wife, Mary LEE; Son, John LEE
Wt: John MASON; Nathan BAY; Ann MASON

AJ-2-401   **Milcah LUSBY**   21 Dec 1790/ 28 Oct 1791
To: Negro Rachel - free from date of my death
    Negro Santy, age 13 - remain slave until age 30
    Negroes Grace & Murrier - serve until age 35
    Two sisters, Sarah & Susannah LUSBY
Ex: Sister, Susannah LUSBY
Wt: Isaac WEBSTER, Junr.; John HARGROVE; Margret TRULOCK

AJ-2-402   **John LITTEN**   4 Jun 1785/ 9 Apr 1793
To: Daughter, Mary ELY
    John ELY, son of Mary ELY
    Wife, Elizabeth LITTEN
    Boy, William JAMES
    Wife's son, John RICHEY - tract 34 a.
    Daughter, Hannah LITTEN
Ex: Daughter, Hannah LITTEN
Wt: Stephen NORTON; Robert MORGAN; John COOK

AJ-2-404   **John LOVE**   27 Mar 1793/ 16 Apr 1793
To: All my children (names unspec.) - balance of land divided
    Daughter, Sarah BULL, wife of Jacob BULL
    Ann MOORE, widow of James MOORE, deceased - house & lot in
      Bellair
    To be sold: land pur. for me by John STUMP, one moiety of land
      on Susquehanna River held with heirs of Thomas SMITH,
      deceased, one moiety of land held with John BARCLAY Esq.
Ex: Col. Ignatius WHEELER; David CLARK; Walter BILLINGSLEA, Junr.
Wt: John ARCHER; Walter BULL; James PRESTON

7 May 1793 - Margaret LOVE, widow of John LOVE, claimed her dower
             or 1/3.

AJ-2-407   **Deborah LEE**   24 Apr 1794/ 19 Aug 1793
To: Nephew, William SAUNDERS
    Ann WILLITS ¦¦ Cassandra WILLITS ¦¦ Nathan RIGBIE
Ex: Samuel WILLITS
Wt: Sarah COX; Peter WILLIAMS; Rachel DIXON

AJ-2-408   **Henry LAMMOT**   5 Jan 1798/ 23 May 1798
To: Wife, Barbara LAMMOT - plantation & land in Baltimore Co.
    Sons, John, Joshua, Jacob, & Henry LAMMOT
    Daughter, Mary WALKER
Ex: Christian HOOFMAN; Son, Jacob LAMMOT
Wt: Christian HOOFMAN; William PERRY; Peter HOOFMAN (or HOOPMAN)

AJ-2-411   **Edward MORGAN**, of Deer Creek   6 Jun 1775/ 28 Jun 1775
To: Son, Samuel MORGAN - Negro lad Hector
    Daughter, Martha PRIGG - Negro man George
    Daughter, Elizabeth LYON
    Son, William MORGAN - tract 170 a. *Arabia Petra* adj. the
        Chapple bought of Robert DUNN; Negro boy Benjamin
    Daughters, Elizabeth & Susanah MORGAN
    Mary WILES, daughter of Sarah WILES which was formerly her
        maiden name
    Granddaughter, Mary PRIGG
    Wife, Elizabeth MORGAN - Negroes James, Priscilla, & Hagar
    Son, Robert MORGAN - plantation with land bought of William
        TILLARD; Negroes Michael & Jane
Ex: Robert MORGAN
Wt: John WILLSON; Josiah LEE; William WELLS

AJ-2-413   **Richard MORRIS**, planter   18 Jul 1775/ 18 Nov 1777
To: Son, Thomas MORRIS ¦¦ Wife, Jane MORRIS
    Daughters, Elizabeth GRANT, Sarah YOUNG, & Mary YOAKLEY
    Sons, Richard, Edward, Michael, John, & William MORRIS
    Three youngest children, Giles, Susannah, & Frances MORRIS
Ex: Wife, Jane MORRIS
Wt: Frances HOLLAND; James TAYLOR; John PERRY

AJ-2-414   **James McNAIR**   1 Sep 1776/ 4 Aug 1778
To: Three sisters, Jennet, Jane, & Elizabeth McNAIR, now living in
        Shire of Argiule, Great Britain
    Two brothers, John, & Archenbald McNAIR
    James MITCHEL
Ex: James CLERK; John DONAHAY
Wt: John DONAHEY; Anne DONAHEY

AJ-2-415   **Benjamin McCOMAS**   4 Sep 1778/ 16 Oct 1778
To: Brother, John McCOMAS
Ex: John McCOMAS, son of William
Wt: Aquilla PACA; Abraham NORRISS, Junr.; Francis DALLAM

AJ-2-416   **James McCRACKEN** (or McCRACKIN) 27 May 1777/ 29 Oct 1778
To: Wife, Mary McCRACKEN
    Nephews, John, James, & David McCRACKEN, sons of brother John
        McCRACKEN
    Nephew, James THOMPSON, son of my sister (name unspec.)

        Natural daughter, Elizabeth (under age 16), begotten upon the
            body of one Elizabeth VANSCYKLE
        Trustee - Amos GARRETT
Ex: Levin MATHEWS; Gerge LITTLE
Wt: Isaac GRIEST; Micajah JAMES; William SPENCER

(undated) - Mary McCRACKEN, widow, refused standing to this will.

AJ-2-418   **Edward MITCHELL, Sen.**   1 Apr 1779/ 22 May 1779
To: Son, Micajah MITCHELL - tract part of *Hughes Choice*, tract part
        of *Eyetrap* bought of Reuben PERKINS joining the River
        Susquehanna
    Son, Aquila MITCHELL - part of 2 tracts *Royal Exchange &
        Paradise*, land pur. of Thomas GILBERT
    Son, Winston MITCHELL - part of 3 tracts *Gravilly Bottom, Wood
        Close, & Cook's Rest*
    Daughter, Ann MITCHELL - part of 2 tracts *Treble Union &
        Eyetrap* not already given away; Negro girl named Cassy
    Daughter, Martha MITCHELL - part of 2 tracts *Betties Lot &
        Derbius Chance*; mulatto boy named Jonas
    Wife, (name unspec.) - mulatto woman named Mary
Ex: Brother, William MITCHELL; Son, Micajah MITCHELL
Wt: George GOODWIN; William PORTER

AJ-2-420   **John MILES**   20 Jun 1779/ 9 Aug 1779
To: Son, Thomas, John, Isuck, James, & Peter MILES
    Daughters, Sarah & Elizabeth MILES ¦¦ Cashandrow MILES
    Wife, Jene MILES - 2 tracts *Miles Beginen & Miles Addition*
Ex: (None named)
Wt: Robert KENNEDY; Joseph GIBBENS

AJ-2-421   **Robert McCLURE**   4 May 1779/ 31 Mar 1780
To: Brothers, Francis & Richard McCLURE, Donegal Co. in Ireland
Ex: John ARCHER
Wt: Mathew McCLINTOKE; John STEPHENSON

AJ-2-422   **Thomas MITCHELL**   5 Apr 1782/ 1 May 1782
To: Wife, Hannah MITCHELL ¦¦ Son, Kent MITCHELL
    Daughter, Mary MITCHELL - dwelling place after my wife's death
    Daughters, Martha & Elizabeth MITCHELL - all land I now possess
    Negro man, Bob - set free after wife's decease
    Grandson, Edward GUYTON, son of Joshua GUYTON
Ex: Wife, Hannah MITCHELL
Wt: Daniel DONOVAN, Sen.; James COLE; William BOSLEY

AJ-2-424   **Solomon McCOMAS**   20 Aug 1781/ 10 Dec 1781
To: Son, William McCOMAS - tract part of *Anns Dowry* with my
        dwelling house on W side of Bynams Run
    Son, Aaron McCOMAS - tract part of *Anns Dowry* on E side of
        Bynam's Run
Ex: Wife, Ann McCOMAS; Son, William McCOMAS
Wt: Daniel MACCOMAS; James MORRISON; James LEACH

                            Codicil: 4 Sep 1781/ 10 Dec 1781
To: Sons, William & Aaron McCOMAS ¦¦ Wife (name unspec.)

  Two daughters, Mary & Hannah McCOMAS
Wt: Daniel MACCOMAS; James MORRISON

10 Dec 1781 - Widow renounced bequests & chose her dower.

AJ-2-426 **James MAXWELL**   30 Jun 1780/ 19 Mar 1782
To: Brother, Moses MAXWELL - half of lands & tenements adj. the
  plantation of John DAY
  Brother, Jacob MAXWELL - rem. half of lands
  Sisters, Phebe MAXWELL, Elizabeth MAXWELL, & Ann DORSEY
  Nephew, James MAXWELL, son of Ann DORSEY - Negroes Prince, Nat,
   & Sal & her issue
  Niece, Frances DORSEY, daughter of Ann DORSEY - Negroes Beck
   & Patt & their issue
Ex: Benedict Edward HALL; John Beale HOWARD
Wt: Aquilla HALL; Ashberry CORD; Aquilla GARRETTSON

AJ-2-428 **John MATHEWS**, gentleman 16 Jun 1783/ 3 Dec 1783
To: Son, Roger MATHEWS - tracts part of *Mathews Enlargement* &
  Covent Garden containing my dwelling, bond for land from
  John HANSON (1769)
  Son, Bennett MATHEWS - rem. parts of *Mathews Enlargement* &
   Covent Garden, bond for land from Richard DALLAM (1775)
  Sons, Josias, Carvil, & James MATHEWS
  Wife (name unspec.) || Half brother, Capt. Bennett MATHEWS
  Daughters, Rebecca, Mary, Hannah, Milcah, Neomy, & Frances
   MATHEWS
  To be sold: tract *Shipping Dock* on Bush River
Ex: Wife, (name unspec.); Son, Roger MATHEWS
Wt: Benedict Edward HALL; Michael GILBERT, Junr.; William LESTER

AJ-2-431 **Daniel McCOMASS**   15 Jul 1785/ 9 Sep 1785
To: Two children, Elizabeth McCOMASS, & Daniel McCOMASS
  Wife, Elizabeth McCOMASS
Ex: Father, William McCOMASS
Wt: John COX; Isaac PARSONS; Frederick McCOMASS

AJ-2-432 **Thomas MONTGOMERY**, planter 19 Jun 1782/ 20 Dec 1785
To: Daughters, Elizabeth WEBB & Jane SMITH
  Two granddaughters, Margaret & Martha MONTGOMERY
  Two sons, Thomas & James MONTGOMERY - plantation & dwelling on
   Brices Endeavor
Ex: Sons, Thomas & James MONTGOMERY
Wt: Bartholomew CANNEL (or CONNEL); James McGEAUGH; Hugh BANKHEAD

AJ-2-434 **Jane MILES**   16 Jun 1785/ 4 Feb 1786
To: Daughter, Cassandra MILES || Sons, Isaac & James MILES
  Trustee: Alexander RIGDON || To be sold: land
Ex: (None named)
Wt: Benjamin McCRERY; Margeret WILSON

AJ-2-435 **Patrick McGACLIN** 30 Jul 1785/ 5 May 1786
To: Wife, Ceartrin McGACLIN
  John GRUDER, son of Jacob GRUDER of Lancaster Co, Pennsylvania
Ex: George PATTERSON of Harford Co.
Wt: Daniel MORRISON; James MORRISON

AJ-2-436 James MATHER 6 Jan 1785/ 22 Jun 1786
To: Wife, Joanna MATHER - Negro woman Jane
    Son, Michael MATHER - all my real estate after my wife's death;
        Negro boy Peter
    Daughters, Joanna MATHER & Mary RUFF
Ex: Wife, Joanna MATHER; Son, Michael MATHER
Wt: Michael GILBERT, Junr.; George YOUNG; John BULL

AJ-2-438 Martha McCOMAS 13 Oct 1785/ 16 Oct 1786
To: Granddaughter, Delilah CARROLL
    Daughter, Elizabeth McCOMAS - Negro Liddy & her issue
    Daughter, Sarah BRADFORD - Negro Phillis & her issue
    Daughter, Martha AMOS - Negro Sam
    Daughter, Hannah McCOMAS - Negro Jacob
    Grandson, James McCOMAS, son of my son John
    Negro man Samson - free
    My 8 children (additional names unspec.)
Ex: Robert AMOS, Esq.
Wt: David STANDIFORD; Thomas THOMAS; Daniel MACCOMAS

AJ-2-439 Sarah McCARTIE _____ 1787/ 5 Sep 1787
To: Son, Jacob Giles McCARTIE - tract 100 a. part of *Robinhoods
    Forrest* now known as *William & Sarah's Inheritance*, tract
    18 a. *Knavery Prevented*
Ex: (None named)
Wt: Solomon ARMSTRONG; Ford ARMSTRONG; James REDEN

AJ-2-440 Benjamin MEAD 20 Nov 1787/ 2 Jan 1788
To: Daughter, Mary MURPHY - Negro girl Rachel about 13 years, &
        Negro girl Hagar about 2 years
    Son, Benjamin MEAD - Negro boy Dennis, Negro girl Hannah & her
        incr.
    Son, Edward MEAD - Negro boy George, girl Grace & her incr.
    Wife, Elizabeth MEAD, called by some prejudice persons
        Elizabeth PARKS - Negro woman Daphne & her incr.
    Guardian of son Benjamin: Samuel LYNCH of Kent Co.
    Brother, William MEAD
Ex: Wife, Elizabeth MEAD
Wt: Moses MAXWELL; Jacob MAXWELL; William SAVORY

AJ-2-443 James MURPHY 5 Aug 1788/ 28 Oct 1788
To: Daughters, Rose, Allice, & Elizabeth MURPHY
    Sons, John & James MURPHY || Wife, Elizabeth MURPHY
    Son, Francis MURPHY || Mother, Rose MURPHY
    Non-beneficiary: Daniel CARTER; Benjamin Bradford NORRIS, Esq.
        - attorney for ex.
Ex: Wife, Elizabeth MURPHY; Son, Francis MURPHY
Wt: Archa HEAPS; James McGREAUGH; Patrick DORAN

AJ-2-444 Bennett MATHEWS of Rumney Neck 27 Sep 1790/ 21 Nov 1790
To: Brother, Joseph MATHEWS - land left by my father; Negroes Ned
        & Amey
    Brother, Carvel MATHEWS - Negroes Aron & Tom
    Brother, Roger MATHEWS; Sisters, Fanny & Neomy MATHEWS

Ex: Brother, Roger MATHEWS
Wt: Leven MATHEWS; Cyrus OSBORN; George CHAUNCEY, Junr.

AJ-2-446   **Margaret MILES**   12 Nov 1790/ 14 Dec 1790
To: Sons, Joshua & Aquila MILES - tract where I live
    Also to son Joshua MILES - tract 40 a. adj. where I live next
        to William NORRIS
    Also to son Aquila MILES - tract 20 a. adj. where I live next
        to Jesse JARRETT
    Son, Thomas MILES || Daughter, Elizabeth HUGHS
    Daughter, Eleanor HUTCHINS - Negro woman Mary
    Grandson, William AMOS
    Daughters, Catharine ROBINSON, Mary AMOS, & Margaret ROBINSON
Ex: Sons, Joshua & Aquila MILES
Wt: Richard BIDDLE; Cornelius GARRISON; John GUYON

AJ-2-448   **Thomas MILLS**   15 Apr 1788/ 3 Jan 1791
To: Wife, Mary MILLS
Ex: (None named)
Wt: Richard CLERKE; William WILSON; Joseph SAUNDERS

AJ-2-449   **James McCOMAS**   17 Feb 1791/ 5 Mar 1791
To: Son, Nathaniel McCOMAS - tract *Osborns Lot*, tract *Littleton*
    Son, Josias McCOMAS - tract part of *Greshams College*
    Son, James McCOMAS - tract rem. part of *Greshams College*
    Wife, Elizabeth McCOMAS
    Six daughters, Martha, Elizabeth, Susannah, Sarah, Charilotte,
        & Mary McCOMAS
    Mentioned: Sawmill in partnership with Daniel McCOMAS
Ex: Brothers, William & John McCOMAS
Wt: Charles ALLEN; William WILSON; Aaron McCOMAS, Junr.

AJ-2-451   **Patrick McCLASKEY**   Verbal: 16 Jun 1791/ 10 Aug 1791
To: Betsy DURHAM
Ex: (None named)
Wt: Elizabeth DURHAM, Senr.; Selah DURHAM; Cynthia THOMPSON;
    Ann DURHAM; Robert MONEY

Recording note: McCLASKEY was tutor at Abingdon College. He died
on June 18, 1791.
Verified: Charles TAIT - I saw McCLASKEY at Capt. THOMPSON's on the
Tuesday before he died.

AJ-2-454   **Hannah McCOMAS**   18 Jun 1792/ 23 Sep 1796
To: Daughter, Martha GOUGH || Granddaughter, Hannah GOUGH
    Daughter, Susanna McCOMAS || Grandson, Zachius McCOMAS
    Daughter, Hannah ONION - Negro girl Julett
    Daughter, Elizabeth ONION - Mulatto girl Miriah
    Daughter, Charity ONION - Negro woman Amy, Negro man London,
        blacksmith
    Husband, William McCOMAS - Negro boy George
    Negro Samson & his wife Jenny - to be manumitted by husband
    Son, Stephen ONION
    Grandson, Thomas ONION of Stephen ONION - Negro boy Joe
    Sons, Thomas Bond ONION, John Barrett ONION, Zachius ONION,

William Francis Heath ONION, & Corbin ONION
Negro Jack the foreman & his wife Lisa - freedom
Negro Sall & Jem my waiting man - freedom
Ex: (None named)
Wt: Thomas BOND; Peggy BOND; Sally BOND

AJ-2-457 **Arthur McCORD**   31 Dec 1792/ 26 Feb 1793
To: Wife, Ann McCORD ¦¦ Daughter, Ann McCORD
    James McKESSON (under age 21), son of Sarah McKESSON
Ex: Wife, Ann McCORD
Wt: Andrew SIMS; Thomas REED; George LUCKEY; Jacob DUNCAN

AJ-2-458 **Kent MITCHELL**   6 Jul 1793/ 27 Sep 1793
To: Grandsons, Parker William, & Kent MITCHELL, son of William
        MITCHELL - tracts *Royal Exchange Division* & *Gravelly Hills*
    Son, William MITCHELL
    Grandson, Edward MITCHELL, son of William - 2 tracts *Harmonds
        Addition* & *Shaws Hunting Ground*
    Son, James MITCHELL - Negro boy Isaac, to be free at age 25
    Daughter, Sarah MITCHELL ¦¦ Housekeeper, Ellenor ROBINSON
    William BREWER, boy that lives with me
    Daughter, Susanna MITCHELL - Negro girl named Sook
    Daughter, Sophia (nee MITCHELL)
    Granddaughters, Charlotte, Elizabeth, Sarah, Clemency, Mary,
        & Hannah (MITCHELL ?)
    To be sold: tract *Cowens Addition*; my land William PORTER now
        occupies
Ex: Sons, William & James MITCHELL
Wt: Gregory BARNES; Aquila MITCHELL; Mathew MOLTON; Micajah
    MITCHELL

AJ-2-460 **Moses McCOMAS**   24 Dec 1793/ 4 Nov 1794
To: Wife, Elizabeth McCOMAS - Negro woman Lydda
    Son, Daniel McCOMAS - half of my land with dwelling house;
        Negro boy Jim
    Son, Josiah Scott McCOMAS - rem. half of my land; Negro boy
        Andrew
    Daughter, Martha McCOMAS - Negro boy Jack
Ex: Wife, Elizabeth McCOMAS
Wt: Daniel MACCOMAS (or McCOMAS); William WILSON; John McCOMAS

AJ-2-462 **James McCOMAS**, son of Aquilla   8 Feb 1794/ 11 Mar 1794
To: Sons, Quilla, Amos, & James Preston McCOMAS - all my lands
    Daughters, Serah & Clemancy McCOMAS
Ex: Wife, Ann McCOMAS; Frederick AMOS; Brother, Alexander McCOMAS
Wt: William SLADE of Ezekiel; James HARPER; Pierse CREAGH

AJ-2-463 **William MORGAN** of Deer Creek   5 Nov 1795/ 23 Nov 1795
To: Daughter, Elizabeth CHEW - tract *New Stadt* pur. of Ralph SMITH
    Daughter, Sarah MORGAN - tract *Now Stadt* pur. of Samuel
        HAWKINS, adj. small field bought of Ralph SMITH
    Daughter, Cassandra MORGAN - tract mortgaged to Edward MORGAN
        by Robert DUNN, land bought of John MOORE of Kent Co.
    Son, Edward MORGAN - plantation where I dwell containing
        Simmons Choice, *Simmons Neglect*, *Addition to Simons Neglect*,

& *Freeland's Mount*, tract part of *Duleys Mistake*, tract *Planters Paradise*, tract part of *Freelands Mount*, tract part of *Arabia Petra* bought of James CALHOUN Esq., tract *Millers Attempt*, grist mill & saw mill

Daughter, Ellinor MORGAN - tract 100 a. part of *Freelands Mount*, tract 50 a. mortgaged from William ALLENDER, deceased, tract small part of *Arabia Petra*, tract 165 a. part of *Arabia Petra* bought of Samual JENKINS

Son, James L. MORGAN - tract *Paas Park*, tract 100 a. part of land bought of Richard DALLAM

Daughters, Mary MORGAN - tract 155 a. *Johnsons Chance*, tract 70 a. *Ashmores Retirement*, tract 21 a. *Griffies Delight*, tract 40 a. *The Meadow Ground*

Daughters, Martha & Margaret MORGAN - tracts *Elberton* & *The Sting*

Wife, Cassandra MORGAN

Grandson, William CHEW - house & lot in Abington bought of Alexander COOK

Negroes to have freedom at expiration of term starting 1 Jan 1796: London & Mary his wife - 10 years each; Priss - 21 years; Fainer - 25 years; Bett - 27 years; Bob - 30 years; Prina - 21 years; Rilla - 22 years; James - 26 years; Joseph - 28 years; Abraham & Jane - 10 years each; Hannah - 30 years; Patty - 21 years; Abraham - 26 years; Peggy - 27 years; Rebecka - 30 years; Ned & Frances - 12 years each; Dutches - 28 years; George - 30 years; Hannah - 12 years; Tower - 26 years; Ann - 28 years; Bill - 30 years; Cate - 15 years; Isaac - 20 years; Jerry - 13 years; Jack - 13 years; Mike - 26 years; Ben - 15 years; Sam - 24 years; Susanna - 20 years; Phillip & Hester his wife, they being advanced in years - to continue as slaves

Thomas & his wife (name unspec.), being advanced in years - to continue as slaves

Brother, Samuel MORGAN ¦¦ Edward PRIGG

To be sold: tract *Tralee*, tract 70 a. part of *Arabia Petra* bought of Aquila MASSEY, tract *Ann's Delight Enlarged*, all land I hold under Sheriffs Title, tract 50 a. on Broad Creek bought of Edward PRIGG

Ex: Robert MORGAN; Edward PRIGG
Wt: P. H. LEE; John BULL of Edmond; William PRIGG

Codicil:(undated)

To: Brother, Robert MORGAN - tract *Spittle Craft*
    Brother, Samuel MORGAN

AJ-2-469   **Milcah MATHEWS**   8 Mar 1795/ 20 Mar 1795
To: Daughter, Neomy MATHEWS - Negroes Jim, Ferreca, & Charles
    Son, Carvel MATHEWS - Negroes Edmond & George
    Daughter, Fanny MATHEWS - Negroes Jacob, Sam, & David
Non-beneficiary: Brother (or son ?), Roger MATHEWS
Ex: (None named)
Wt: Samuel W. FOWLER; William FRISBY

AJ-2-470   **Levin MATHEWS**   14 Feb 1795/ 17 Mar 1795
To: Sisters, Ann & Elizabeth MATHEWS - tract *Penny Come Quick* that

```
          I live on
          Cousin, Frances MATHEWS
     Ex:  Cousin, Roger MATHEWS
     Wt:  David CANE, Junr.; Nicholas GASSAWAY; Charlotte DAY
```

AJ-2-471   **Samuel McMATH**   12 Jun 1797/ 3 Oct 1797
To: Wife, Mary McMATH ¦¦ Daughter, Mary McMATH
Ex: William McMATH
Wt: Sarah McMATH; John ELLIS; Abraham CURRY

AJ-2-472   **Mathew McCLINTICK**   21 Feb 1797/ 1 Apr 1797
To: Wife, Ann McCLINTICK - tract 10 a. my dwelling place & then to
     grandson Mathew McCLINTICK; all Negroes, to be free after
     Ann's death & after age 25
    Grandson, William McCLINTICK
    Grandson, Mathew McCLINTICK, now living in Philadelphia - house
     & lot at Cross Roads
Ex: Samuel SMITH
Wt: James WEBSTER; Samuel WEBSTER; Richard WEBSTER

AJ-2-474   **Jacob MAXWELL**   22 Mar 1798/ 20 Aug 1798
To: Wife, Elizabeth MAXWELL - all lands I now possess
    Child my wife may be carrying
    Brother, Moses MAXWELL ¦¦ James Maxwell DORSEY
    Sister, Ann Maxwell DORSEY & husband, John Hammond DORSEY -
     part of plantation on which they now live
    Negro man Sam - free 3 years after my decease
Ex: Wife, Elizabeth MAXWELL; Brother, Moses MAXWELL; Lambert
     WILMER; John Hammond DORSEY
Wt: Thomas Howell BIRCKHEAD; Samuel HOOPER; Joseph GAFFORD

AJ-2-476   **John MILLER**   2 Mar 1800/ 25 Mar 1800
To: Youngest son, Edward MILLER
    All my children in England (names unspec.)
Ex: Brother, Joseph MILLER
Wt: Michael CARRELL; William B. WILSON

AJ-2-477   **Alexander McCOMAS**   8 Feb 1790/ 8 Apr 1800
To: Grandson, Alexander McCOMAS, son of Edward Day McCOMAS
    Wife, Mary McCOMAS
    Son, Edward Day McCOMAS - tract 112 a. *Edinborough*
    Son, Alexander McCOMAS - tract 50 a. part of *Horse Range*
     currently belonging to son Nicholas DAY
    Children, Elizabeth LYTLE, Nicholas Day McCOMAS, Mary McCOMAS,
     & George McCOMAS
Ex: Sons, Nicholas Day & George McCOMAS
Wt: William SMITH; George McCOMAS; Nicholas Day McCOMAS

AJ-2-479   **James MOORES**, tanner   4 Jun 1791/ 15 Nov 1791
To: Wife (name unspec.) - Negro woman Peg & her youngest child
    Son, Daniel MOORES - tract *Paca's Meadows*, tract part of *Scotts
     Close* & *Majors Choice* to the SE of the road from my dwelling
    Son, John MOORES - rem. part of my lands where my dwelling
     house stands with all the land adj., grist mill & dam
    Daughter, Deliverance HANNAH, wife of William HANNAH - all

      Negro children that have been or may be born with her of
      Negro women who are my property
  Daughter, Sarah BRYERLY, wife of Robert BRYERLY - all Negro
      children that have been or may be born with her of Negro
      women who are my property
  Two grandchildren, Elizabeth & James GLASGOW ¦¦ Son, James
      MOORES
  To be sold: tract purchased of William HORTON
Ex: Sons, John & Daniel MOORES
Wt: Michael DENNY; Thomas WRIGHT; John ARCHER, Senr.

                            Codicil: 14 Jun 1791/ 15 Nov 1791
To: Wife (name unspec.) ¦¦ Children (names unspec.)
Wt: Thomas WRIGHT; Michael DENNY; John ARCHER, Senr.

                            Codicil: 15 Oct 1791/ 15 Nov 1791
To: Sons, John & James MOORES ¦¦ Wife (name unspec.)
  Grandson, James GLASGOW - to be educated in the learned
      languages
Wt: Joseph WOOLSEY; Charles HEDRECK; William HAMBY; John ARCHER

AJ-2-482   **Joseph NORRIS** of Baltimore Co. 6 Oct 1772/ 18 Oct 1795
To: Children or heirs of my brother John NORRIS, deceased
  Children or heirs of my brother Benjamin NORRIS, deceased
  Children or heirs of my brother Thomas NORRIS, deceased
  Brother, Abraham NORRIS
  Sisters, Elizabeth HUGHS, Sarah NORRIS, & Hannah HENDON
  Wife, Christian NORRIS - tracts *Everly Hills*, & *Addition to*
      Gibsons Ridge
Ex: Wife, Christian NORRIS
Wt: Elizabeth BOND; Jacob BOND; Jacob BOND, Jr.

AJ-2-485   **Sarah NORRIS** of Baltimore Co. 20 Oct 1770/ 13 Jun 1780
To: Daughter, Mary NORRIS, wife of James NORRIS, son of Edward
      NORRIS, deceased - tract 68 a. *Addition to Shepherds Range*
      in His Lordship's Reserve, tract 50 a. *Enlargement* in the
      same reserve, 5 tracts 118 a. given by my father (still
      living)
Ex: James NORRIS
Wt: Elizabeth BOND; Edward NORRIS; Jacob BOND

AJ-2-487   **Rachel NEVILL** of Kent Co.   13 Oct 1787/ 28 Nov 1787
To: Capt. John McGOWAN - Negroes Nan & Sam, to be freed 3 months
      after my death
  John McGOWAN, son of Capt. James McGOWAN - Negroes Fann,
      Rachell, & Ann
  Elizabeth McGOWAN, daughter of Capt. James McGOWAN
Ex: Capt. John McGOWAN
Wt: Judith McGOWAN; Rebekah DAVIS

AJ-2-488   **Mary NORRINGTON**   29 Dec 1791/ 17 Apr 1792
To: Daughters, Mary POTEET, Hannah & Sarah NORRIS
  Ann THOMPSON ¦¦ Sons, John, Isaac, & Abraham NORRINGTON
  Daughters, Frances THOMPSON, Cassandra THOMPSON, Priscilla LION
      (or LYON), & Temperance LONG

         Three daughters, Rachel, Martha, & Susannah NORRINGTON
Ex: John LYON
Wt: Elijah NORRIS; William SINCLAIR; Aran (or Aron) NORRIS

AJ-2-490   **Edward NORRIS**   16 Aug 1793/ 25 Sep 1793
To: Wife, Elizabeth NORRIS
    Son, Edward NORRIS - half my farm including mansion house
    Son, Oliver NORRIS - other half of lands
    Sons, John & William NORRIS (both under age 21)
    Five daughters, Hannah, Elizabeth, Susanna, Mary, & Ann NORRIS
       (all under age 21)
Ex: Wife, Elizabeth NORRIS; Aquila NORRIS; James AMOSS
Wt: John MASON; William AMOS; Samuel CALWELL

AJ-2-493   **James NORRIS**   21 Aug 1798/ 22 Nov 1798
To: Wife, Elizabeth NORRIS
    Sons, James & Henry NORRIS - Negro man Minggo, Negro woman
       Thamer after my wife's death
    Also son James NORRIS - tract 100 a. *Expectation*
    Also son Henry NORRIS - tract 50 a. *Norris Venter*
    Children of my daughter, Sarah WHITE
    Negro man Affrick - freedom after my wife's death
    Daughters, Ann & Elizabeth (nee NORRIS)
Ex: (None named)
Wt: James LEACH; Gidion BAKER; David STANDEFORD; Stephen WATTERS

AJ-2-494   **William OSBORN**, farmer   23 Jun 1774/ 27 Feb 1779
To: Cousin, James OSBORN, son of James OSBORN - land conveyed from
       my Uncle William HOLLIS, tract *Owlets Nest* bought of William
       HOLLIS; Negroes Old Peter, Moll, Sam, Isaac, Will, & Doll
    Cousin, William OSBORN, son of James - Negro wench Dinah &
       three children Bridget, Hannah, & Pompey
    Cousin, Martha OSBORN, daughter of my brother James - Negro
       boys Neo & Tom
    Sister, Martha HOLLIS - Negro girl Fan
    Cousin, Cyrus OSBORN - Negro girl Cance at Robert JEFFRYS
    Cousin, Benjamin OSBORN - Negro boy Jack
Ex: Cousin, James OSBORN
Wt: George CHAUNCY; Joseph PREWETT; Zebede BENETT

AJ-2-496   **James OSBORN**   6 Apr 1779/ 28 Mar 1780
To: Eldest son, James OSBORN - tract 60 a. *Common Garden Corrected*,
       all my lands E of Rumney Creek; Negro fellow Harry
    Second son, William OSBORN - tract part of *Common Garden
       Corrected*
    Second (third ?) son, Cyrus OSBORN - tract part of *Common
       Garden Corrected*; Negro girl Peg
    Fourth son, Benjamin OSBORN - tract part of *Common Garden
       Corrected*; Negro boy George
    Daughter, Mary OSBORN - Negro boy Jack
    Second daughter, Martha OSBORN - Negro girl Bess
    Patty GREENFIELD
Ex: Son, James OSBORN
Wt: William HANSON; Benjamin CHAUNCEY; John HANSON; James
    WETHERALL

AJ-2-498 **Zachius ONION** 3 Nov 1781/ 4 Dec 1781
To: Wife, Hannah ONION - half of lower Merchant Mill on the Little
    Falls at *Onion Works*, half of tract 400 a. *Onions
    Inheritance*; Negroes Jack, Landon, Jem the waiter, Big Sam,
    Sampson, Lydia, Sall, Big Jenny, & Amia
  Eldest son, Stephen ONION - half of tract *Hethcode Cottage*
    where my dwelling house stands, half tract *Thompsons Choice*;
    Negro boys George & Lem, Negro girl Nance
  Second son, Thomas Bond ONION - lower Mill, dwelling house
    where Mr. SMITH resides, tract 400 a. *Onions Inheritance*
    after mothers death; mulatto man Neo, Negro boy Isaac, Negro
    girl Jen
  Son, John Barrett ONION - Negro boys Sam & Ben, Negro girl Cass
  Son, Zachius ONION - mulatto boy Peter, Negro man Dick & boy
    Tom
  Son, William Frances Heath ONION - Negro boys Bob & Jack, Negro
    child Lidd
  Also sons Zachius & William ONION - upper Mill & rem. of
    Onion's Inheritance
  Son, Corbin ONION - tract *Jerusalem* where Thomas HUTCHINS
    resides, tract *Rebecas Lot*; Negro boy Jacob, Negro Job, &
    Negro girl Peheb
  Daughter, Martha ONION - tract 226 a. *Onions Pasture Ground*
    near Joppa known by the name *Gugeons*; Negro girl Poll
  Daughter, Susannah ONION - tract 300 a. *Betts Prosperty* where
    Thomas DONTHEY now resides; Negro girl Phillis
  Daughter, Hannah ONION - tract 300 a. including place where
    Theophilus BAKER has resided for some time; Negro girl Jenny
  Daughter, Elizabeth ONION - tract *Prospect Hills* in fork of
    Gunpowder, Baltimore Co., my house & lots in Joppa; Negro
    woman Grace
  Daughter, Sarah ONION - tract 300 a. adj. MASON's land; Negro
    girl Ruth
  Daughter, Charity ONION - tract *Turkey Hills* where James
    HUGGINS resides, tract *Onions Defence* adj. Givins Mill on
    the Little Falls; Negro girl Rose
  To be sold: all other lands in Md, Penn, or other states
Ex: Wife, Hannah ONION; Son, Stephen ONION
Wt: J. Beale HOWARD; Alexander COWAN; Thomas Gasway HOWARD; William
    SMITH; Buckler BOND; Thomas BOND

AJ-2-502 **Jane OSBORN** 19 Sep 1787/ 26 Nov 1787
To: Daughter, Martha (nee OSBORN)
  Grandchildren, the sons & daughters of son James OSBORN
  Grandchildren, the sons & daughters of son William OSBORN
  Grandchildren, the sons & daughters of daughter Martha (nee
    OSBORN)
  Grandchildren, the son & daughter of daughter Mary (nee OSBORN)
  Son, Benjamin OSBORN
Ex: Son-in-law, James GARRETTSON
Wt: William HILL; Giles KIMBLE; Mary McCLAIR

AJ-2-504 **Lawrence OSBORN** Verbal: __ Feb 1789/ 20 Feb 1789
To: Phrisby DORSEY - all my estate

Ex: (none names)
Verified: Nathan HUGHS & Lewis HANSON

AJ-2-504　**Cyrus OSBORN**　　　　　　18 May 1793/ 10 Dec 1798
To: Five children, Nancy, Martha, Sharlot, Mary, & Lennard OSBORN
　　Semelia OSBORN, wife of my brother James OSBORN, deceased -
　　　Negroes I bought of brother James
　　Wife, Susannah OSBORN
Ex: Wife, Susannah OSBORN
Wt: Cyrus OSBORN; George HENDERSON

AJ-2-506　**William PRESBURY**　　　　11 Nov 1772/ 12 Apr 1774
　　of Baltimore Co.
To: Eldest son, James PRESBURY ¦¦ Youngest son, Greenberry PRESBURY
　　Wife, (name unspec.)
　　Children, Sarah, Clemency, Elisabeth, William, & Joseph
　　　PRESBURY
Ex: John WILSON, Senr.
Wt: Henry WETHERALL; William Robinson PRESBURY; Mary Ann WETHERALL

AJ-2-507　**Ann PRESTON**　　　　　　　22 Dec 1774/ 24 Jan 1775
To: Son, James PRESTON
　　Trustee: Brother Joseph LUSBY
Ex: Brother, Joseph LUSBY
Wt: Henry WETHERALL; John DURHAM; Avarilla SMITH

AJ-2-508　**Lewis PUTTEE** of Baltimore Co.　　1 Apr 1772/ 7 Aug 1779
To: Daughters, Rebeckah POLLARD, Ann PUTTEE, Mary CAVENER,
　　　Catharine WHITACRE, Elizabeth JAMES, Martha NORRIS, Frances
　　　PUTTEE, & the children of my daughter Sarah WEIR,
　　Son, Peter PUTTEE - tract 100 a. inc. dwelling plantation part
　　　of *Bin* after mother's death, rem. 100 a. of *Bin*, tract 125
　　　a. *Bonds Last Shift*
　　Wife, Sarah PUTTEE
　　Son, Peter PUTTEE (under age 21)
　　Grandsons, Francis & Isaac, sons of daughter Frances PUTTEE
Ex: Jacob BOND
Wt: Wiliam CUTHBARN; Jacob BOND, Junr.; Jacob BOND

AJ-2-510　**John PATRICK**　　　　　　　18 Jan 1783/ 11 Mar 1783
To: Brother, James PATRICK
Ex: Brother, James PATRICK, Robert CONN, & David HARRY
Wt: John CONN; Edward CUNARD

AJ-2-511　**Joseph PRESBURY**　　　　　16 Apr 1783/ 19 Jun 1783
To: Son, Joseph PRESBURY - all my real estate
　　Sons, William PRESBURY & Thomas Pycraft PRESBURY
　　Daughters, Elin (or Elinor) MORRISS & Mary PRESBURY
　　Children, James PRESBURY, & Henry PRESBURY
Ex: Son, Joseph PRESBURY
Wt: James WETHERALL; Henry WETHERALL; Charles WATTERS

AJ-2-513　**Aquila PACA, Junr.**　　　　8 Nov 1783/ 17 Nov 1783
To: Dr. James LEE, son of Samuel LEE - tract *Mould & Success* which
　　　I now live on, tract *Pacas Conveniency*, tract part of

Palmers Points, house where John STEEL now lives; to manumit all Negroes as specified; use of Negro Simon until age 30
Parker Hall LEE, son of Samuel LEE, Samuel LEE, son of Josiah LEE, & James Lee MORGAN, son of William MORGAN - tract *Pacas Park* near Harford Town
Richard & Corbin LEE, sons of James LEE - tracts *Delph,Delph Neglect, Neawsams Meadows*, tract part of *Goldsmiths Hall*
William WILSON, son of Samuel WILSON
Margaret DOWNING, wife of Richard DOWNING, & Priscilla (WEBB ?), daughters of William WEBB
Elizabeth & Mary VANCLEAVE, daughters of Dr. VANCLEAVE
Henry JOHNS ¦¦ Josias HALL
Negro Jenny - freedom at my decease
Negroes Bob & Grace his wife, Bet & Milcah - freedom at the finish of the crop now in the ground, tract 40 a. adj. house where John STEELE now lives
Negroes Jack, Jo, & Hagar, wife of Jo - freedom after 7 years
Negro Hagar - freedom after serving 5 years
Negroes Patience, Grace the younger, Phillis, Sucky, Fan, Pompey, & Tom - freedom at age 21
Negro Nace - freedom after serving 15 years
Negro Simon - freedom at age 30
Negro children born during above periods - males free at 21, females free at 16
Any children of James, Josiah, or Samuel LEE, & of William MORGAN & Samual WILSON, not already having a legacy appointed above
To be sold: tracts *Water Mill* & *Addition to Water Mill*
Ex: William MORGAN; William WILSON; Parker Hall LEE
Wt: Francis DALLAM; Henry JOHNS; John ARCHER

AJ-2-516 **Susey PLUNKET**   14 Oct 1783/ 6 Dec 1784
To: John REDDILL
Ex: (None named)
Wt: William MUNK; Marey MECOUN

AJ-2-517 **John PACA**   5 Sep 1781/ 31 Dec 1785
To: Son, Aquilla PACA - tracts *Maidens Bower Secured* & *Pacas Search* on Thomases Run & Deer Creek, tract part of *Pacas Park*, tracts *Security, Water Mill*, & *Addition to Water Mill*, tract *Chilberry Hall* on Winters Run
Daughter, Mary PACA - Negro Peg, wife of Negro Shins (already belonging to her)
Son, William PACA - lots in Abingdon & Washington, tracts *Swan Harbour, Pacas Bit, Pacas Meadow, Pacas Meadow Resurveyed* & *Island*
Daughter, Martha PHILLIPS - Negro Harry bought of her husband James PHILLIPS; also Rachel & her children, & Amynta
Daughters, Frances, & Susannah PACA
Also daughters Martha PHILLIPS, & Frances, & Susannah PACA - lots in Washington, tracts *Askins Hope* & *Middlemores Defence*
Ex: James PHILLIPS; Richard DALLAM; William SMITH
Wt: George CHAUNCEY, Junr.; John Hall HUGHES; John RUFF

Codicil: 24 Mar 1782/ 31 Dec 1785
To: Daughter, Mary PACA
   Daughter, Frances PACA - lots in Abingdon #43, 44, 32 & 33, lots in Washington 2-13 marked RD on plat
   Daughter, Martha PHILLIPS - lots in Abingdon #42, 21, 22, 10, & 11, lots in Washingtpon #2-4 marked I+P on plat
   Daughter, Susannah PACA - lots in Abingdon # 64, 65, 53 & 54, lots in Washington # 2-6 marked WS on plat
   Son, William PACA - lot in Abingdon #52, two lots in Washington next adj. W. of Richard DALLAM's Brew house
   Aquilla PACA & John DALLAM; Richard DALLAM
Wt: Sarah MAGEE; Loyd MARSH; George CHAUNCEY, Junr.

AJ-2-521   **George PRESBURY**   23 Apr 1783/ 19 Jun 1786
To: Son, George Gouldsmith PRESBURY - lands in Baltimore Co. on Gunpowder River & on W side; Negroes including Sophia
   Grandson, James Tolley PRESBURY - lands in Gunpowder Neck & on or near Gunpowder River & on the E side
   Grandson, George PRESBURY, son of William - rem. of lands on or near Gunpowder River; Negro Andrew
   Granddaughter, Mary PRESBURY, daughter of the late George Beedle PRESBURY - Negroes Sam & Isaac
   Granddaughter, Isabella PRESBURY, daughter of the late George Beedle PRESBURY - Negroes Hagar & Geofray
   Granddaughter, Ann PRESBURY (under age 16), daughter of George Gouldsmith PRESBURY
   Granddaughters, Sophia PRESBURY, Barthea PRESBURY, & Isabella PRESBURY, daughters of William PRESBURY
   Daughter-in-law, Elizabeth PRESBURY, in case her husband should predecease me
Ex: George Gouldsmith PRESBURY
Wt: Edward YORK; William YORK; Benjamin RUMSEY

AJ-2-524   **John PRESTON**   20 Aug 1785/ 20 Feb 1787
To: Brothers, William & Corbin PRESTON - all my lands
Ex: Brothers, William & Corbin PRESTON
Wt: William JOHNSON; James PRESTON; Sarah PRESTON; John LOVE

AJ-2-525   **Bever PAIN**, gentleman   26 Jan 1788/ 17 Mar 1788
To: Sons, Thomas, James, Barnet, & William PAIN
   Wife, Elizabeth PAIN
   Son, Jacob PAIN - all my real estate after his mother's death
Ex: Wife, Elizabeth PAIN; Son, Jacob PAIN
Wt: John LITTON; William TAYLOR; William WEST

AJ-2-526   **Walter PERDUE**   23 Jul 1792/ 20 Nov 1792
To: Wife, Mary PERDUE || Nephew, Walter PERDUE || Rachel JAMES
Ex: Nephew, Walter PERDUE; Wife, Mary PERDUE
Wt: James ENLOWS; John MASH; Daniel CURTIS

AJ-2-528   **Bernard** (or **Barnard**) **PRESTON**   2 Jan 1789/ 14 Oct 1794
To: Wife, Sarah PRESTON || Eldest son, Barnard PRESTON
   Children, Mary JOHNSON, Anna RUFF, & Daniel PRESTON
   Son, James PRESTON - dwelling plantation
Ex: Wife, Sarah PRESTON; Son, James PRESTON

Wt: John LOVE; John FORWOOD; Bernard PRESTON of Daniel; Margaret LOVE; Ann LOVE JOHNSON

AJ-2-530 **James PRITCHARD**   12 Mar 1793/ 24 Aug 1796
To: Son, Samuel PRITCHARD - tract 98 a. part of *Hughes Enlargement Resurveyed*
    Son, Benjamin PRITCHARD - tract 80 a. part of *Hughes Choice & Hughes Enlargement Resurveyed*
    Granddaughter, Elizabeth PRITCHARD, daughter of son Daniel PRITCHARD
Ex: Sons, Samuel & Benjamin PRITCHARD
Wt: Richard BARNES; Ephraim ARNOLD; Gregory BARNS, Junr.; Ford ARMSTRONG

AJ-2-531 **Samuel PRIGG**   28 Feb 1799/ 7 May 1799
To: Father, William PRIGG - all my real estate
Ex: Brother, Edward PRIGG
Wt: Robert MORGAN; Barnett JOHNSON of John; James ANDERSON

- END OF WILL BOOK -

WILL BOOK "AJ-R"
HARFORD COUNTY, Md.

AJ-R-001 Thomas RENSHAW   30 Apr 1774/ 18 Jun 1774
To: Son, Thomas RENSHAW - tract 82 a. *Thomases Desire* between Deer
    Creek & Broad Creek
    Sons, Robert & Martin RENSHAW - land on which my father Thomas
    RENSHAW lived
    Sons, James, Bennett, & Hosia RENSHAW (all under age 21)
    Daughters, Frances, & Salinah RENSHAW & Elizabeth WEBSTER
    Wife, Mary RENSHAW - home plantation; Negro Tom until age 21
    Stepdaughter, Mary BRICE
Ex: Wife, Mary RENSHAW
Wt: John LOVE; John JOHNSON; Sias BILLINGSLY; Thomas BRICE

AJ-R-003 William RICHARDSON   23 Dec 1774/ 17 Feb 1775
To: Nathaniel RICHARDSON; Wife, Tabitha RICHARDSON
Ex: Wife, Tabitha RICHARDSON
Wt: Henry WETHERALL; James LITTLE

AJ-R-004 Robert RUSSELL   19 Jul 1775/ 24 Aug 1775
To: Wife, Mary RUSSELL - my plantation
    Sons, James & Thomas RUSSELL (both under age 21), born of said
    Mary
    My other children: Hugh RUSSELL, blacksmith living in Fogs
    Mannor; Andrew RUSSELL, blacksmith of Lancaster Co, Penn;
    John RUSSELL in the Barrens of York Co, Penn.
    Son-in-law, David McCULLOGH; Daughter, Jean SYMS
Ex: (None named)
Wt: Isaac BUSH; Sylvester COGGINS

AJ-R-006 Richardson ROBERTS   14 Feb 1777/ 28 Jun 1777
To: Wife, Clorinda ROBERTS
Ex: Wife, Clorinda ROBERTS; Benjamin RICHESON
Wt: Charles CUMMINGS; Irwin ROBERTS

AJ-R-007 William ROBINSON   8 Jun 1776/ 14 Apr 1778
To: Son, William ROBINSON - tract 42 a. part of *Thomas Bond's Gift*,
    tract 65 a. *Robinsons Meadows*
    Son, Richard ROBINSON - tract 100 a. *Wilsons Retreat*
    Son, Archabald ROBINSON - tract 100 a. *Better Hope*; tract 46
    a. part of *Carlisles Parcks*
    Daughter, Elizabeth ROBINSON - Negro girl Lusey
Ex: Wife, Temperance ROBINSON; Son, Richard ROBINSON
Wt: Charles BAKER; Bennet BUSSEY; John PARKER

AJ-R-008 Sabina RIGBIE   16 Oct 1776/ 18 Sep 1779
    late of Cecil Co., now of Harford Co.
To: Son, John RUMSEY - the family Bible; Negro man slave Pompey
    bought of Col. Benjamin YOUNG
    Sons, Charles & Benjamin RUMSEY ¦¦ Son, William RUMSEY
    Oldest son, (named unspec.) & his heirs in Bohemia (Cecil Co.)
    Granddaughter, Sabina RUMSEY - Negro girl Nell bought of Hugh
    DEAN

Mrs. Cassandra PEARCE - pair of gold sleeve buttons formerly
belonging to Col. Nathan RIGBIE, her deceased father
Granddaughter, Amelia BOYER
Ann WILLETT, wife of Samuel WILLETT
Non-beneficiaries: John RIGBIE (apparent 2nd husband of Sabina
RIGBIE who pre-deceased her), his Will signed 20 July 1766;
Ann RIGBIE, sister of John RIGBIE, married Samuel WILLETT;
Henrietta RIGBIE, (first) wife of John RIGBIE; Philip
RIGBIE, brother of John RIGBIE; Nathan RIGBIE, son (only
child) of John RIGBIE by Henrietta; both Nathan & Henrietta
died shortly after birth of Nathan; Benjamin RUMSEY,
administrator of estate of John RIGBIE
Ex: Son, John RUMSEY
Wt: Alexander COWAN; Moses HASLETT; Margaret McCOY

AJ-R-010 **John ROBERTS**   28 Mar 1760/ 19 Jan 1780
of St. Johns Parish, Baltimore Co.
To: Brother-in-law, John ALLINDER & his wife Lucina ALLINDER - 3
lots in town of Joppa, numbers 6, 16, 17 & this lot, 1/2 a.
each; plantation *Fosters Neck Woolfs Harbor* & *Arthers Delay*
Brother, Stephen ROBERTS
Ex: John ALLINDER & Lucina, his wife
Wt: Roderick CHEYNE; John SKINNER; Elizabeth CHEYNE

AJ-R-011 **Moses RUTH**   18 Sep 1780/ 15 Jan 1781
To: Wife, Esther RUTH
Second daughter, Ruthea McCANDLESS - tract 40 a. *St George's
Neighbor*, tract 400 a. N end of *Brooms Bloom*; Negro girl
Beck & Negro boy Peter
Daughters, Jean BLAIR, wife of Thomas BLAIR & Sarah
KIRKPATRICK, wife of William KIRKPATRICK - tract rem. part
of *Brooms Bloom*
Daughter, Jean BLAIR - Negro woman Cate
Esther HAYS, wife of John HAYS
James ARCHER || Doctor John ARCHER
Moses M. QUISTON, eldest son of daughter Jean
Grandson, Moses KIRKPATRICK, eldest son of daughter Sarah
Granddaughters, Ruthea THOMPSON & Jean NELSON
Grandchildren, Alexander, James, William, Esther, & Sarah
McCANDLESS, issues of daughter Ruthea McCANDLESS
Grandchildren, issues of daughter Sarah KIRKPATRICK
Thomas ARCHER, son of Dr. John ARCHER
Ex: James McCANDLESS; Dr. John ARCHER
Wt: Benjamin Bradford NORRIS; David GLENN; Nathaniel McCLURE

                                          Codicil: 18 Sep 1780
To: Negro Sam - set free; Negro Root - set free
Negro girl Rachel, age 6 on May 19, 1780 - set free at age 31
Negro boy Steven, age 2 on Sep 12, 1780 - set free at age 31

                                  Codicil: 1 Jan 1781/ 15 Jan 1781
To: Thomas HAYS; Joseph HAYS; Moses M. QUISTON; Moses KIRKPATRICK
Alexander McCANDLESS; Wife,Esther RUTH; James SHEREDINE
Wt: James SHERIDINE; Rachel E. LEE

Renunciation: 4 Feb 1781/ 24 Feb 1781
Ester RUTH, widow of Moses RUTH, quitted her claim to bequests
    except for dowry.
Wt: Andrew HOWLETT; William REED

AJ-R-015 **Stephen ROBERTS**   2 Feb 1782/ 18 Mar 1782
To: Sister, Lucy or Lucina ALLINDER, wife of John ALLENDER - tract
    Persons Outlett, Ogg King of Bashan, & *Wetharals Addition*
Ex: Lucina ALLENDER
Wt: John WANE; Ann JERVIS; Nathanell PHIPPS

AJ-R-016 **Thomas RENSHAW**   9 Feb 1784/ 30 Mar 1784
To: Wife, Hannah RENSHAW - Negro Dick
    Edward PRIGG || Six children (names unspec.)
Ex: Wife, Hannah RENSHAW
Wt: Stephen Ricketts PRICE; John FARMER; James DAVIDSON

AJ-R-018 **Nathan RIGBIE**   8 Dec 1783/ 10 Jun 1784
To: Grandson, Nathan Rigbie SHERIDINE
    Daughter Hannah's children (names unspec.)
    Daughter, Hannah (nee RIGBIE)
    Male issue of sister, Elizabeth SMITH
    Child or children of sister, Anna (nee RIGBIE) || Deborah LOWE
    To be sold - tract 475 a. *Rigbies Chance,* tract 230 a. part of
        Rigbies Hope on Deer Creek
Ex: Isaac WEBSTER; Daniel SHEREDINE
Wt: Samuel GOVER; E. Gittings GOVER; Andrew WALLACE

AJ-R-020 **Thomas RICHARDSON**   28 Mar 1784/ 9 Nov 1784
To: Son, Thomas RICHARDSON - tract 65 a. in Harford Co. bought of
        John BOND; Negro fellow Jack
    Daughter, Sally RICHARDSON - Negro wench Jude & Negro girl Cash
    Daughter, Elizabeth RICHARDSON - Negro wench Cloe & Negro girl
        Briget
    Grandson, Thomas CALWELL, son of Samuel CALWELL - Negro boy
        Charles
    Sons, Benjamin, Samuel, & William RICHARDSON
Ex: (None named)
Wt: J. Beale HOWARD; Elizabeth HOWARD; Blanch HOWARD

                                                 Codicil: 7 Aug 1784
To: Negro Jude, left to daughter Sally, full freedom
Wt: J. Beale HOWARD

AJ-R-021 **Benjamin RICHENSON**   15 Nov 1784/ 11 Jan 1785
          (or **RICHARDSON**)
To: Housekeeper, Hannah ARLET, wife of Thomas ARLET
    Winston RICHENSON (or RICHARDSON), 2nd son of Hannah ARLET -
        tract 800 a. part of *Richensons Outlet,* tract 232 a.
        Richensons Barrons
    Elizabeth NORRIS, wife of Benjamin Bradford NORRIS
Ex: Winston SMITH
Wt: James MURPHY; Alexander OSBORN

AJ-R-023 **Barny RILLY** (or **RILEY**)   5 Feb 1785/ 8 Mar 1785
To: Wife, Jane RILLY - my estate lands
    Sons, James, Charles, William, & John RILLY
    Daughter, Routh RILLY ¦¦ Daughter, Peggy RILLY, alias REARDON
Ex: Wife, Jane RILLY; Eldest son, James RILLY; Isaac WEBSTER
Wt: Jane McGAW; James McGAW; John McGAW

AJ-R-025 **Ester RUTH**   24 Mar 1781/ 20 Jun 1786
          widow of the late Moses RUTH, Sr.
To: Granddaughters, Sarah & Ester McCANDLESS
    Grandson, Dr. John ARCHER ¦¦ Son, James ARCHER
    Daughter, Ester HAYS, wife of John HAYS
    Daughter, Jean BLAIR, wife of Thomas BLAIR
    Daughter, Sarah KIRKPATRICK, wife of William KIRKPATRICK
    Daughter, Ruthia McCANDLESS, wife of James McCANDLESS - Negro
      girl Rachel
Ex: Son-in-law, James McCANDLESS
Wt: Andrew HOWLETT; William REED; James REED

AJ-R-027 **Edward ROBINSON**   Verbal: 9 Feb 1786/ 18 Feb 1787
To: Wife, Margret ROBINSON ¦¦ Nephew, James TAYLOR
    Son, Richard ROBINSON
Ex: (None named)
Wt: Charles TAYLOR; John ROCKHOLD; Bathia STANDIFORD

AJ-R-028 **Thomas Baker** (or Bacor) **RIGDON**   18 Dec 1784/ 9 Aug 1789
To: Eldest son, Alexander RIGDON - tract 44 a. part of *Rock
      Quarter*, tract 28 a. part of *Crookett Ridg*, tract *Long Ally*
    2nd son, Thomas Bacor RIGDON - tract 77 a. part of *Crooked Ridg*
    3rd son, William RIGDON - tract 61 a. part of *Crooked Ridg*,
      tract *Rigduns Lookout*
    4th son, Steven RIGDON - tract 115 a. part of *Rock Quarter*,
      tract 52 a. part of *Crooked Ridg*
    5th son, Bencemond (or Benjamond) RIGDON - tract 41 a. part of
      Rock Quarter, tracts *Ye Fathers Safe Guard* & *Bacors Choyse
      Inlarged*, tract 24 1/4 a. part of *Roberts Center Inlarged*;
      Negro boy Steven
    Thomas WEST - tracts *Maryes Delite* & *Ye Charmin Spot*
    Daughters, Ann PRESTON & Margrate CLARK ¦¦ Wife, Ann RIGDON
    3rd Daughter, Elizabeth (nee RIGDON) - Negro girl Ann & her
      incr., & Negro boy Lisha
Ex: (None named)
Wt: George McATEE; John ASHMORE; William ASHMORE

AJ-R-031 **James RIGBIE**   3 Oct 1788/ 24 Jan 1791
To: Son, James RIGBIE - tract 12 a. with saw mill
    Daughter, Sarah WALLACE ¦¦ Daughter Mercy (nee RIGBIE)
    Daughters Anna, Sarah, Cassandra Elizabeth, & Susannah RIGBIE
    Nephew, William SMITH - power of attorney
    Non-beneficiaries: Brother, Nathan RIGBIE, deceased; John
      WILSON; Dr. John ARCHER; Joseph MILLER; Father, Nathan
      RIGBIE
    Sisters, Elizabeth SMITH, Cassandra WEBSTER, & Ann WILLETT
    Kinsman, Isaac WEBSTER - tract in Anne Arundel Co. adj. Friends
      Meeting House on West River; tract on which Herrion Creek

```
        Church stands
Ex: Son, James RIGBIE; Son-in-law, Isaac MASSEY
Wt: John DALLAM; Joseph WILSON; James TASKER; Isaac MASSEY

24 Jan 1791 - Isaac MASSEY refused executorship.
```

AJ-R-034 **Ann RIGDON**   4 Feb 1796/ 3 Oct 1797
To: Son, Alexander RIGDON
    Grandson, Thomas RIGDON, son of Alexander RIGDON - Negro boy
      Brise until age 30 & then to be set free
    Son, Thomas RIGDON - Negro woman Nanny & her son Neff
    Son, William RIGDON - Negro boy Elisha, son of Negro woman
      Nanny, & Negro boy Davey, son of Negro woman Hanna, upon
      death of Negro man Mingo
    Negro boy Davey, to be retained by whomsoever of my children
      Negro man Mingo may please to live with
    Daughter, Margret (nee RIGDON) ¦¦ Son, Stephen RIGDON
    Negro woman Hanna & her daughter Sabina - set free
    Son, Benjamin RIGDON ¦¦ Granddaughter, Elizabeth CLARK
Ex: Son, Alexander RIGDON
Wt: James HOWLETT; Samuel SMITH; Henry MACATEE; Lyle SMITH

AJ-R-036 **Samuel RICKETTS, Sen.**   9 Sep 1794/ 2 Jan 1799
To: Son, Samuel RICKETTS
Ex: Son, Samuel RICKETTS
Wt: John Hammon DORSEY; James WETHERALL

AJ-R-037 **William RICHARDSON**   17 Nov 1799/ 24 Dec 1799
To: Sons, Vincent, Benjamin, Samuel, & Joshua RICHARDSON - all my
      lands
    Son William's children (names unspec.) - Negro man (name
      unspec.)
    Wife, Mary RICHARDSON ¦¦ Sons, Henry & William RICHARDSON
    Daughter, Martha AMOS, wife of Mordecai AMOS - Negro woman Suck
    Daughters, Elizabeth RICHARDSON & Mary RICHARDSON - Negroes
      (names unspec.), formerly the estate of Sarah BOND
Ex: Son, Benjamin RICHARDSON; Wife, Mary RICHARDSON
Wt: John BOND; Charles BAKER; George RUSH

AJ-R-040 **John RUFF**   1 Jan 1799/ 19 Feb 1800
To: Negroes to go free after following servitude: Sauney - 2 years;
      Poppy - 4 years; Moses - 6 years; Ester - 6 years; Benjamin,
      Sen - 8 years; John - 10 years; William - 12 years; Cyrus -
      24 years; Benjamin, Jr. - 22 years; Allexander - 28 years;
      Ann - 2 years; Priscilla - 2 years; Prianna - 20 years
    Wife (name unspec.)
    Rebecca MUNROW, young woman now living with me
    Brother, Daniel RUFF ¦¦ Brother Daniel RUFF's children
Ex: Wife, (name unspec.); Nephew, John RUFF
Wt: William COALE; James OSBORN; Samuel COALE

AJ-R-044 **Ruth SMITH**   17 May 1774/ 24 May 1774
To: Children, Sarah, Benjamin, Ruth & Mary SMITH (all minors)
Ex: James WALKER
Wt: Garsham SILVER; John ARCHER

AJ-R-045 **Jeremiah SHEREDINE**   22 Jul 1775/ 7 Aug 1775
To: Wife, Cassandra SHEREDINE - Negroes Jupiter, Jacob, Aron,
      Peter, Samuel, & Mary
    Son, Nathan SHEREDINE (under age 21)
    Sister, Tabitha RICHARDSON
Ex: Brother, Upton SHEREDINE
Wt: Nathan RIGBIE; William COALE; Shipwith JOHNS; Daniel
    SHEREDINE

                                       Codicil: 22 Jul 1775
To: Sister, Tabitha RICHARDSON - Negro man Aron, set free at age
      31

AJ-R-046 **Cassandra SHEREDINE**   20 Apr 1776/ 10 Jun 1776
To: Deborah LOWE; Son, Nathan SHEREDINE (under age 21)
    Tabitha RICHARDSON, sister of my husband Jeremiah SHEREDINE,
      deceased
    Daniel SHEREDINE & his heirs || Aunt, Ann WILLETT
    Sister Hannah's (nee RIGBIE) children (names unspec.)
Ex: Father, Nathan RIGBIE
Wt: William COALE, Jun.; Isaac MASSEY; James RIGBIE, Junior

AJ-R-048 **Samuel SMITH**   5 May 1776/ 10 Jun 1776
To: Wife, Catharin SMITH - land where I live on east side of Main
      from Farmers Ford on Deer Creek to Doctor ANDREWS
    John PACA || Ezekial VANHORN - rem. of my lands
Ex: (None named)
Wt: Nathan RIGBIE; Thomas ANDREWS; John HOPKINS; John SCATTIN

AJ-R-049 **Robert SMITH**   29 Aug 1776/ 13 Sep 1776
To: Robert MILLS || John MILLS || Susannah MILLS || Margret DUNAVON
    Uncle, David OWENS in Bon Water, Ireland, & his children
Ex: Robert MILLS
Wt: James HARRIS; John DAVIDSON; John MILLS

AJ-R-051 **William SMITH**   28 Apr 1777/ 18 Jun 1777
To: Wife (name unspec.) - half of 3 tracts viz. 2 bought from
      William FEW & other from Thomas BOND, half of tract on W
      side of Little Creek excluding 20 a.
    Richard & Josias Wm. DALLAM - tract 20 a. on W side of Little
      Creek
    To be sold - 2 mills & lands concerned with Richard & Josias
      Wm. DALLAM
    Son, Thomas SMITH - cleared land on E side of Deer Creek, land
      after wife's decease
    Son, Winstone SMITH - 2 tracts bought from William McCOMAS,
      tract part of *Deavers Neighbor* on W side of Deer Creek,
      tract part of *Rigdons Range* on W side of Deer Creek,
      tract between Little Creek & Deer Creek
    Son, John SMITH - residue of land: 2 small tracts formerly the
      seat of Dr. Josias MIDDLEMORES; *Aarons Spring Neck*, &
      Websters Enlargement to be divided with brother Thomas SMITH
    Son, William SMITH - tract part of *Rigdons Range* on E side of
      Deer Creek, tract part of *Deavers Neighbor* on E side of Deer
      Creek, half of tract adj. *Rigdons Range*

       Son, Nathan SMITH - tract *Bryerly Grove*, half tract adj.
          Rigdons Range
       Daughters, Martha & Harriott (nee SMITH) (under age 16)
       Daughter, Sarah DALLAM ¦¦ Granddaughter, Frances HENDERSON
       Faithful slave, old Will - set free
Ex: Wife (name unspec.); Son, William SMITH
Wt: Benjamin RICHARDSON; Samuel RICHARDSON; William LACKHARD

AJ-R-055   **Alse SIMS**   4 May 1780/ 20 May 1780
             widow of Robert SIMS
To: Oldest daughter, Elizabeth SIMS ¦¦ Daughters, Jean & Margret
       SIMS
    Son, Robert SIMS - the family Bible
    Sons, William & Francis SIMS
    Walter ROBISON ¦¦ Henry BENINTON
Ex: George ANDERSON; Robert COOK
Wt: William WILLIAMS; Sam McKISSON

AJ-R-056   **Elizabeth SLACK**   30 Apr 1779/ 27 Mar 1781
To: Daughter, Elizabeth (SLACK or BULL ?)
    Sons, John & Richard BULL
Ex: Son, John BULL
Wt: Joanna MATHER; John BARBEY; Isaac WEBSTER

AJ-R-058   **James STEWART**   7 Oct 1781/ 11 Oct 1781
To: Daughter, Ann, wife of Edward PARKER ¦¦ Daughter, Sarah STEWART
Ex: Edward PARKER
Wt: Bennet BUSSY; Leonard GREENLAND; William BAKER

20 Oct 1781 - Sarah STEWART, wife of James STEWART, refused
              standing to or abiding by her said deceased husband's
              will, but chooses in lieu thereof such part as she is
              by law entitled.

AJ-R-059   **Benjamin SCOTT**   5 Jan 1781/ 25 Jun 1782
To: Brothers, James & Aquila SCOTT
    Mother, Ann SCOTT ¦¦ Sisters, Ann SCOTT & Elizabeth BOND
    Non-beneficiary: Sister, Martha SCOTT, deceased
Ex: Mother, Ann SCOTT; Brother, James SCOTT
Wt: William BOND, son of Joseph; Benjamin GREEN

AJ-R-061   **Ann SCOTT**   26 Dec 1782/ 21 Jan 1783
To: Daughter, Elizabeth BOND
    Granddaughter, Casandra SCOTT ¦¦ Sons, James & Aquila SCOTT
Ex: Son, Aquila SCOTT
Wt: William BOND, son of Joseph; John CALDER

AJ-R-062   **William STEPHENSON**   3 May 1783/ 11 Jul 1783
             (or **STEVENSON**)
To: Three sons, George, William & James STEPHENSON - tract 500 a.
       on which I dwell to be divided equally by Daniel SHEREDINE
       & Stephen JAY
    Daughters, Mary, Rachel, & Ann STEPHENSON
    Wife, Rachel STEPHENSON
    Negroes, (names unspec.) - to be divided among my children

Ex: Wife, Rachel STEPHENSON; John RUMSEY
Wt: Samuel BAYLESS; John BUCKALOW; Jacob HALL Junr.

AJ-R-064 Zaccharias SPENCER, planter   13 Aug 1782/ 16 Dec 1783
To: Wife, Charity SPENCER
    Children, Elizabeth McGEAUGH, Zaccharia SPENCER, Rachel KENT,
    James SPENCER, Charity ROBINSON, William SPENCER, John
    SPENCER, Margaret CRAIL
Ex: Son, James SPENCER; Jesse KENT
Wt: Bartholomew CONNELL; Henry DICKSON; Jacob LUKENS

AJ-R-066 Robert SCOTT (or **SCOT**)   11 Aug 1779/ 21 Feb 1784
To: Son, Robert SCOTT, Junr. - plantation 130 a. *Coothill*
    Son, Walter SCOTT & daughter, Sarah SCOTT
    Grandson, John SCOTT
Ex: Son, Robert SCOTT
Wt: Benjamin SCAFF; Ann SCAFF; William BAILEY

AJ-R-068 Robert Young STOKES   10 Feb 1784/ 13 Jul 1784
To: Sister, Rebecca YOUNG - lot 2 & half of lot 1 in W. Presbury
        GOULDSMITH Plat of 4 a. in Baltimore Town given to me by my
        Grandfather YOUNG
    Sister, Clare (nee STOKES) - lot 3 & half of lot 1 in W.
        Presbury GOULDSMITH Plat
    Sister, Ann (nee STOKES) - lot 4 in W. P. GOULDSMITH Plat
    Sister, Mary (nee STOKES) - lot 5 in W. P. GOULDSMITH Plat
    Brother, William STOKES - lot 6 in W. P. GOULDSMITH Plat
    Brother & 4 sisters - one lot each in Havre de Grace
    Heirs of William HALL, heir-at-law to John HALL of Speutia -
        tract part of *Cohiers Lott* bonded to my father by John HALL
        upon pur. from his Uncle John STOKES
    Gabriel CHRISTIE || Grandmother, Clare YOUNG
    Mother, Rebecca YOUNG
    Wife, Sarah STOKES || Daughter, Eleanor ROGERS
    Son, William Brooks STOKES - residue of land
    Non-beneficiaries: Daniel DULANEY, Esq., advisor to son
Ex: Clement BROOKE
Wt: Benedict Edward HALL; Daniel DURBIN; James White HALL

                              Codicil: 11 Feb 1784/ 13 Jul 1784
To: Individuals with leases on lots in Havre de Grace (names
    unspec.)
Wt: Amos BARNS; John DONN; Richard RUTTER

AJ-R-073 William SMITH   3 Nov 1784/ 11 Jun 1796
To: Son, Jacob Giles SMITH (under age 21) - half of rents from
        plantation at Bay Side leased to Mathey RIDLEY, Samuel
        HUGHES, & Mark PRINGLE
    Wife, Susanna SMITH, step-mother of Jacob Giles SMITH & mother
        of Paca SMITH - dwelling & plantation *Blenhum* during her
        widowhood
    Sons, Winstone & Paca SMITH (both under age 21)
    Daughter, Frances SMITH
    Susannah RISTEAU, grandmother of my 2 sons Jacob Giles & Paca
        SMITH

Ex: (None named)
Wt: James W. HALL; Samuel JAY

23 Dec 1784 - Wt: Gabriel CHRISTIE, after arriving in America from a trip to England.

18 Sep 1795, Baltimore Co. Wills
29 Apr 1796, Harford Co. Wills
Susannah SMITH, widow of William SMITH, late of Harford Co., quitted her claim to the will.

AJ-R-078 **Robert SAUNDERS**   2 Jul 1785/ 27 Jul 1785
To: Wife, Elizabeth SAUNDERS
Ex: Wife, Elizabeth SAUNDERS
Wt: James PRICE; James DULEY; James WILSON

AJ-R-079 **John STEWART**   17 Jan 1787/ 14 Mar 1787
To: Mother, Martha BIRUM ¦¦ Son, George STEWART
    Non-beneficiary: Wife (name unspec.), deceased
Ex: Jacob MAXWELL
Wt: J. Hamond DORSEY; Moses MAXWELL; John WILSON

AJ-R-081 **Kent STALLIONS**   21 May 1785/ 21 Apr 1787
To: Grandson, Edward STALLIONS (under age 21)
    Children, Jacob, John, Richard, & Mary STALLIONS
    Daughters, Elizabeth DENNY, Martha HAMMILTON, Susanna MURNAHAN, Sarah DOBBINS, & Ann WOTTON
    Son, Thomas STALLIONS ¦¦ Wife, Elizabeth STALLIONS
Ex: Sons, Jacob & John STALLIONS
Wt: Richard RUFF; Godfrey WATTERS

AJ-R-083 **Robert SMITH**   28 Mar 1783/ 1 Jan 1788
          of Deer Creek Middle Hundred
To: Wife, Jean SMITH
    Son, William SMITH - plantation *Williams Discovery*
    Son, John SMITH - plantation *Franksfort*
    Daughter, Sarah RIGDON, wife of Baker RIGDON
    Daughter, Elizabeth LINDSEY, wife of Andrew LINDSEY
    Sons, Samuel & Robert SMITH ¦¦ Daughter, Jean SMITH
    Grandson, Lyle SMITH, son of Samuel SMITH
Ex: Wife, Jean SMITH; Son, William SMITH
Wt: Ralph PYLE; John THOMAS; James BARNETT

AJ-R-085 **James SAUNDERS**   17 Apr 1790/ 25 May 1790
To: Son, William SAUNDERS ¦¦ Wife, Mary SAUNDERS
    Daughters, Sarah McKAY & Charlotta NICHOLS
Ex: Wife, Mary SAUNDERS
Wt: William DITTO; William GORDON

AJ-R-086 **Thomas SAUNDERS**   3 Feb 1790/ 15 Mar 1790
To: Brothers, Joseph & William SAUNDERS
    Sisters, Elizabeth LYNCH & Kathren TREDWAY
Ex: Brothers, Joseph & William SAUNDERS
Wt: Isreal MORRIS; John HAYES; Rebecca HAYES

AJ-R-087 **Joseph STILES**   2 Dec 1790/ 10 Dec 1790
To: Wife (name unspec.) - lot with house, lot used for tavern, lot
    on which stables stand near the mill, lot adj. Henry RUFF,
    1/2 a. lot pur. of Col. WHITE
    Sons, George & John STILES; Child my wife now pregnant with.
Ex: Son, George STILES
Wt: John Thomas RICKETTS; William LUCKIE; John ARCHER

AJ-R-090 **Thomas SMITH**   11 Apr 1791/ 19 Dec 1791
To: Wife, Hannah SMITH - tract bought of John STUMP & Richard
    DALLAM on SE side of Elbow Branch now in possession of James
    SMITH; 3 Negroes, Jacob, Jean & Rachal
    Sons, James, William, & Nathaniel SMITH - tract on SE side of
    Elbow Branch upon wife's death, tracts *Smith's Mistake* &
    Neighbors Good Will
    Son, Nathaniel SMITH - Negro Jacob at wife's death
    Daughter, Mary McCRACKIN - Negro wench Rachal at wife's death
    Daughter, Hannah SMITH - 1/2 a. land & fishing ground pur. of
    Benjamin JOHNSTON; Negro wench Jean at wife's death
    Sons, Ralph, Hugh, Thomas, & John SMITH
    Daughters, Susanna GARRETT (or GORRELL), Olivia INGRAM, &
    Elizabeth GARRETT (or BARRETT)
    Youngest children are Mary, Hannah, William, Nathaniel, & James
    To be sold - tract pur. with John LOVE from Micajah MITCHELL
Ex: John CHRESWELL; James SMITH
Wt: John Hall HUGHS; Andrew COCHRAN; Robert BONER

AJ-R-093 **Frederick SWAN**   13 Apr 1794/ 13 May 1793 (?)
To: Wife, Catherine SWAN
    Daughters, Mary GLADDEN & Susannah MURRAY ‖ Son, Jacob SWAN
    Daughter, Catherine FOSTER, wife of John FOSTER who has left
    her & her child
    Children, Elizabeth, Margaret, & John SWAN
Ex: Wife, Catherine SWAN; Son, Jacob SWAN
Wt: George AMOSS; James McCOMAS of Daniel; James HARPER

AJ-R-095 **Samuel SUTTON**   Verbal: 29 Jul 1793/ 13 Aug 1793
To: Granddaughter (name unspec.), a child of William MOOBERRY
Ex: (None named)
Wt: David FORD; Nicholas HORNER

AJ-R-096 **William STANDIFORD**   27 Sep 1793/ 7 Jan 1794
To: 2nd Son, Edmon STANDIFORD - dwelling & 85 1/4 a. plantation
    No 23 in Maladys Manor (My Lady's Manor)
Ex: (None named)
Wt: John DEMOSS, Junr.; Jesse DAWNS; Daniel POWCOCK; James LYTLE

AJ-R-097 **Susannah SMITH**   18 Sep 1795/ 7 Oct 1795
          widow of William SMITH   (20 Apr 1796 ?)
To: Daughter, Frances SMITH ‖ Son, Paca SMITH - all real estate
Signed by: John DALLAM for Susannah SMITH
Ex: Brother, William PACA
Wt: Eliza P. PHILLIPS; Eliza GILES; William PACA

AJ-R-098 **Thomas SMITHSON**   14 Jun 1795/ 27 Oct 1795
To: Son, Nathaniel SMITHSON - plantation 100 a. part of *Beals Camp*
    Son, Archibald SMITHSON - tract 100 a. part of *Beals Camp* where
        son Nathaniel SMITHSON now lives
    Wife, Mary SMITHSON || Sons, William & Daniel SMITHSON
    Daughters, Margaret BARTIN & Cassander GREEN
    Deceased son Thomas SMITHSON's 3 children (names unspec.)
    Daughters, Ann, Elizabeth, & Sarah DURHAM
    Grandson, Benjamin SMITHSON
    Negro woman Hannah - to be free
    Negro man Caesar & Negro boy Jack - free when they arrive at
        age 30 years or, if wife is still living, serve until her
        death
Ex: Son, Nathaniel SMITHSON
Wt: James PRESTON; William GREENFIELD; Joshua GREEN

AJ-R-101 **John STUMP, Sen.** of Cecil Co.   23 Aug 1794/ 17 Mar 1797
To: Granddaughter, Ann JOHNSON (under age 16)
    Grandsons, John JOHNSON & Joseph COULSON (both under age 21)
    Negroes that are age 21 (names unspec.) - to be free
    Negroes under age 21 (names unspec.) - to be at the
        disposal of my executors until age 21, then to be free
    Children, John STUMP, Herman STUMP, & Hannah STUMP
    To be sold - all real estate
Ex: Sons, John & Herman STUMP
Wt: Nathan NORTON; Edward JACKSON; William TAYLOR

AJ-R-103 **Ann STANDIFORD**   9 Mar 1797/ 9 May 1797
To: Martin PARKER - lease to 100 a. part of *Bonds Forris*, tract
        9 1/4 a. *Addition to Poverty Inclosed* conveyed from Robert
        AMOSS
    Ann PARKER & Elizabeth PARKER, daughters of Martin PARKER
    Loyd STANDIFORD || Elizabeth STANDIFORD
    Bethia TAYLOR, wife of Charles TAYLOR
Ex: Martin PARKER
Wt: Francis CLARK; David CLARK; George CLARK (or CHALK)

AJ-R-105 **Enoch SPENCER**   17 May 1799/ 28 May 1799
To: Wife, Sarah SPENCER - half plantation & dwelling
    Son, Mahlon SPENCER - half plantation & dwelling
    Daughters, Hannah BURNET & Ann ELY
Ex: Son, Mahlon SPENCER
Wt: Thomas BOND of John; Thomas ELY; Ezra SPENCER

AJ-R-107 **Susanna SCOTT**   25 Oct 1797/ 28 Mar 1798
                                               (11 May 1800 ?)
To: Winston SMITH, son of William SMITH, Bayside - all my Negroes,
        to wit, Dan, big Tom, little Tom, & Poll, for the time they
        have to serve
    Isabella IRELAND, daughter of the Rev. John IRELAND
Ex: Winston SMITH
Wt: Ezra DENISON; John ARCHER

AJ-R-110 **David THOMAS**   3 Mar 1776/ 20 May 1776
To: Daughters, Mary McDANIEL, Martha THOMAS, & Rebecca THOMAS

```
          Wife, Mary THOMAS
          John, James, Isaac, & Owen THOMAS, my 3 (4 ?) sons
      Ex: Sons, John & James THOMAS
      Wt: Robert COOK; Charles BEAVER; David SWEENEY, Jr.
```

AJ-R-111 **Mary TREDWAY**   (Undated)/ 31 May 1779
```
      To: Son, James GITTINGS (or GITTING); Sarah ANDREW
          Daughter, Mary LYNCH, who is married to a TAYLOR - Negro Diner
             & Joshua
          Thomas TREDWAY - all the other Negroes
          Mr. TREDWAY - Negroes Diner & Joshua
          Mary GITTINGS, daughter of Asal GITTINGS
          Mary ANDREW - Negro woman Jane
          Ann & Mary COUNIGIN ¦¦ James WEBSTER
      Ex: (None named)
      Wt: James GITTINGS, son of Thomas; Elizabeth GITTINGS, daughter
             of same; Thomas LUCAS

      7 Jun 1779 - Verified by Micajah GREENFIELD since there was a
                   question of Mary TREDWAY not being of sound mind.
```

AJ-R-113 **Benjamin THOMAS**   18 Aug 1780/ 10 Oct 1780
```
      To: My 3 children, Mary, Joseph, & youngest son Francis
             THOMAS
          Joseph MATTINGLY, son of James, deceased
          Edward GREEN
      Ex: Alexander RIGDON
      Wt: Stephen RIGDON; Benjamin RIGDON; John MILES
```

AJ-R-114 **Rachel THORPE**   8 Aug 1781/ 7 Sep 1781
```
      To: Brother, John WILLMOTT - Negro man James, bought of Thomas
             CHINWORTH, deceased; Negro boy Harry, Negro Sam, & Negro
             girl Bine
          Sister, Hannah MOOR (or MOORE), wife of James MOOR - Negro
             woman Nan, during her (Hannah's) life, & afterwards to
             Hannah's son John MOORE
          Niece, Sarah, daughter of my brother John WILLMOTT - Negro girl
             Sall
          Kindsman, John WILLMOTT, son of brother John - Negro Tom
          Sister, Dinah TOWSON ¦¦ Brother, Richard WILLMOTT
          Kindswoman, Ruth WILLMOTT, daughter of brother John
          Rachel BOSLEY, Hannah WILLMOTT, & Mary WILLMOTT, daughters of
             brother John
          Elizabeth THOMPSON ¦¦ Brothers, Richard & John WILLMOTT
          Elizabeth GILL, daughter of William GILL
      Ex: Brother, John WILLMOTT
      Wt: Thomas FRANKLIN; Thomas LOVE
```

AJ-R-117 **Thomas TREDWAY**   22 May 1782/ 13 Aug 1782
```
      To: Son, Daniel TREDWAY - half of real estate
          Grandchildren, Thomas, George, James, Daniel, & Chrispin
             CUNNINGHAM - half of real estate
      Ex: Son, Daniel TREDWAY
      Wt: Daniel TREDWAY, Junr.; James MEAD, Junr.; Aram HUGHES
```

AJ-R-118 **Henry THOMAS**   17 Dec 1780/ 13 Aug 1782
To: Son, Henry THOMAS - lands on S side of Stout Bottle Branch,
       half of cleared lands on N side of Stout Bottle Branch
    Son, John THOMAS - half of cleared lands on N side of Stout
       Bottle Branch
    Sons, James & David THOMAS
Ex: (None named)
Wt: John LOVE; Mathew McELHINNEY; Margaret LOVE

AJ-R-119 **Henry THOMAS**   2 Mar 1783/ 14 Jun 1783
To: Three daughters, Sarah, Hannah, & Anna THOMAS (all minors) -
       all lands
    Three brothers, David, James, & John THOMAS
    Wife, Betty THOMAS
Ex: (None named)
Wt: John LOVE; Amos DAVIS; John PYLE; John FORWOOD

14 Jun 1783 - Betty FORD renounced the several bequests made to her
       & chose instead her dower or third part.

AJ-R-121 **John TIMMONS**   15 Jun 1785/ 11 Apr 1787
To: Sons, Thomas & Edward TIMMONS - tract 300 a. *Friendship*
    Heirs of my daughters Mary DORNEY & Sarah STRICKLING
    Daughters, Jane COSTLY, Elizabeth STRICKLING & Susanna SMITH
Ex: Son, Thomas TIMMONS
Wt: Jacob BOND; Robert DUTTON; Richard CHEW

AJ-R-124 **Adam TOLAND**   5 Feb 1787/ 23 Apr 1787
To: Brothers, Haly, Isaac, Jacob, & Benjamin TOLAND
    Sister, Ester TOLAND
Ex: Brother, Benjamin TOLAND
Wt: James MADEN; John Taylor HUGHES; Aram HUGHES

AJ-R-126 **Abraham TAYLOR**, shoemaker   5 Sep 1788/ 19 Dec 1788
To: Eldest son, Aquila TAYLOR (under age 21) - tract 65 a. *Cowans
       Addition*
    Wife, Isabella TAYLOR
    Sons, George TAYLOR, & Bennett TAYLOR (both under age 16)
Ex: Wife, Isabella TAYLOR; Joseph FORD
Wt: Francis NEILL; Mitchel STEWART; Francis Loveill PITT

AJ-R-129 **Thomas TURNER**   31 Jan 1789/ 17 Mar 1789
To: Wife, Martha TURNER - tract on which I live
    Son, Andrew TURNER - tract as described in metes & bounds of
       Nov 2, 1785 wit. by John McDONALD & John JOHNSTON
    Son, Samuel TURNER
    Daughters, Sarah, Catharine, Martha, Margaret, & Arabella
       TURNER
    Non-beneficiaries: William JOHNSON; Robert GILLIS of Baltimore
       Co.
    To be sold - other parts of land upon wife's death
Ex: Sons, Andrew & Samuel TURNER
Wt: John BELL; John VANCE; William OLDHAM

AJ-R-132 **David THOMPSON**   17 Jan 1791/ 24 Feb 1791
To: Son, John THOMPSON - Negro fellow Tom CUDGA
    Son, James THOMPSON - Negro boy Clenes
    Son, David THOMPSON - Negro girl Dinah
    Son, Henry THOMPSON- Negro boy Bill
    Daughter, Anna THOMPSON - Negro girl Mint
    Daughter, Mary THOMPSON; Wife, Sarah THOMPSON
Ex: Wife, Sarah THOMPSON; Brother, James THOMPSON
Wt: John RUFF; Thomas SHAY

AJ-R-134 **Edmond TALBOTT**   16 May 1794/ 8 Dec 1794
To: Wife, Elizabeth TALBOTT - third part of land I live on; Negro
        boy Jacob, Negro girl Priscilla
    Daughter, Hannah SCAFF - all land except 100 a. I live on;
        Negro girl Pegg, during her (Hannah's) life, & Negro man
        Will
    Granddaughter, Mary SCAFF, daughter of John SCAFF - Negro girl
        Pegg, afterwards
    Daughter, Mary TALBOTT - tract 100 a. part of *Bonds Gift* where
        I live
    Grandson, Thomas TALBOTT, of Thomas TALBOTT, deceased - Negro
        boy Jesse
    Grandsons, Edward OLDHAM & Henry OLDHAM, sons of William OLDHAM
    Granddaughters, Mary GORSUCH & Nancy BOND, daughters of Thomas
        TALBOTT, deceased
Ex: John SCAFF
Wt: Benjamin AMOS of James; Robert WHITFORD; John CROSSMORE

AJ-R-136 **John THOMAS**   18 May 1797/ 27 Jun 1797
To: Youngest son, William THOMAS
    Three youngest sons (names unspec.) - bound out until age 15
    Wife & my children (no names unspec.)
Ex: Barnet JOHNSON, son of Barnet; William PYLE
Wt: Thomas CREAL; Margaret CREAL; John FORWOOD; Willaim PYLE

AJ-R-140 **John VANCE**   15 Jun 1782/ 20 Jul 1782
To: Wife, Agnes VANCE
    Sons, John & Andrew VANCE (both not of lawful age) - all landed
        property
    Daughters, Alice, & Eleanor (or Eleoner) VANCE (both not of
        lawful age)
    Son, William VANCE ¦¦ Daughters, Jane TURNER & Rebecca HANNA
Ex: Wife, Agnes VANCE
Wt: John SMYTH; John BROWN; John BROWN, Junr.

AJ-R-142 **James VOGAN**   23 Dec 1783/ 13 Jan 1784
To: Mother (name unspec.) - tract 60 a. *Browns Delight*
    Sister, Mary VOGAN - tract 60 a. *Browns Delight* at mother's
        death, tracts 25 a. *Browns Look Out*, 18 a. *Riley's Addition*,
        & 24 a. *Riley's Long Meadow*
    Sister, Elizabeth AMOSS & brother, George VOGAN
    Elizabeth WEBB
Ex: James CLENDENHAN; Robert KIRKWOOD
Wt: Daniel McCOMAS; Esram HUGHES; Patrick DORAN

AJ-R-146 **Charles WORTHINGTON, Senior** 22 Nov 1773/ 24 Mar 1774
    of Baltimore Co.
To: Son, John WORTHINGTON - dwelling plantation 354 a. *Worthington Dividend*; 2 Negro men Poatswain & Pompay
    Son, Charles WORTHINGTON - 2 tracts 300 a. part of *Phillips Purchase* bought of Henry COALE & Thomas JOHNES; 2 Negro men Ben & Harry
    Son, Samual WORTHINGTON - tract 200 a. *Well's Lott* being part of *Phillips Purchase* bought of Thomas WELLS; 2 Negro boys Davey & Ceasor, & Negro girl Pegg
    Daughter, Sarah WORTHINGTON - Negro girl Poll & Negro boy Mitway
    Daughter, Mary WORTHINGTON - Negro girl Priss & Negro boy Ben
Ex: Sons, John & Charles WORTHINGTON
Wt: Joseph HOPKINS, Sen.; Joseph HENLEY; Skipwith COALE

AJ-R-148 **John WATTERS**, planter 16 Feb 1774/ 26 Mar 1774
    of Baltimore Co.
To: Daughter, Hannah WATTERS - the old family Bible; Negro woman Luc, Negro girls Pheby, & Cloe
    Son, Charles WATTERS - Negro boy Sam, Negro girl Isabele
    Daughter, Sarah WATTERS
    Wife, Mary WATTERS || Child my wife is with
Ex: Wife, Mary WATTERS; Brother, Stephen WATTERS
Wt: Joseph PRESBURY; Nathan HORNER; Robert SCOTT

AJ-R-150 **Charles WARD** 17 Feb 1776/ 16 Apr 1776
To: Wife (name unspec.)
    Martha CAMPBELL || Sons, Reubin, Moses, & James WARD
    Daughters, Mary, Rebecca, & Ann WARD
    To be sold - land
Ex: Robert BRYARLY; William HILL
Wt: John McCLURE; William McCULLOUGH; David BROWN

AJ-R-152 **Mildred WHEELER** 3 Sep 1776/ 14 Oct 1776
To: Rev. John LEWIS of Cecil Co.
    Niece, Mildred GREENWELL of St. Marys Co. - Negroes Charity & Will
    Godson, Francis TIRE, son of William TIRE of Charles Co. - Negro boy Jarret
    Elenor GREEN, daughter of Benjamin GREEN of Harford Co. - Mallatto girl Helen
    Nephew, John NEAL, son of William NEAL late of Charles Co. - Negroes Ned, Jack, & Abner
    Nephew, Francis NEAL, brother to above John NEAL - Negroes Toney & Rachel
    Niece, Elizabeth McTEE of Charles Co. - Negroes Coock, Betty, & Bennet
    Nephew, Joseph NEAL, brother to John & Francis NEAL - Negroes Augustus & Vance
    Niece, Mary Ann BOWMAN - Negro woman Darkis, to be free at death of niece
    Susanna WHEELER, daughter of Thomas WHEELER
    Rose BRADY of Charles Co.
    Sarah NEAL, sister to John, Francis, & Joseph, my brothers, all

       of Charles Co.
Ex: John NEAL of Charles Co.; Benjamin GREEN of Harford Co.
Wt: John CRETIN; Josias WHEELER; John WOODARD

AJ-R-154 **Isaac WOOD**   29 Apr 1776/ 23 Jun 1777
To: Son, Isaac WOOD ¦¦ Wife, Elizabeth WOOD
    Son, James WOOD - tract 65 a. rem. from land sold to Thomas
      SHEARER
    Daughters, Hannah & Mary (nee WOOD) & Granddaughters, Hannah
      COWAN & Elizabeth HAYES - 2 1/2 a. each from 10 a. tract on
      Spesutia Church Road & the Quaker Road
    To be sold - tract 25 a. *Isaacs Lot*, tract 61 a. previously
      intended for son, Isaac WOOD
    Sons, William, Benjamin, & Moses WOOD - rem. tracts after
      wife's death
Ex: Wife, Elizabeth WOOD
Wt: Andrew MEEK; Daniel ANDERSON

AJ-R-157 **John WILSON, Senr.**   7 Oct 1775/ 16 Aug 1777
To: Son, Benjamin WILSON - Negro lad Clitus
    Daughter, Margret CRAWFORD
    Son, William WILSON, Junr. - Negro boy Tom
    Daughter, Sarah LOGHLIN - Negro woman Hagar
    Daughter, Johanna CALBERT (or CALVEAT) - Negro girl Ginny
Ex: Sons, Benjamin & William WILSON
Wt: John PATRICK; Winston Smith DALLAM; William COALE, Jun.

AJ-R-159 **Samuel WORTHINGTON**   26 Aug 1777/ 25 Sep 1777
To: Brother, John WORTHINGTON - half of tract *Welses Lott* with
      dwelling being part of *Phillips Purchase*
    Negroes Sesor, Pall, Davey, Sesor, Hector, Lovor - set free at
      age 25
    Brother, Charles WORTHINGTON - tract residue of *Welses Lott*
      being part of *Phillips Purchase*
    Charles LEE, son of Josiah & Sarah LEE ¦¦ Joseph HENLY
    Mary LITTEN ¦¦ Solomon REES
    Christian M. WILLIAMS (or McWILLIAMS)
    Henry WORTHINGTON, son of John & Presila WORTHINGTON
    Sarah WORTHINGTON, daughter of Charles & Mary WORTHINGTON
Ex: Brothers, John & Charles WORTHINGTON
Wt: Skipwith COALE; Gidion PERVEIL; Elizabeth BONER

AJ-R-161 **Robert WILLIAMSON**, farmer   5 Oct 1777/ 3 Nov 1777
          of Deer Creek Upper Hundred
To: Wife, Sarah WILLIAMSON - house with 10 a.
    Martha CROSSON ¦¦ Jean, Samuel, William, & John CROSSON
    To be sold - rem. of land
Ex: James BARNET; Wife, Sarah WILLIAMSON
Wt: James BARNET; Henry CROOKS; Samuel LOCKHERD

AJ-R-163 **James WILSON**   9 May 1777/ 6 Jan 1778
To: Brothers, John & Archibald WILSON
    Nephew, Andrew WILSON, son of John WILSON
    Andrew WILSON, oldest son of brother Archibald WILSON
    Wife, Isabel WILSON ¦¦ Nephew, Mathew CLARK, son of James CLARK

Ex: Wife, Isabel WILSON
Wt: John MONTGOMERY; William MONTGOMERY

AJ-R-164 **Henry WETHERALL**   13 Mar 1778/ 26 Aug 1778
To: Son, Henry WETHERALL - tract 167 a. *Linen Manufacture*, tract
    50 a. *Johns Interest*, tract part of *Lewis' Purchase Improved*
    adj. *Whitely*
    Son, James WETHERALL - tract rem. part of *Lewis' Purchase
    Improved*, tract 45 a. *Hills Hill*
    Son, William WETHERALL - tract 100 a. *Locust Neck*, tract 60 a.
    Hansons Neglect
    Wife, Mary Ann WETHERALL
Ex: Wife, Mary Ann WETHERALL
Wt: Samuel Groome OSBORN; William OSBORN; Roger BOYCE; Robert
    SAUNDERS

AJ-R-167 **Thomas WHITE**   15 Apr 1773/ 4 Oct 1779
    age 68 about Mar 15, 1773, of Philadelphia, Pa.,
    but formerly of Baltimore Co.
To: Wife (name unspec.) - house & lot on Walnut Street,
    Philadelphia pur. of Isreal MORRES, ground rent on lot on
    Second Street leased to Mordecai YARNALL; girl Rachel & boy
    Jesse
    Daughters, Sophia (HALL ?) & Sarah Charlotte WHITE - tracts
    Dairy Enlarged & *Addition to Simmons Neglect*; tract 100 a.
    part of *Mourieat (Monreal ?)* adj. *Halls Plains*, *Brownes
    Entrance* & *Paca's Stoney Ridge*
    Son, Willaim WHITE - tracts *Rumney Royal*, except that sold to
    Samuel GRIFFITH, *Delf Island*, & *Swansbury*; tract part of
    Hammonds Hope; tract part of *Paradise* between part conveyed
    to Col. John HALL & *Head of Swansbury*; tract small part of
    Royal Exchange Resurveyed Especially at the Hollow Bottum
    Daughter, Mary MORRIS - tract *Leigh of Leighton*
    Also to daughter, Sarah (or Sharah) Charlotte WHITE - tract
    Eaton pur. of James PHILLIPS & adj. small tracts *Eatons
    Addition*, & *Eatons Second Addition*; tract part of *Montserada*
    pur. of Mary STOKES with small tract *Little Worth* surveyed
    by James CALDER which adj. *Montserada* & the River; 2 tracts
    Gays Enlargement & *Gays Favour* at head of Back River; tract
    Jones Addition at head of Bush River & part of *Hathaways
    Hazard* pur. of John HUGHES & Martha GARRATTSON; tract 130
    a. part of *Monreal* between *Sophia's Dairy*, *Deavers Stoney
    Ridge* & *Hathaways Hazard*; 2 tracts 690 a. parts of *Monreal*
    adj. *Hathaways Hazard*, *Abbotts Forest*, *Halls Plains*,
    Whiteakers Ridge, land sold to Robert PATTERSON, *Miles
    Hill the Addition*, & *Come by Chance Jones Addition*; also
    tract part of *Monreal* rem. unsold between the *Agreement* &
    land sold to Thomas BROWN, Kent MITCHEL, & James COLE; lot
    & storehouses at Bush Town & tract *Wood Yard*; Negro woman
    Rachel & all her children, & Ester & all her children
    Aquila HALL ¦¦ Robert MORRIS
    Two sisters in England , son's wife, & sister (no names
    specified)
    Also to daughter, Sophia (HALL ?) - five tracts near Deer
    Creek: *Halls Rich Neck*, *First Addition to Halls Rich Neck*,

Second Addition to Halls Rich Neck, Wind Mill Hill, & part of *Aquila's Inheritance;* tracts near Winter Run: *Ah Ha Indeed,* the *Outlet,* parts of *Constant Friendship, Neighbors Affinity,* & *Hathaways Trust* with *Harrisons Resolution* & *Hickory Ridge;* tract 864 a. part of *Abbotts Forest* conveyed from Isaac WEBSTER; tract parts of *Monreal* on both sides of Humphreys Run except parts contracted to Daniel DONAWIN & William ARNOLD; tracts on S side of Winters Run: *Constatinople, Lacedeman, Antrim, Kilkenny, Londonderry,* & *Little Hopewell;* all residue of Negroes except Rachel & Ester
    Daughter Sophia's son, Thomas HALL
    Grandson, William HALL - parts of land (given to Sophia ?) on N side of Rock Branch with parts towards Aquila HALL's mill on Binam Run
    Grandson, Edward HALL - parts of land 1425 a. (given to Sophia ?) *Ah Ha Indeed* adj. *Ah Ha the Cow Pasture, Edenburg,* Rock Branch, & the W branch of Bush River; tract 888 a. S of Rock Branch adj. *Edenburg*
    Granddaughter, Charlotte HALL - Negro woman Moll & all her children, mulatto girls Dinah & Lucy
    W. Thomas HARRISON
    Mary FAWCETT (who died between the writing & executing of this will)
    Servant, Rachel - set free
    Contract with Solomon ARMSTRONG for 60 a. part of *Monreal*
    Contract with Thomas HENDERSON for 10 a. part of *Monreal* & *Jones Addition*
Ex: Wife (name unspec.); Son, William WHITE; Robert MORRIS
Wt: James MATHEWS; Benedict Edward HALL; Aquilla HALL, Jun.; John CLARKE; Edward Carvel TOLLEY

                                                    Codicil: 5 Nov 1776
To: Daughter, Sarah Charlotte WHITE

                              Codicil: 26 Mar 1778/ 8 Sep 1780
To: Wife (name unspec.) - mulatto girl Lucy previously given to Charlotte HALL
    Daughter, Sarah Charlotte WHITE, now deceased - ground rents pur. of Joseph & James MORRIS & previously willed lands to be divided between wife, son (William), & daughters Sophia & Mary
    To be sold - tract in Pennsylvania pur. of Doctor William SMITH
Wt: Thomas ANDREWS; Jacob GILES, Jun.; Edward GILES

                                  Codicil: 19 May 1778/ 4 Oct 1779
To: Son, Rev. William WHITE
Wt: George PATTERSON; William HALL

<u>AJ-R-180</u> **William WILLSON** (or **WILSON**)   18 Feb 1774/ 23 Jun 1780
        of Baltimore Co.
To: Wife, Cassandra WILLSON - Negro woman Sarah
    Youngest son, Samuel WILLSON - dwelling plantation 300 a. *Aquillas Inheritance;* tract 189 a. part of *Good Neighborhood Enlarged* adj. *Aquilas Inheritance* bought of John HARRIS; 12

       Negroes, viz. Harry, Cloe, Bobb, Henry, Faney, Clem, Sarah,
       Betty, Saune, Agram, Sukey, & Landon
    Daughter, Rachel WILLSON - tract 200 a. part of *Gibsons Park*;
       9 Negroes, viz. Jane, Hagar, Floro, Ben, Poll, Pheeby,
       Jacob, Rachael, & Adam
    Son, William WILLSON - tract 400 a. rem. part of *Gibsons Park*;
       6 Negroes, viz. David, Leanda, Charles, Dinah, Betty, & Jane
    Five Negroes set free, viz. Bristol & Fanney, Adam & Affee, &
       Tower
    John HARRIS
Ex: (None named)
Wt: Nathan RIGBIE; James WALKER; William WILSON

AJ-R-183 **John WATKENS** (or **WATKINS**)   13 Oct 1780/ 25 Jan 1781
To: Three oldest sons, John, William, & Amos WATKENS
    Wife & my young children, (names unspec.)
Ex: Wife (name unspec.)
Wt: Benedict Edward HALL; Francis GARRETT

AJ-R-185 **Grace WALLIS**   18 Sep 1780/ 3 Sep 1781
To: Daughters, Sarah HOPKINS & Frances HOPKINS
    Granddaughter, Grace JACOB || Sons, Thomas & Joseph WALLIS
    Non-beneficiary: Uncle, Joseph JACOB, deceased, of New Port
    Negro woman Dinah - set at liberty
Ex: Sons, Joseph & Thomas WALLIS
Wt: James RIGBIE; Joseph WARNER; Cuthbert WARNER

AJ-R-187 **Abraham WERAM**   8 May 1781/ 14 Jun 1782
       (or **WEREAM** or **WAREAM**)
To: Wife, Cristiana WERAM || Thomas MATSON
    My children (names unspec.)
Ex: Wife, Cristiana WERAM; Thomas MATSON
Wt: Theophilus JONES; Samuel CROW

AJ-R-188 **Henry WOOD**   9 Apr 1781/ 10 Aug 1782
To: Wife, Susanna WOOD
Ex: Wife, Susanna WOOD
Wt: James LYTTLE; John JOHNSON; James SKEVINTON

AJ-R-189 **Richard WELLS, Sen.**   3 Oct 1782/ 24 Oct 1782
To: Eldest son, Richard WELLS - tract 150 a. at N end of my land
    Youngest son, William WELLS - tract rem. part of *Arabia Patra*;
       Negro man Isaac
    Daughter, Cassandra WARD - Negro girl Cate
    Richard WARD, son of Cassandra WARD
    Daughter, Susanna DOWNING - Negro girl Pat
    Richard DOWNING, son of Susanna DOWNING
    Daughter, Frances HENLEY - Negro man Lordon
    Daughter, Elizabeth RENSHAW
Ex: Son, William WELLS; Edward WARD
Wt: Joseph WILSON, Jun.; Jacob WALLIS; Thomas WALLIS

AJ-R-191 **Richard WELLS**   13 Jan 1784/ 29 Jun 1784
To: Wife, Jane WELLS - Negro girl Jane
    Son, Richard WELLS - half of real estate; Negro man Jack

```
     Son, Samuel WELLS - residue of real estate
     Daughter, Cassandra HAWKINS - Negro girl Rachael
     Daughter, Drusilla WELLS - Negro girl Cate
     Daughter, Mary WELLS - Negro girl Hannah & Negro boy Bobb
     Daughters, Luranah HAWKINS, Elizabeth BARNES, & Susanna PRIGG
Ex:  Wife, Jane WELLS
Wt:  Joseph WALLIS; William ELLIS; James FISHER
```

AJ-R-193 **Abraham WHITAKER**   (undated)/ 20 Jul 1784
```
To:  Four sons, Abraham, Thomas, George, & Josias WHITAKER - all
     real estate to be divided equally
     Daughter, Susanna WHITAKER - Negro girl named Hannah
     Wife, Elizabeth WHITAKER - Negro girl named Sall
Ex:  Wife, Elizabeth WHITAKER
Wt:  Robert HARRIS; Alexander CRAWFORD; Daniel McFILTON (or
     McJILTON)
```

AJ-R-195 **John WOOD**   5 Oct 1784/ 8 Nov 1784
```
To:  Amos BARNES
     Non-beneficiary: Rebecca, deceased wife of Amos BARNES
     Daughters, Mary & Susannah WOOD || Sons John & Hudson WOOD
     Son, Joshua WOOD - all my real estate
Ex:  Wife, Sarah WOOD
Wt:  Henry JOHNS; Mitchel STEWART; Greenberry DORSEY
```

AJ-R-197 **Samuel WEBSTER**   26 Nov 1785/ 3 Jan 1786
```
To:  Son, Samuel WEBSTER - part of plantation he lives on being the
     NE part
     Son, Richard WEBSTER - tract SW part of the plantation
     adj. James Run, Websters Forest, land sold to Robert
     ADAIR, & Christophers Camp
     Son, Michael WEBSTER - plantation 100 a. he lives on being part
     of Howard's Forest
     My six children (other names unspec.)
Ex:  Three sons, Samuel, Richard, & Michael WEBSTER
Wt:  John ARCHER; Daniel BAYLES; Isaac WEBSTER
```

AJ-R-199 **Ignatius WHEELER**   1 Dec 1784/ 9 Nov 1786
```
To:  Eldest son, Ignatius WHEELER - all my lands on N side of Deer
     Creek; tract 1/3 of Childrens Rowling House
     Son, Bennett WHEELER - tract part of Brotherly Care adj.
     Wheeler & Clarks Contrivance, tract 1/3 of Childrens Rowling
     House; Negro man Tom, his wife Sall, his sons Joe & Tom, &
     his daughters Nan, & Sarah
     Son, Joseph WHEELER - rem. part of tracts Wheeler & Clarks
     Contrivance, Brotherly Care, & Benjamins Camp, tract Persons
     Range, tract 1/3 of Childrens Rowling House; Negro man
     Harry, his wife Hester, & their 2 eldest children Bet & Peg,
     & Negro boy Ralph
     Daughter, Monica WHEELER - Negro man Frank, & his wife Suck,
     Negro boys Jack & Paul, Negro girls Cate, Beck, Gin, &
     Clarke, Negro man James & Hannah his wife
     Daughter, Elizabeth MITCHEL - Negro boy Stephen, Negro girls
     Nan, Suck, & Mary
```

Daughter, Mary GIBSON - Negro man Davy & Rachel his wife, Negro
woman Christian, Negro girl Fan, Negro boys Gabriel, Neo,
& Will, Negro girls Gin & Sall, Negro girl Terry, Rachel's
daughter
Son, Joseph WHEELER - Negro boy Jerry, after wife's death
Wife, Elizabeth WHEELER - Negro boy named Jerry
Ex: Elizabeth WHEELER
Wt: Josias WHEELER; Thomas WHEELER; David CLARKE

AJ-R-203 **Hugh WHITEFORD**   21 Jun 1786/ 30 Jun 1786
To: Wife, Anna WHITEFORD - Negro girl Fann
Son, John WHITEFORD
Daughters, Anna GIBSON, wife of Jacob & Mary COOPER, wife of
Alexander
Grandson, Hugh WHITEFORD, son of John - tract *Whiteford's
Desire*, tract 73 a. *Wats Disapointment*
Son, Hugh WHITEFORD - dwelling plantation 184 a. *Whiteford's
Adventure*, land in Pennsylvania, certificate land in
Maryland; Negroes Dina, Gess, Jean, & Jack
Ex: Son, Hugh WHITEFORD
Wt: Nathaniel WYLIE; Aquila JONES; Hugh WHITEFORD, son of Michael;
Jacob GIBSON; Alexander COOPER

AJ-R-205 **Samuel WEBB**   2 Dec 1787/ 4 Mar 1788
To: Son, Samuel WEBB - tract 18 1/2 a. *Webbs Spot*, meadow *Diggins
Meadow* adj. *Webbs Spot*, mill dam & race, *High Field*,
Spittle Craft, *Giles & Websters Discovery*, Joseph DAVIS
land, Jacob ALBERT's land, & *Rice Patch Runn*; molatto waggon
driver Ned & his mother Bett, old yellow Negro man Jim
Grandson, William WEBB, son of William WEBB, deceased
Daughter, Sarah WEBB, alias CARROLL
Doctor John ARCHER on brother William WEBB's account
Son-in-law, Jacob FORWOOD ¦¦ Margaret WEBB, alias BRIERLY
Margaret Lee WEBB, alias DOWNING ¦¦ Elizabeth WEBB, alias HALL
Constant Priscilla WEBB, alias DOWNING
Non-beneficiary: George & Elizabeth WEIR, deceased
To be sold - residue of real estate
Ex: Son, Samuel WEBB
Wt: Edward ELLETT; Samuel ELLETT; Thomas FLAHARTY

AJ-R-209 **William WHITEFORD**   11 Oct 1788/ 4 Nov 1788
To: Brother, Hugh WHITEFORD
William WHITEFORD, son of Hugh WHITEFORD
Mary WHITEFORD, daughter of Hugh
William BEAN (under age 21), son of John BEAN
William PARKS (under age 21), son of John PARKS
John MUNN ¦¦ Jean GORDON ¦¦ Ann PARKS
Ex: Brother, Hugh WHITEFORD
Wt: John MONTGOMERY; John CLARK; Hugh WHITEFORD, Junr.

AJ-R-211 **Mary WATTERS**   14 Nov 1789/ 13 Apr 1790
To: Son, Godfrey WATTERS - my land
Godfrey's brothers, Henry WATTERS & William WATTERS
Ex: (None named)
Wt: Henry RUFF, Sr.; Henry RUFF, Jr.; Daniel PRESTON

AJ-R-212 **Elizabeth WALTHAM**   Verbal: 2 May 1790/ 15 Jun 1790
To: John DUTTON - Negro woman Sook, to have freedom
    My brothers & sisters excluding brother Carlton WALTHAM's
        children
Ex: (None named)
Wt: Ann YEATES; Margret YATES; Edeth (or Eady) EVERETT

AJ-R-213 **Josiah WHEELER**   22 Jan 1791/ 7 Feb 1791
To: Wife (name unspec.) - Negroes until daughter Susanna is 18
    To be sold - land to discharge debt
    Daughter, Susanna WHEELER (under age 18) - rem. lands; Negroes
        given to her mother
    Cousin, Thomas HILLEN
    Money toward finishing the Roman Chapel near Hickory Tavern.
Ex: Cousin, Thomas HILLEN; Cousin, Thomas WHEELER
Wt: Thomas ARCHER; Joseph WHEELER; John FORWOOD

1 Mar 1791 - The widow (name unspec.) renounced in form.

AJ-R-215 **Edward WARD**   19 Jul 1774/ 27 May 1791
To: Son, Richard WARD - half of land, other half after wife's death
    Wife, Cassandra WARD - half of land
    Daughter, Avis WARD - Negro Rachel & her incr.
    Youngest daughter, Margret WARD (under age 16) - Negro Liddia
        & her incr.
    Daughters, Mary & Elizabeth WARD
    Eldest son, Edward WARD - cut off because he treated father so
        badly
Ex: Wife, Cassandra WARD
Wt: William RAE; John STUMP; Peter WILSON - Quaker

27 May 1791 - Cassandra WARD quit her claim & elected her dower or
        1/3.

AJ-R-217 **Col. Ignatius WHEELER**   13 Jul 1793/ 13 Aug 1793
To: Daughters, Monica, Treacy, Henrietta, Mary Ann, & Elizabeth
        WHEELER, sons, Francis Ignatius, Bennett & Ignatius WHEELER
        - balance of estate to be divided
    Wife, Henrietta WHEELER - one third of land
    Trustees: John Lee GIBSON, Esq.; Joseph WHEELER
Ex: Wife, Henrietta WHEELER; John Lee GIBSON, Esqr.; Joseph WHEELER
Wt: John ARCHER; David CLARK; Thomas WHEELER

                                         Codicil: 14 Jul 1793/ 13 Aug 1793
To: Joseph STOKES - small tract to be conveyed which was sold to
        him
Wt: Francis NEIL; John ARCHER; Bennet WHEELER

AJ-R-221 **James WEBSTER**   27 Dec 1791/ 26 Jan 1792
To: Two daughters, Susanah & Mary WEBSTER, & Son, James WEBSTER -
        lands to be divided equally
    Negro man Bob - freed in 6 years
    Wife, Mary WEBSTER || My mother, Mary SIMS
Ex: Wife, Mary WEBSTER; James LYTLE
Wt: George McLAUGHLIN; John BULL of Edmund; William STALLINGS

AJ-R-223 **Rachel WILSON**   3 Dec 1790/ 11 Jun 1793
To: Negroes & their children - to be free, males at age 21, females
    at age 18
    My mother & my 2 brothers (names unspec.)
Ex: Two brothers (names unspec.)
Wt: William COX; Jehu KEIN; Henry WILSON, the elder

                                Codicil: 4 Dec 1790/ 11 Jun 1793
To: Uncle, Henry WILSON - all above Negroes, if above Will cannot
    legally give them their freedom
Wt: Hannah RICHARDSON; John CRAIGE

AJ-R-225 **James WARD**   3 Sep 1793/ 12 Nov 1793
To: Wife, Ann WARD
    Son, William WARD (under age 14)
    Eldest sons, Richard & James WARD (both under age 21)
    Daughters, Elizabeth & Ann WARD
    Two oldest Negroes, James & Dido - free in 6 years
    Youngest Negroes, Hannah, Jacob, & Joe - free at age 35
Ex: Wife, Ann WARD
Wt: Elisha BRYARLY; John WARD; Samuel RAINE

18 Nov 1793 - Ann WARD, widow, resigned right of executorship.

AJ-R-228 **Hannah WEBSTER**   13 Oct 1790/ 8 May 1795
To: Two sisters, Mary & Margaret WEBSTER
Ex: Sisters, Mary & Margaret WEBSTER
Wt: William HALL; Sabina HALL BAYER

AJ-R-229 **John Lee WESBTER** of Spesutia   4 Mar 1795/ 19 Aug 1795
To: Son, John Skinner WEBSTER (under age 21) - lands & plantation
    at Spesutia Creek, lands on the Cranberry Swamp at the long
    bridge; Negro man James until free
    Second son, Isaac Lee WEBSTER (under age 21) - residue of lands
    in Harford Co., lands in Pennsylvania & Virginia
    Surviving son if only one - lands at *Forrest Plantation* called
    Best Endeavor
    To be sold - other lands
    Daughters, Elizabeth & Ann WEBSTER (both under age 16)
    Sister, Ann JEWETT
    Brother-in-law, John WILSON - supervise education of my minor
    children
    Negroes - manumitted according to list recorded in Harford Co.
    Records
Ex: Brother-in-law, John WILSON; Son, John Skinner WEBSTER
Wt: William COCHRON; Mitchel STEWART; William WILLIAMS; Jacob
    BROWN

                                Codicil: 28 May 1795/ 19 Aug 1795
To: Nephews, John JEWETT & Thomas JEWETT, discharge from
    apprenticeship to master, Joshua HUSBAND
    Son, Isaac WEBSTER - principal of bond from Col. William
    FITZHUGH & Col. George PLATOR
    Sister, Elizabeth ROBERTSON
Wt: Jacob BROWN; Mitchel STEWART; William COCHRAN; John ARCHER

Codicil: 8 Jun 1795
To: Negro girl Becky - given to her mother
    Son, John WEBSTER ‖ Brother, Isaac WEBSTER
Wt: John WILSON; Ann JEWETT; John S. WEBSTER

AJ-R-238 **John WINEMAN**   30 Mar 1788/ 13 Oct 1795
To: Ignatius WHEELER - tracts *Williams Delight*, *Milers Point*,
    Georges Interest; tract *Dallams Fancy* where I live & grist
    mill stands
Ex: Ignatius WHEELER
Wt: Jonathan HAMMILTON; Ann MORRISON; Robert HAMMILTON

    Presented for recording by executors of Ignatius WHEELER's
    estate: Henrietta WHEELER, John Lee GIBSON, & Joseph WHEELER

AJ-R-240 **Anna WHITEFORD**   10 Feb 1791/ 17 Nov 1795
To: Daughters, Anna GIBSON & Mary COOPER
    Grandson, Hugh GIBSON; Granddaughter, Anna COOPER
    Children of daughter Mary COOPER & her husband Alexander COOPER
    Children of daughter Anna GIBSON & her husband Jacob GIBSON
    Granddaughter, Anna GIBSON; Son, Hugh WHITEFORD
Ex: Alexander COOPER
Wt: Patrick DORNEY; Simon GILLESPIE

AJ-R-242 **Richard WALDRON**   22 Jun 1796/ 2 May 1797
To: Son, David WALDRON - money due me in state of New York; tools
    he carried to Kentucky
    Wife, Phebey WALDRON - lot part of *Majors Choice*
    All my daughters (names unspec.)
Ex: Wife, Phebey WALDRON
Wt: Joseph BARNES; John BARNES; Daniel SCOTT

AJ-R-244 **Richard WILMOTT**   12 May 1794/ 13 Jun 1797
To: Daughter, Elizabeth MATTHEWS, wife of Bennet MATHEWS - tract
    Deep Valley in Baltimore Co. on Morgans Run
    Daughter, Mary HALL, wife of Dr. Jacob HALL
    Grandson, Richard Wilmott HALL - Negro boy Abram
    Grandson, William Wilmott HALL - Negro girl Priss
    Grandson, Thomas Parry HALL - Negro girl Hanna
    Granddaughter, Mary HALL - Negro girl Peg
    My relation, Ruth WILMOTT, daughter of John WILMOTT
    My relation, Sarah WILMOTT, daughter of John WILMOTT
Ex: Dr. Jacob HALL
Wt: Joseph STOKES; John CRETIN; John ARCHER

AJ-R-246 **James WETHERALL** of Abingdon   20 May 1797/ 24 Aug 1797
To: Children of Daniel RUFF of Philadelphia: John RUFF, Hannah
    RUFF, Daniel RUFF, Jr., Henry RUFF, & James RUFF
    Land for burying ground - 20 square feet of ground in Abingdon
    where wife is buried
Ex: Daniel RUFF
Wt: William SMITH; John MONKS; Ben NOWLAND

Codicil: 20 May 1797/ 24 Aug 1797
To: Daniel RUFF's children
Wt: William SMITH; John MONKS; Ben NOWLAND

AJ-R-249 **Joseph WEST**   23 Oct 1798/ 4 Dec 1798
To: Wife, Ann WEST - all of real estate
    Niece, Frances TRICE ǁ Niece, Polly WEST, alias CUNNINGHAM
    Thomas TRICE, son of Hermon & Frances TRICE
Ex: Phillip ALBERT; John FORWOOD of William
Wt: John McLAUGHLIN, Sr.; James McLAUGHLIN; John McLAUGHLIN, Jr.

AJ-R-250 **Isaac WEBSTER**   2 Sep 1799/ 30 Sep 1799
To: Wife, Elizabeth WEBSTER ǁ Son, Thomas WEBSTER
    Surviving children (names unspec.)
    John S. WEBSTER ǁ Son, Isaac WEBSTER
    Friend, Daniel SHEREDINE
Ex: Sons, Isaac & Thomas WEBSTER
Wt: Samuel WEBSTER - Quaker; John W. WILSON - Quaker; Isaac Lee
    WEBSTER

AJ-R-252 **Joseph WOOLSEY**   20 Nov 1799/ 28 Jan 1800
To: Wife, Sarah WOOLSEY - 1/3 of real estate
    Son, Henry WOOLSEY - 1/3 of real estate
    Son, George WOOLSEY - 1/3 of real estate
    Daughter, Deborah MOORE, wife of Jason MOORE
    Son, Joseph WOOLSEY
Trustees: Samuel BAYLESS & John MOORES
Ex: Wife, Sarah WOOLSEY; Sons, Henry & George WOOLSEY
Wt: Alexander YOUNG; John CUMANS; Matthew DENISTON

AJ-R-255 **Charles WORTHINGTON**   20 Sep 1799/ 9 Feb 1802
          of Deer Creek
To: Son, Joseph WORTHINGTON - tract 300 a. *Philips his Purchase*;
    Negro boy Jim, to be set free on the first day of 1812
    Six children, Sarah, Charles, Ann, Margarett, Mary, & Elizabeth
       WORTHINGTON
    To be sold - plantation or farm 100 a. near the River
       Susquehanna willed from brother, Samuel WORTHINGTON
    Negroes to be free on the first day of the year indicated:
       boy Bill - 1804, girl Priss - 1806, Jim - 1812, Ness - 1815,
       boy Mike - 1817, Arringe - 1817, Charles - 1820, Prince -
       1822, Sall - 1823, Harry - 1824
Ex: Son, Joseph WORTHINGTON; Son-in-law, James JOHNSON
Wt: Peter WILSON; Joseph HARRIS; Nathaniel HARPLEY

AJ-R-258 **John WILSON**   11 Jul 1792/ 11 Jun 1793
To: My children, James, Hugh, Mary, John, Jean, & Elizabeth WILSON
    Son, Robert WILSON
    To be sold - all real estate
Ex: Sons, James & John WILSON
Wt: James DAGG; Lemuel HENLEY (or Samuel KENLY); Robert CRISWELL

AJ-R-260 **Ann WARD**   5 Jan 1800/ 11 Feb 1800
To: Daughters, Hannah FALLS, Jane JOHNSON, Elizabeth WARD, & Ann
    WARD

```
    Sons, Richard, James, & William WARD
    Negro Tom - freedom at the year 1830
    Negro Primes - freedom at the year 1832
    Robert BRYARLY
Ex: Daughter, Elizabeth WARD
Wt: William BAY; David THOMAS
```

AJ-R-264 **Robert YOUNG**, farmer   8 Feb 1777/ 3 Nov 1777
```
To: Eldest son, Alexander YOUNG - upper half of plantation
    Youngest son, Hugh YOUNG - lower half of land adj. Cristifers
       Camp (Christophers Camp ?)
    Eldest daughter, Agness YOUNG ¦¦ Second daughter, Sarah YOUNG
    Third daughter, Mary YOUNG
Ex: Addam MEGAW; Hugh KIRKPATRICK
Wt: Hugh DEVER; Samuel WEBSTER, son of Isaac; John McADOW
```

AJ-R-266 **Edward YORK**   7 Mar 1790/ 16 Apr 1793
```
To: Wife, Mary YORK ¦¦ Mary RABURG
    Negro boy, Abraham - set free at age 25
    My brothers' & sisters' children (names unspec.)
Ex: Wife, Mary YORK
Wt: Thomas Howell BIRCKHEAD; Hannah DEBRULER
```

AJ-R-268 **Oliver YORK**   12 Sep 1784/ 18 Apr 1785
```
To: Wife, Sarah YORK - dwelling plantation 112 1/2 a. part of
       Bridewell Dock & York Chance
    Child if wife is now with child ¦¦ Brother, Edward YORK
Ex: Wife, Sarah YORK
Wt: J. Hammond DORSEY; James HILL; Thomas STRONG
```

AJ-R-270 **John YORK**   20 Feb 1783/ 17 Mar 1783
```
To: Wife, Hannah YORK
Ex: Wife, Hannah YORK
Wt: Lambert WILMER; James HILL; James SPENCER
```

                    - END OF WILL BOOK -

INDEX OF TRACT NAMES & GEOGRAPHIC LOCATIONS

Name	Ref
Aarons Spring Neck	R-051
Abbots Forest	2-280
Abbotts Forest	R-167
Abingdon	2-211,463,517;R-246
Abingdon College	2-451
Ables Lott	2-040
Abraham's Inheritance	2-378
Abrahams Spot	2-340
Addition to Brothers Lott	2-237
Addition to Gibsons Ridge	2-482
Addition to Joshua's Choice	2-002
Addition to Poverty Inclosed	R-103
Addition to Shepherds Range	2-485
Addition to Simmons Neglect	2-280, 463;R-167
Addition to Water Mill	2-513, 517
Agreement	R-167
Ah Ha Indeed	R-167
Ah Ha the Cow Pasture	R-167
Amos Fancy	2-002
Andersons Lot	2-010
Ann's Delight Enlarged	2-463
Anne Arundel Co.	R-031
Anns Dowry	2-424
Antioch	2-024
Antrim	2-280;R-167
Aqua Demnum	2-292
Aquila Hall's Mill	R-167
Aquila's Inheritance	R-167
Aquilas Begining	2-274
Aquilas Inheritance	2-274
Aquillas Inheritance	2-092;R-180
Arabia Patra	2-202;R-189
Arabia Petra	2-346,411,463
Argiule, Shire of	2-414
Arthers Delay	R-010
Arthurs Lott	2-150
Ashmores Retirement	2-463
Askins Hope	2-517
Atkinsons Purchase	2-237
Back River	R-167
Bacors Choyse Inlarged	R-028
Baltimore	2-103,176,312
Baltimore Co.	2-024,027,136, 140,150,194,213,215, 237,252,268,271,274, 335,378,391,408,482, 485,498,506,508,521;
Baltimore Town	R-010,073,129,146, 148,167,180,244 2-021,062, 312,340;R-068
Barrens	R-004
Barton's Chance	2-111
Batchelars Quarter	2-391
Bay Side	2-204;R-073
Bayside	R-107
Beals Camp	R-098
Bears Neck	2-027
Beaver Dams	2-062
Beaver Neck	2-268
Bellair	2-404
Benjamin's Choice	2-237
Benjamins Camp	R-199
Benjamins Choice	2-249
Best Endeavor	R-229
Better Hope	R-007
Betties Lot	2-418
Betts Prosperity	2-498
Bin	2-508
Binam Run	R-167
Black Island	2-204
Blacksmiths Lot	2-340
Blenhum	R-073
Blue Rocks	2-340
Bohemia	R-008
Bon Water	R-049
Bond's Lot	2-336
Bonds Forest	2-021,040
Bonds Forris	R-103
Bonds Gift	R-134
Bonds Gratuety	2-291
Bonds Inheritance	2-064
Bonds Last Shift	2-033,508
Bonds Pleasant Hills	2-021,040
Boston	2-009
Branters Ridge	2-340
Bread and Cheese Branch	2-062
Brices Endeavor	2-432
Bridewell Dock	R-268
Broad Creek	2-378,463;R-001
Brook Cross	2-252
Brookers Cross	2-340
Brooms Bloom	R-011
Brother's Discovery	2-188
Brother's Lott	2-237
Brotherly Care	R-199
Brownes Entrance	R-167
Browns Delight	R-142
Browns Look Out	R-142
Bryerly Grove	R-051

A-1

Bryerlys Refuse	2-340	Cross Roads	2-472
Buchanans Deer Park	2-340	Cuba	2-176
Bucks Co.	2-146	Culvers Entrance	2-079
Buford	2-031	Cumberland Forge	2-237
Bush River	2-428;R-167	Dairy Enlarged	R-167
Bush River Neck	2-316	Dallams Fancy	R-238
Bush River Upper Hundred	2-051	Daniels Land	2-340
Bush Town	2-274;R-167	Days Double Purchase	2-150,171
Bynams Run	2-424	Days Meadows	2-150
Calvert Co.	2-391	Days Priviledge	2-150,171
Carlisles Parcks	R-007	Deavers Compulsion	2-167
Carolina	2-190,266	Deavers Enlargement	2-167
Cecil Co.	R-008,101,152	Deavers Goodwill	2-340
Cecils Adventure	2-062	Deavers Neighbor	R-051
Cedar Swamp	2-374	Deavers Pleasure	2-167
Chapple	2-411	Deavers Project	2-167
Charles Co.	R-152	Deavers Stoney Ridge	R-167
Charles Town	2-276	Deep Valley	R-244
Chestnut Spring	2-167	Deer Creek	2-092,237,333,352,
Chilberry Hall	2-517		357,374,379,384,
Childrens Rowling House	R-199		394,411,463,517;
Christophers Camp	R-197,264		R-001,018,048,
Clark's Tobacco	2-263		051,167,199,255
Clarksons Purchase	2-040	Deer Creek Hundred	2-120
Clear Fountain	2-141	Deer Creek Middle Hundred	R-003
Cley Hill Inlarged	2-085	Deer Creek Upper Hundred	R-161
Coffee House	2-021	Delf Island	R-167
Cohier's Lot	2-204;R-068	Delph	2-513
Colerain	2-008	Delph Neglect	2-513
Colletts Points	2-204	Derbius Chance	2-418
Combine's Chance	2-237	Derry, County	2-008
Combs Adventure	2-237	Diary Improved	2-280
Come by Chance Jones Addition	R-167	Diggins Meadow	R-205
Common Garden Corrected	2-496	Dismall Swamp	2-268
Constant Friendship	R-167	Donegal Co.	2-421
Constantinople	2-280	Dooleys Mistake	2-384
Constatinople	R-167	Double Loan	2-263
Cook's Rest	2-418	Drew's Inlargement	2-184
Coothill	R-066	Drews Inlargement	2-155
County Derry	2-008	Duleys Mistake	2-463
Covent Garden	2-428	Dunbo Mill	2-008
Cowans Addition	R-126	Dunboe, Parish of	2-008
Cowens Addition	2-458	Durbin's Beginning	2-340
Cox's Chance	2-092	Durbins Beginning	2-134
Coxes Mill	2-274	Durbins Chance	2-134
Cramberry	2-249	Eaton	R-167
Cranberry	2-276,306	Eatons Addition	R-167
Cranberry Hall	2-306	Eatons Second Addition	R-167
Cranberry Meadows	2-237	Eden Town	2-107
Cranberry Swamp	R-229	Eden's Addition	2-223
Cranbury Hall	2-276	Edenburg	R-167
Cristifers Camp	R-264	Edinborough	2-477
Crooked Ridg	R-028	Egham Hithe	2-092
Crookett Ridg	R-028	Elberton	2-463
		Elbow Branch	R-090

Eling	2-301	Great Britain	2-109,249,414
Ellburton	2-237	Great Road	2-037,276
Elling	2-301	Green Spring Forest	2-268
Ellinor's Choice	2-340	Greshams College	2-449
Elliots Refuse	2-340	Griffies Delight	2-463
Elliott's Run	2-037	Gugeons	2-498
England	2-031,092,476;	Guinea	2-176
	R-073,167	Gunpowder (River)	2-150,498
Enlargement	2-485	Gunpowder Falls	2-340
Everly Hills	2-482	Gunpowder Neck	2-150,258,
Expectation	2-111,493		263,521
Eyetrap	2-418	Gunpowder River	2-066,171,521
Farmers Ford	R-048	Guyton's Addition	2-340
Fates Neighbor	2-340	Hall & Bones Discovery	2-268
Fells Point	2-021	Halls Chance	2-276,306
Ferry	2-123	Halls Chance Addition	2-268
First Addition to Halls		Halls Meadows	2-274
Rich Neck	R-167	Halls Park	2-268
Fogs Mannor	R-004	Halls Plains	2-276;R-167
Forrest Plantation	R-229	Halls Purchase	2-268
Fosters Neck Woolfs		Halls Rich Neck	R-167
Harbor	R-010	Hammonds Hope	R-167
Fountain Copper Mines	2-021	Hansons Neglect	R-164
Fountain Copper Mines		Harford Town	2-513
Resurvey	2-021	Harmonds Addition	2-458
France	2-176	Harrises Trust	2-040
Franksfort	R-083	Harrisons Resolution	R-167
Frederick Co.	2-021,280	Hathaways Hazard	R-167
Free Land's Mount	2-357	Hathaways Trust	R-167
Freeland's Mount	2-463	Havanna	2-176
Freelands Mount	2-384	Havre de Grace	R-068
Friends Discovery	2-128	Hawks Nest, The	2-167
Friends Meeting House	R-031	Hawthawas Hazard	2-280
Friendship	R-121	Head of Swansbury	R-167
Frisby's Conveniency	2-204	Herrion Creek Church	R-031
Gays Enlargement	R-167	Hethcode Cottage	2-498
Gays Favour	R-167	Hickory Ridge	R-167
George & Josephs Farm	2-340	Hickory Tavern	R-213
Georges Interest	R-238	High Field	R-205
Gibsons Park	R-180	Hills Hill	R-164
Gilberts Pipe	2-263	His Lordships Reserve	2-017,
Giles & Websters			028,485
Discovery	R-205	Hog Pen Branch	2-021
Giles Addition	2-237	Hogs Neck	2-237
Giles Angles	2-237	Hollis Refuse	2-311
Givins Mill	2-498	Hollow Bottom	R-167
Goldsmiths Hall	2-513	Holly Hill	2-311
Good Neighborhood		Holmwood	2-150
Enlarged	R-180	Homer Resurveyed	2-124
Gordon's Meadows	2-340	Horse Range	2-477
Graftons Entrance	2-213	Howard's Forest	R-197
Gravelly Bottom	2-227	Howards Harbour	2-016
Gravelly Hills	2-458	Howels Nest	2-301
Gravilly Bottom	2-418	Hugh's Inheritance	2-010
Great Barrington	2-031	Hughes Choice	2-418,530

A-3

Hughes Enlargement Resurveyed	2-530	Little Hopewell	2-280;R-167
Humphreys Run	R-167	Little Worth	2-141,280;R-167
Iles of Caparee	2-014,053	Littleton	2-449
Iles of Capere	2-053	Locust Neck	R-164
Improved Venture	2-134	Londonderry	2-280;R-167
Improved Venture, The	2-263	Long Ally	R-028
Ireland	2-008,421;R-049	Long Bridge	2-258
Isaac's Double Purchase	2-384	Long Island	2-031
Isaac's Inheritance	2-384	Lower Mill	2-498
Isaacs Lot	R-154	MacCarteys Neighbors	2-237
Isles of Caperea	2-340	Maidens Bower Secured	2-517
Islington	2-301	Majors Choice	2-479;R-242
Jacks Purchase	2-263	Maladys Manor	R-096
Jacobs Delight	2-340	Maple Ford Branch	2-021
Jacobs Mount	2-340	Margarets Purchase	2-079
James Addition	2-280	Margins Grove	2-333
James Park	2-237,249	Margrets Mount	2-092
James Run	R-197	Maryes Delite	R-028
Jarretsburg	2-340	Mary's Delight	2-100,340
Jarrett's Fatigue	2-340	Mathews Enlargement	2-428
Jarretts Discovery	2-340	Maxwell's Conclusion	2-150
Jerusalem	2-498	Maxwells Conclusion	2-171
John's Forest	2-340	Meadow Ground, The	2-463
Johns Interest	R-164	Meeting House	2-179
Johns Third Addition	2-167	Merchant's Mill	2-092,498
Johnson's Choice	2-333	Middle Borough	2-204,268
Johnson's Enlargement	2-340	Middlemores Defence	2-517
Johnsons Chance	2-463	Middlesex	2-092
Jones Addition	R-167	Milers Point	R-238
Joppa	2-331,397,498;R-010	Miles Addition	2-420
Joshua's Choice	2-002	Miles Beginen	2-420
Joshua's Forest	2-002	Miles Hill the Addition	R-167
Joshua's Meadow	2-002	Mill on Swan Creek Run	2-268
Joshua's Meadow Enlarged	2-040	Millers Attempt	2-463
Kent Co.	2-303,440,463,487	Minorea (Island)	2-237
Kentucky	R-242	Mohongehala River	2-163
Kilkenny	2-280;R-167	Monreal	2-280;R-167
Kimble Addition	2-369	Montreal	2-280
Kimbles Debble Purchis	2-369	Montserada	2-280;R-167
Knavery Prevented	2-439	Montserada Addition	2-237
Knight's Increase	2-379	Morgan's Hog Pen	2-037
Lacedeman	2-280;R-167	Morgan's Lott	2-071
Lady Baltimore's Manner	2-053	Morgans Run	R-244
Lancaster Co.	2-435;R-004	Mould & Success	2-513
Land of Promise	2-237	Mount Felix Seat	2-237
Leases Habitation	2-017	Mount Real	2-276
Leases Herbitation	2-017	Mount, The	2-167
Leigh of Leighton	R-167	Mountain	2-352,384
Levels Addition	2-237	Mountserada	2-237
Lewis' Purchase Improved	R-164	Mourieat	R-167
Linen Manufacture	R-164	Mow Meadow	2-340
Lingans Adventure	2-391	Murdaugh's Chance	2-092
Little Creek	R-051	Murpheys Hazard	2-274
Little Falls	2-498	Muscator Creek	2-268
		Musketo Creek	2-204

My Lady's Manor	2-037;R-096	Park Hill	2-099
My Lords Gift	2-040	Parkers Chance	2-237
Myladies Manner	2-037	Parson's Lot	2-340
Nams Run	2-274	Partners Hills	2-062
Narrow Neck	2-316	Patapsco River	2-237
Nats Island	2-237	Pattersons Chance	2-340
Neawsams Meadows	2-513	Pattersons Regulation	2-340
Negro Joe's cabin	2-368	Pearsons Outlet	2-340
Neighbors Affinity	R-167	Peeled Egg	2-092
Neighbors Good Will	R-090	Pennsylvania	2-056,141,146,
Netter Wills Addition	2-106		344,435,498;
New Jersey	2-146		R-004,167,203,
New Port	R-185		229,246
New Stadt	2-463	Penny Come Quick	2-470
New West Wood	2-092	Perrimans Revise	2-227
New Westwood	2-274	Persons Outlett	R-015
New York	2-031;R-242	Persons Range	R-199
Newstead	2-292	Philadelphia	2-092,472;
No 23 in Maladys Manor	R-096		R-167,246
No Name	2-369	Philips his Purchase	R-255
Norris Venter	2-493	Phillips Purchase	2-298;
North Carolina	2-331		R-146,159
North Union	2-301	Planter's Delight	2-204
Noth Wales	2-340	Planter's Paradise	2-384
Now Stadt	2-463	Planters Neglect	2-301
Oakington Agreeable		Planters Paradise	2-463
Settled	2-064	Popular Neck	2-040
Obediahs Venture	2-134,263	Pork Hill	2-099
Oblong	2-394	Port Lewis	2-176
Ogg King of Bashan	R-015	Potees Industry	2-340
Old Joe's Spring Branch	2-021	Preston's Deceit	2-024
Onion Works	2-498	Primrose Hill	2-047
Onions Defence	2-498	Prospect	2-021
Onions Inheritance	2-498	Prospect Hills	2-498
Onions Pasture Ground	2-498	Purgetary	2-369
Osborns Lot	2-449	Quaker Road	R-154
Osborns Lott	2-040	Rangers Range	2-071
Other Centre	2-024	Rebecas Lot	2-498
Outlet	R-167	Rice Patch Runn	R-205
Overshott	2-021	Rich Neck	2-316
Owlets Nest	2-301,494	Richards Retirement	2-167
Oxford	2-031	Richensons Barrons	R-021
Oxfordshire	2-031	Richensons Outlet	R-021
Paas Park	2-463	Rick Bottom Corrected	2-237
Paca's Meadows	2-479	Rigbies Chance	R-018
Paca's Stoney Ridge	R-167	Rigbies Hope	2-237;R-018
Pacas Bit	2-517	Rigdons Range	R-051
Pacas Conveniency	2-513	Rigduns Lookout	R-028
Pacas Meadow	2-517	Riley's Addition	R-142
Pacas Meadow Resurveyed	2-517	Riley's Long Meadow	R-142
Pacas Park	2-513,517	River Susquehanna	2-067,418;
Pacas Pleasure	2-167		R-255
Pacas Search	2-517	Road's Necessity	2-340
Palmers Points	2-513	Roberts Center Inlarged	R-028
Paradise	2-188,268,418;R-167	Robinhoods Forrest	2-439

Robinsons Meadows	R-007	Spring Branch	2-037,368
Robinsons Outlett	2-062	St. George's Neighbor	R-011
Roches Choice	2-340	St. Johns Parish	R-010
Rock Branch	R-167	St. Lucia	2-176
Rock Quarter	R-028	St. Lucie	2-176
Romney Creek	2-268	St. Marys Co.	R-152
Royal Exchange	2-418	Staines	2-092
Royal Exchange Division	2-458	Standiford Meadows	2-340
Royal Exchange Resurveyed Esp.	R-167	Sting, The	2-463
Ruffs Chance	2-016	Stoney Batter	2-340
Rumney Creek	2-327,496	Stoney Ridge	R-167
Rumney Neck	2-258,444	Store, The	2-171
Rumney Royal	R-167	Stout Bottle Branch	R-118
Rumsey Creek	2-237	String of Good Luck, The	2-340
Rumsey Marsh	2-237	Surry	2-092
Rupalta	2-067	Surveyor's Point	2-099
Saint Albins	2-099	Susquehanna River	2-067,237, 404,418;R-255
Saint Martins Ludgate	2-237	Sussex Co.	2-146,344
Sam Halls	2-024	Swampipoint	2-301
Sarah's Garden	2-167	Swan Creek	2-258,263,268
Scotts Close	2-479	Swan Creek Run	2-268,274
Scotts Modesty	2-040	Swan Harbour	2-517
Second Addition to Halls Rich Neck	R-167	Swansbury	R-167
Second Adventure	2-394	Talbots Addition	2-340
Second Long	2-394	Taylors Good Half	2-268
Second Runn	2-085	Tarry's Choice	2-340
Second Street	R-167	Taylors Good Hass	2-268
Second Thought	2-021	Thames Street	2-021
Second Thought Improved	2-021	Thomas Bonds Gift	R-007
Security	2-517	Thomas Smiths Aqua Demnum	2-292
Shaws Hunting Ground	2-458	Thomas's Orchard	2-053
Shepherd's Choice	2-237	Thomases Desire	R-001
Shepherds Adventure	2-237	Thomases Run	2-517
Sheriffs Hall	2-268	Thompsons Choice	2-498
Shipping Dock	2-428	Three Sisters	2-340
Simmonds Choice	2-384	Timber Neck	2-268
Simmons Choice	2-463	Tobago, Island of	2-176,312
Simmons Neglect	2-280,463	Tralee	2-463
Simmonses Choice	2-352	Trap	2-340
Smith's Mistake	R-090	Trapley Neck	2-258
Smiths Folley Resurveyed	2-268	Treble Union	2-418
Smiths Folly Resurveyed	2-204	Tricks & Things	2-340
Smiths Mistake	2-257	Turkey Hills	2-498
Sons Addition	2-340	Union	2-263
Sophia's Dairy	R-167	Upper Cross Roads	2-364
Sophias Dairy	2-280	Upper Mill	2-498
South Union	2-311	Valentine's Choice	2-106
Spesutia	R-229	Virginia	R-229
Spesutia Church Road	R-154	Walkers Desire	2-333
Spesutia Creek	R-229	Walnut Street	R-167
Speutia	R-068	Washington	2-517
Spittle Craft	R-205	Water Mill	2-513,517
Spittle Creek	2-463	Wats Disapointment	R-203
		Weatheralls Last Addition	2-340

Webbs Spot	R-205
Websters Enlargement	R-051
Websters Forest	R-197
Well's Lott	R-146,159
Wells Denu	2-340
Welses Lott	R-159
West Jersey	2-374
West River	R-031
West Wood	2-092,263
Wests Beginning Improved	2-092
Wetharals Addition	R-105
Whealing (River)	2-107
Wheeler & Clarks Contrivance	R-199
Whitacres Delay	2-340
Whiteakers Ridge	R-167
Whiteford's Adventure	R-203
Whiteford's Desire	R-203
Whitely	R-164
Whitemarsh	2-340
Wilburns Adventure	2-274
Wild Cat Denu	2-340
William & Sarah's Inheritance	2-439
Williams Delight	R-238
Williams Discovery	R-083
William's Swamp	2-258
Wilsons Retreat	R-007
Wind Mill Hill	R-167
Winters Run	2-517;R-167
Wood Close	2-418
Wood Yard	R-167
Woods Close	2-090,227
Worthington Dividended	R-146
Ye Charmin Spot	R-028
Ye Fathers Safe Guard	R-028
York	2-141
York Chance	R-268
York Co.	2-056,340;R-004
Young Man's Addition	2-268

INDEX OF SLAVES BY FIRST NAME

Name	Owner	Ref
Abigail	<GRIFFITH>	2-258
Abigail	<HALL>	2-288
Abigal, girl	BRADFORD	2-055
Abner <NEAL>	<WHEELER>	R-152
Abraham, boy	<BOND>	2-038
Abraham	<DREW>	2-155
Abraham, man	<GREEN>	2-252
Abraham	<MORGAN>	2-463
Abraham, boy	<YORK>	R-266
Abram, boy	<HALL>	
	<WILMOTT>	R-244
Aby, man	<HALL>	2-288
Adam	<WILLSON>	R-180
Affee	<WILLSON>	R-180
Affey, woman	<JOHNS>	
	<RIGBIE>	2-348
Affrick, man	<NORRIS>	2-493
Agram	<WILLSON>	R-180
Allexander	<RUFF>	R-040
Amey, woman	<BOND>	2-038
Amey	<MATHEW>	2-444
Amia	<ONION>	2-498
Amy, woman	<McCOMAS>	
	<ONION>	2-454
Amynta	<PACA>	
	<PHILLIPS>	2-517
Andrew, man	<LINGAN>	2-391
Andrew, boy	<McCOMAS>	2-460
Andrew	<PRESBURY>	2-521
Ann	<MORGAN>	2-463
Ann <McGOWAN>	<NEVILL>	2-487
Ann, girl	<RIGDUN>	R-028
Ann	<RUFF>	R-040
Archibald, boy	<BAKER>	2-059
Aron	<MATHEW>	2-444
Aron	<SHEREDINE>	R-045
Arringe	<WORTHINGTON>	R-255
Augustus	<HALL>	2-286
Augustus	<NEAL>	
	<WHEELER>	R-152
Averilla, girl	<DORSEY>	2-153
Bacchus	<HALL>	2-276
Barnett	<BAKER>	2-024
Bash, man	<BIDDLE>	2-012
Beck, girl	<BAKER>	
	<WHITAKER>	2-024
Beck	<DORSEY>	2-426
Beck	<HALL>	2-276
Beck, girl	<JOLLEY>	2-350
Beck	<MAXWELL>	2-426
Beck, girl	<McCANDLESS>	
	<RUTH>	R-011
Beck, girl	<WHEELER>	R-199

Name	Owner	Ref
Becky, girl	<WEBSTER>	R-229
Belinda	<HALL>	2-306
Bell, girl	<BOND>	
	<MORRIS>	2-038
Bell, wench	<BULL>	2-028
Bellily	<HALL>	2-306
Ben, boy	<ANDERSON>	2-010
Ben, boy	<BAKER>	2-024
Ben, boy	<BARNES>	2-067
Ben	<DALE>	2-142
Ben	<DREW>	2-184
Ben, boy	<FISHER>	2-202
Ben, boy	<HALL>	2-276
Ben	<HALL>	2-288
Ben	<JAY>	2-368
Ben	<MORGAN>	2-463
Ben, boy	<ONION>	2-498
Ben	<WILLSON>	R-180
Ben, man	<WORTHINGTON>	R-146
Ben, boy	<WORTHINGTON>	R-146
Bendow, man	<HOLLIS>	2-301
Benjamin, boy	<MORGAN>	2-411
Benjamin, Jr	<RUFF>	R-040
Benjamin, Sr	<RUFF>	R-040
Bennet	<McTEE>	R-152
Bennet	<WHEELER>	R-152
Bess, wench	<AMOS>	2-001
Bess	<BAKER>	2-024
Bess, girl	<OSBORN>	2-496
Bet	<GREEN>	2-252
Bet	<PACA>	2-513
Bet, child of Harry	<WHEELER>	R-199
Betsy, daughter of Ester <GILBERT>	<MORGAN>	2-263
Bett	<CRETIN>	2-116
Bett	<HOLLAND>	2-324
Bett, girl	<LEE>	2-384
Bett	<MORGAN>	2-463
Bett girl	<VANCLEAVE>	2-384
Bett, mother of Ned	<WEBB>	R-205
Betty, girl of Dinah	<BAKER>	2-059
Betty, girl	<COOPER>	
	<GREEN>	2-261
Betty <HALL>	<RUMSEY>	2-286
Betty <McTEE>	<WHEELER>	R-152
Betty	<WILLSON>	R-180
Bess <HALL>	<RUMSEY>	2-286
Bill, boy	<BARNES>	2-067
Bill	<DREW>	2-184
Bill	<EVATT>	2-198

B-1

Name	Owner	Ref
little Bill	<GRIFFITH>	2-258
Bill, boy	<HALL>	
	<RUMSEY>	2-286
Bill, boy	<HALL>	2-288
Bill	<MORGAN>	2-463
Bill, boy	<THOMPSON>	R-132
Bill, boy	<WORTHINGTON>	R-255
Billie, child of Dinah		
	<JOHNS> <RIGBIE>	2-348
Bine, girl	<THORPE>	
	<WILLMOTT>	R-114
Bob, man	<BROWNE>	2-064
Bob	<KITLEY>	2-381
Bob, man	<MITCHELL>	2-422
Bob	<MORGAN>	2-463
Bob, boy	<ONION>	2-498
Bob	<PACA>	2-513
Bob, man	<WEBSTER>	R-221
Bobb	<BROWN>	2-066
Bobb, boy	<GALLION>	2-215
Bobb, boy	<WELLS>	R-191
Bobb	<WILLSON>	R-180
Bridget, child	<OSBORN>	2-494
Briget, girl		
	<RICHARDSON>	R-020
Brise, boy	<RIGDON>	R-034
Bristol	<WILLSON>	R-180
Caesas, man	<SMITHSON>	R-098
Cance, girl	<JEFFRY>	
	<OSBORN>	2-494
Cas, child of Judgeth		
	<KIMBLE>	2-369
Cash, girl	<RICHARDSON>	R-020
Cass, girl	<HALL>	2-276
Cass	<HOLLAND>	2-324
Cass, girl	<ONION>	2-498
Cassandra, girl		
	<HOPKINS>	2-321
Cassy, girl	<MITCHELL>	2-418
Cate, woman	<BLAIR>	
	<RUTH>	R-011
Cate	<MORGAN>	2-463
Cate, girl	<WARD>	
	<WELLS>	R-189
Cate, girl	<WELLS>	R-191
Cate, girl	<WHEELER>	R-199
Catharine, woman		
	<GRAFTON>	2-213
Cathrine, woman	<DESSAA>	
	<LETANG>	2-176
Cato, boy	<BRICKHEAD>	2-070
Cato	<GILES>	2-219
Cato, young	<HOPKINS>	2-318
Ceasar, man	<ALLENDER>	2-005
Ceaser	<JAY>	2-368
Ceasor, boy	<BAKER>	
	<GARRETT>	2-024
Ceasor, boy		
	<WORTHINGTON>	R-146
Ceesar	<GILES>	2-219
Celeste, woman	<DESSAA>	
	<LETANG>	2-176
Chance, man	<BROWNE>	2-064
Chaney, girl	BRADFORD	2-055
Charity	<GREENWELL>	
	<WHEELER>	R-152
Charles, boy	<CALWELL>	
	<RICHARDSON>	R-020
Charles, boy	<HALL>	
	<RUMSEY>	2-286
Charles	<MATHEWS>	2-469
Charles	<WILLSON>	R-180
Charles	<WORTHINGTON>	R-255
Chloe <ALLENDER>	<WANE>	2-005
Christian, woman		
	<GIBSON> <WHEELER>	R-199
Cisiah, young	<BRYARLY>	2-076
Cissera	<GILES>	2-219
Claire, woman	<DAY>	2-171
Clarke, girl	<WHEELER>	R-199
Clem, man	<BRICKHEAD>	2-070
Clem	<WILLSON>	R-180
Clenas, boy	<DREW>	
	<THOMPSON>	2-158
Clenes	<DREW>	2-155
Clenes, boy	<THOMPSON>	R-132
Clitus, lad	<WILSON>	R-157
Cloe, girl	<CUMMINS>	2-130
Cloe	<LEE>	2-384
Cloe, wench	<RICHARDSON>	R-020
Cloe, girl	<WATTERS>	R-148
Cloe	<WILLSON>	R-180
Cloe	<WILSON>	2-384
Coffee	<BAKER>	2-024
Coock	<McTEE>	
Coock	<WHEELER>	R-152
Corbin	<HALL>	2-306
Cudgoe, man	<HALL>	2-274
Cuff, boy	<GARRETTSON>	2-223
Cuff	<HALL>	2-276
Cuff, aged	<HAWKINS>	2-292
Cumbo, woman		
	<GARRETTSON>	2-223
Cupid	<HALL>	2-276
Cupid	<HALL>	2-306
Cyrus	<RUFF>	R-040
Dafney, young	<HOPKINS>	2-298
Dampiere	<JOLLEY>	2-350

Name	Owner	Ref
Dan	<SCOTT> <SMITH>	R-107
Daniel, son of Dinah		
	<ALLENDER> <WANE>	2-005
Daniel, man	<FISHER>	
	<JOLLEY>	2-202
Daniel, boy	<GALLION>	2-215
Daniel	<JOLLEY>	2-350
Daphne, wench	<GRIFFITH>	2-227
Daphne, woman	<MEAD>	2-440
Dark, girl	<DAY>	
	<WETHERALL>	2-165
Dark	<EVATT>	2-198
Darke, child of Judgath		
	<KIMBLE>	2-369
Darkey	<HALL> <RUMSEY>	2-286
Darkey	<KITLEY>	2-381
Darkis, woman	<BOWMAN>	
	<WHEELER>	R-152
Darkus, girl	<BAKER>	
	<DENNEY>	2-059
Dave	<HOLLAND>	2-324
Davey, boy	<BOND>	2-014
Davey, boy, son of Hanna		
	<RIGDON>	R-034
Davey, boy	<WORTHINGTON>	R-146
Davey	<WORTHINGTON>	R-159
David, boy	<CRAWFORD>	2-100
David, young	<HOPKINS>	2-298
David	<MATHEWS>	2-469
David	<WILLSON>	R-180
Davy, man	<GIBSON>	
	<WHEELER>	R-199
Deck, boy	<DREW>	
	<HENDERSON>	2-174
Dembo	<BOYCE> <COWAN>	2-027
Dembo	<COWAN>	2-027
Dennis, boy	<MEAD>	2-440
Diamond	<HALL>	2-276
Dick, man	<ONION>	2-498
Dick	<RENSHAW>	R-016
Dido	<WARD>	R-225
Dina	<WHITEFORD>	R-203
Dinah	<ALLENDER> <WANE>	2-005
Dinah, woman	<ANDERSON>	2-010
Dinah	<BAKER>	2-024
Dinah, woman	<BAKER>	2-059
Dinah	<HALL>	2-286
Dinah, girl	<BOND>	2-014
Dinah, girl	<BROWNE>	2-064
Dinah, girl	<CRAWFORD>	
	<DAVIS>	2-100
Dinah, female	<DALE>	2-142
Dinah, girl	<DENNY>	2-163
Dinah	<DREW>	2-155
Dinah, wench	<GALLION>	2-215
Dinah, girl	<HALL>	2-274
Dinah, girl of Judah		
	<HALL>	2-274
Dinah, girl	<HALL>	2-276
Dinah, woman	<HALL>	2-288
Dinah, girl	<HALL>	
	<WHITE>	R-167
Dinah	<HOLLAND>	2-324
Dinah, woman	<JOHNS>	
	<RIGBIE>	2-348
Dinah	<LEE> <WILSON>	2-384
Dinah, girl	<LYON>	2-389
Dinah, wench	<OSBORN>	2-494
Dinah, girl	<THOMPSON>	R-132
Dinah, woman	<WALLIS>	R-185
Dinah	<WILLSON>	R-180
Diner or Dinah, wench		
	<HALL>	2-286
Diner	<LYNCH> <TAYLOR>	
	<TREDWAY>	R-111
Dip, girl	<BROWNE>	2-064
Dipp, female	<BROWN>	2-066
Dole	<GREEN>	2-252
Doll, girl	<HALL>	
	<TOLLEY>	2-288
Doll	<OSBORN>	2-494
Dorcas or Darkey, woman		
	<HALL> <RUMSEY>	2-286
Duke, man	<LEE>	2-384
Dutches, woman	<BROWNE>	
	<THOMPSON>	2-055
Dutches	<MORGAN>	2-463
Dutchess, wife of Forest		
	<LEE>	2-384
Easter, girl	<BAKER>	2-024
old Easter	<DREW>	2-155
Easter	<DREW>	2-184
Easter, girl	<HALL>	2-274
Easter	<LYTTLE> <RUFF>	2-394
Edmond	<MATHEWS>	2-469
Elisha	<JAY>	2-368
Elisha, boy, son of Nanny		
	<RIGDON>	R-034
Elizabeth or Bett, girl		
	<HALL> <RUMSEY>	2-286
Emanuel, boy	<HALL>	2-274
Ester, woman	<CROCKETT>	2-103
Ester, woman	<GILBERT>	
	<MORGAN>	2-263
Ester	<GREEN>	2-252
Ester	<LYTTLE> <RUFF>	2-394
Ester	<RUFF>	R-040
Ester, woman	<WHITE>	R-167
Fainer	<MORGAN>	2-463
Fan, woman	<BOND>	2-014

Name	Owner	Ref
Fan, girl	<GARRETTSON>	2-223
Fan, girl	<GIBSON> <WHEELER>	R-199
Fan, girl	<HANSON> <LANCASTER>	2-327
Fan, girl	<HOLLIS> <OSBORN>	2-494
Fan	<PACA>	2-513
Faney	<WILLSON>	R-180
Fann, woman	<ALLENDER> <DAY>	2-150
Fann <McGOWAN>	<NEVILL>	2-487
Fann, girl	<WHITEFORD>	R-203
Fanney	<WILLSON>	R-180
Fanny	<DELAPORTE>	2-181
Fanny <HALL>	<RUMSEY>	2-286
Fany, woman	<DELAPORTE>	2-181
Ferreca	<MATHEWS>	2-469
Fie	<DAY>	2-150
Fill	<KIMBLE>	2-369
Flora	<WILLSON>	R-180
Floria, girl	<BROWNE>	2-064
Forest, man	<LEE>	2-384
Frances	<MORGAN>	2-463
Frank, boy	<BULL>	2-028
Frank, girl	<DAY>	2-150
Frank, man	<WHEELER>	R-199
Freeborn	<KITLEY>	2-381
Gaberial, young	<HOPKINS>	2-318
Gabriel, boy	<GIBSON> <WHEELER>	R-199
Gain, woman	<CRAWFORD>	2-100
Geofray	<PRESBURY>	2-521
George	<BAKER>	2-024
George, boy	<BOND>	2-014
George, fellow	<DREW> <NELSON>	2-174
George, boy	<GILES>	2-237
George	<HALL>	2-288
George, young	<HOPKINS>	2-298
George, young	<HOPKINS>	2-318
George, boy	<HOPKINS>	2-321
George, man	<JOHNS> <RIGBIE>	2-348
George, boy	<LYTTLE>	2-394
George	<MATHEWS>	2-469
George, boy	<MEAD>	2-440
George, man	<MORGAN>	2-411
George	<MORGAN>	2-463
George, boy	<McCOMAS>	2-454
George, boy	<ONION>	2-498
George, boy	<OSBORN>	2-496
Gess	<WHITEFORD>	R-203
Gill	<HALL>	2-306
Gin, girl	<GIBSON>	R-199
Gin, girl	<WHEELER>	R-199
Ginny, girl	<CALBERT>	R-157
Ginny, girl	<WILSON>	R-157
Grace, girl	<GARRETTSON>	2-223
Grace	<GILES>	2-237
Grace, girl	<HOLLIS>	2-301
Grace	<LUSBY>	2-401
Grace, girl	<MEAD>	2-440
Grace, woman	<ONION>	2-498
Grace, wife of Bob	<PACA>	2-513
Grace, the younger	<PACA>	2-513
Gustus, boy	<HALL>	2-274
Gustus or Augustus	<HALL>	2-286
Guy, man	<BOND>	2-014
Gwin	<HALL>	2-288
Hagar, woman	<LEE>	2-384
Hagar, woman	<LOGHLIN> <WILSON>	R-157
Hagar, girl	<MEAD>	2-440
Hagar	<MORGAN>	2-411
Hagar, girl	<MURPHY>	2-440
Hagar, wife of Jo	<PACA>	2-513
Hagar	<PACA>	2-513
Hagar	<PRESBURY>	2-521
Hagar	<WILLSON>	R-180
Hager, wench	<BRYERLY>	2-033
Hager, girl	<CRAWFORD>	2-100
Hager	<DREW>	2-155
Hager, girl	<GALLION> <GILBERT>	2-215
Hager, girl of Pegg	<HALL>	2-274
Hager, girl	<HALL>	2-274
Hager, girl	<HALL>	2-288
Hager, woman	<LYTTLE> <RUFF>	2-394
Hager, girl	<TOLLEY>	2-288
Hagor	<KIMBLE>	2-369
Han, girl	<LYTTLE>	2-394
Hanna, girl	<HALL> <WILMOTT>	R-244
Hanna, girl	<JOLLEY>	2-350
Hanna, woman	<RIGDON>	R-034
Hannah, girl	<ANDERSON>	2-010
Hannah, young	<BRYARLY>	2-076
Hannah	<DREW>	2-155
Hannah, girl	<GARRETTSON>	2-223
Hannah, girl of Rachiel	<HALL>	2-274
Hannah, woman	<HALL>	2-274

Name	Surname	Ref
Hannah	<HALL>	2-276
Hannah	<HALL>	2-286
Hannah	<HALL>	2-288
Hannah	<HANSON>	2-316
Hannah, girl	<HOPKINS>	2-313
Hannah, young	<HOPKINS>	2-318
Hannah	<KITLEY>	2-381
Hannah	<LEE>	2-384
Hannah, girl	<MEAD>	2-440
Hannah	<MORGAN>	2-384
Hannah	<MORGAN>	2-463
Hannah, child	<OSBORN>	2-494
Hannah, woman	<SMITHSON>	R-098
Hannah	<WARD>	R-225
Hannah, girl	<WELLS>	R-191
Hannah, wife of James	<WHEELER>	R-199
Hannah, girl	<WHITAKER>	R-193
Harriot, girl	<HOPKINS>	2-321
Harriot, girl	<WATERS>	2-321
Harriott	<JAY>	2-368
Harry, boy	<DORSEY>	2-153
Harry, man	<HALL>	2-274
Harry	<LYTTLE>	2-394
Harry, fellow	<OSBORN>	2-496
Harry <PACA>	<PHILLIPS>	2-517
Harry, boy	<THORPE> <WILLMOTT>	R-114
Harry, man	<WHEELER>	R-199
Harry	<WILLSON>	R-180
Harry, man	<WORTHINGTON>	R-146
Harry	<WORTHINGTON>	R-255
Hary	<DREW>	2-155
Hector	<LUSBY>	2-393
Hector, lad	<MORGAN>	2-411
Hector	<WORTHINGTON>	R-159
Helen, girl	<GREEN> <WHEELER>	R-152
Henry	<WILLSON>	R-180
Hester, wife of Phillip	<MORGAN>	2-463
Hester, wife of Harry	<WHEELER>	R-199
Ignatius, boy	<AMOS>	2-001
Isaac, boy of Dinah	<BAKER>	2-059
Isaac, boy	<BARNES>	2-067
Isaac, boy	<BIDDLE>	2-012
Isaac, boy	<BROWNE>	2-064
Isaac, boy	<HALL>	2-274
Isaac	<HALL>	2-288
Isaac	<HOLLAND>	2-324
Isaac, man	<HOPKINS>	2-313
Isaac	<KITLEY>	2-381
Isaac, boy	<MITCHELL>	2-458
Isaac	<MORGAN>	2-463
Isaac, boy	<ONION>	2-498
Isaac	<OSBORN>	2-494
Isaac	<PRESBURY>	2-521
Isaac, man	<WELLS>	R-189
Isabele, girl	<WATTERS>	R-148
black Jack, boy	<ALLENDER> <WANE>	2-005
Jack, man	<CLARK> <COLEGATE>	2-082
Jack, boy	<GREEN>	2-261
Jack, son of Abigail	<GRIFFITH>	2-258
Jack	<HALL>	2-286
Jack, man	<HOLLIS>	2-301
Jack, son of Polly	<JOHNS> <RIGBIE>	2-348
Jack, child of Dinah	<JOHNS> <RIGBIE>	2-348
Jack	<KITLEY>	2-381
Jack	<LUSBY>	2-393
Jack	<MORGAN>	2-463
Jack, foreman	<McCOMAS>	2-454
Jack, boy	<McCOMAS>	2-460
Jack	<NEAL>	R-152
Jack	<ONION>	2-498
Jack. boy	<ONION>	2-498
Jack, boy	<OSBORN>	2-494
Jack, boy	<OSBORN>	2-496
Jack	<PACA>	2-513
Jack, fellow	<RICHARDSON>	R-020
Jack, boy	<SMITHSON>	R-098
Jack, man	<WELLS>	R-191
Jack	<WHEELER>	R-152
Jack, boy	<WHEELER>	R-199
Jack	<WHITEFORD>	R-203
Jacob, boy	<DAY>	2-150
Jacob	<DREW>	2-174
Jacob, young	<GARLAND> <HITCHCOCK>	2-222
Jacob, boy	<HALL>	2-274
Jacob	<HALL>	2-296
Jacob	<HALL>	2-306
Jacob	<HOLLAND>	2-324
Jacob	<LYON>	2-389
Jacob	<MATHEWS>	2-469
Jacob	<McCOMAS>	2-438
Jacob, boy	<ONION>	2-498
Jacob	<SHEREDINE>	R-045
Jacob	<SMITH>	R-090
Jacob, boy	<TALBOTT>	R-134
Jacob	<WARD>	R-225
Jacob	<WILLSON>	R-180
Jacque	<HALL>	2-288

```
little Jame, boy
                       <GALLION>  2-215
James, son of Dinah
              <ALLENDER> <WANE>   2-005
James, boy of Dinah
                       <BAKER>    2-059
James, boy             <BOND>     2-074
James, man             <BROWN>    2-066
James, man    <CHINWORTH>
                       <THORPE>   R-114
James, boy <GARRETTSON>           2-230
James                  <GREEN>    2-252
James, or Jem          <HALL>     2-286
James, son of Jem      <HALL>     2-286
James                  <HORNER>   2-325
James                  <MORGAN>   2-411
James                  <MORGAN>   2-463
James                  <WARD>     R-225
James, man             <WEBSTER>  R-229
James, man             <WHEELER>  R-199
James, man             <WILLMOTT> R-114
James                  GWINN      2-324
James                  RACO       2-324
Jane, woman            <ANDREW>
                       <TREDWAY>  R-111
Jane, girl             <BOND>
                       <MORRIS>   2-074
Jane, woman            <CRAWFORD> 2-121
Jane, girl             <HALL>     2-276
Jane or Jen            <HALL>     2-286
Jane                   <HOPKINS>  2-313
Jane, girl             <JOLLEY>   2-350
Jane                   <KIMBLE>   2-369
Jane, woman            <MATHER>   2-436
Jane                   <MORGAN>   2-411
Jane                   <MORGAN>   2-463
Jane, girl             <WELLS>    R-191
Jane                   <WILLSON>  R-180
Jane, woman            BRADFORD   2-055
Jantee                 <HALL>     2-288
Jarret, boy            <TIRE>
                       <WHEELER>  R-152
Jean, girl    <DAUGHERTY>         2-149
Jean, girl             <FISHER>   2-202
Jean                   <GREEN>    2-252
Jean, girl             <GREEN>    2-261
Jean, wench            <SMITH>    R-090
Jean          <WHITEFORD>         R-203
big Jem                <DAY>      2-150
Jem                    <HALL>     2-286
Jem                    <HALL>     2-288
Jem, waiting man
                       <McCOMAS>  2-454
Jem, the waiter <ONION>           2-498
Jemmy, man             <HALL>     2-288

Jen                    <HALL>     2-286
Jen, girl              <ONION>    2-498
Jeney, girl of Hannah
                       <HALL>     2-274
Jenny <ALLENDER> <WANE>           2-005
Jenny, girl            <HALL>     2-274
Jenny, girl            <LEE>
                       <VANCLEAF> 2-384
Jenny, wife of Samson
                       <McCOMAS>  2-454
Big Jenny              <ONION>    2-498
Jenny, girl            <ONION>    2-498
Jenny                  <PACA>     2-513
Jerry, boy             <HAWKINS>  2-292
Jerry     <LEE> <MORGAN>          2-384
Jerry                  <LYTTLE>   2-394
Jerry                  <MORGAN>   2-463
Jerry, boy             <WHEELER>  R-199
Jesse, boy             <TALBOTT>  R-134
Jesse, boy             <WHITE>    R-167
Jim, boy               <ANDERSON> 2-010
yellow Jim             <DREW>     2-155
Jim                    <KITLEY>   2-381
Jim                    <LYON>     2-389
Jim                    <MATHEWS>  2-469
Jim, boy               <McCOMAS>  2-460
old yellow Jim man
                       <WEBB>     R-205
Jim, boy <WORTHINGTON>            R-255
Jimeney, aged <HAWKINS>           2-292
Jo, boy                <HALL>     2-274
Jo, lad or boy         <HALL>
                       <RUMSEY>   2-286
Jo                     <PACA>     2-513
Jo    <CRISEWLL>       <EDGAR>    2-120
Job                    <ONION>    2-498
Joe    <ALLENDER>      <DAY>      2-150
Joe                    <CRETIN>   2-116
Joe                    <DREW>     2-155
Joe, boy               <GALLION>  2-215
Joe                    <HALL>     2-288
Joe                    <JOLLEY>   2-350
Joe, boy               <McCOMAS>
                       <ONION>    2-454
Joe                    <WARD>     R-225
Joe, son of Tom
                       <WHEELER>  R-199
John, man              <BOND>     2-014
John, young child
                       <HOPKINS>  2-313
John, young            <HOPKINS>  2-318
John                   <RUFF>     R-040
John, servant boy WRIGHT          2-137
Jonas, boy     <MITCHELL>         2-418
big Jonn, man  <GALLION>          2-215
```

Name	Owner	Ref
Joseph	\<MORGAN\>	2-463
Joshua	\<LYNCH\>	R-111
Joshua	\<TAYLOR\>	R-111
Joshua	\<TREDWAY\>	R-111
Josias, boy	\<GREEN\>	2-261
Judah, girl	\<HALL\>	2-274
Judah, woman	\<HALL\>	2-274
Judah	\<HALL\>	2-276
Judath	\<JOLLEY\>	2-350
Jude, wench	\<RICHARDSON\>	R-020
Judgath	\<KIMBLE\>	2-369
Judy	\<EVATT\>	2-198
Julett, girl	\<McCOMAS\> \<ONION\>	2-454
Julia, woman	\<HOLLIS\>	2-301
Jupeter, man	\<GALLION\> \<GILBERT\>	2-215
Jupiter, boy	\<GARRETTSON\>	2-230
Jupiter	\<SHEREDINE\>	R-045
Kate	\<GREEN\>	2-252
Kate	\<HALL\>	2-276
Kate, woman	\<HALL\>	2-296
Kate	\<HALL\>	2-306
Kater	\<LEE\> \<MORGAN\>	2-384
yellow Katre	\<HALL\>	2-276
Lamer, house wench	\<LEE\>	2-384
Lancaster Tom	\<GILES\>	2-219
Landon	\<ONION\>	2-498
Landon	\<WILLSON\>	R-180
Lanney	\<LYON\>	2-389
Leanda	\<WILLSON\>	R-180
Leander, man	\<HALL\>	2-274
Lem, boy	\<ONION\>	2-498
Lemon	\<LYTTLE\>	2-394
Letticia, girl	\<BOND\> \<MORRIS\>	2-074
Liberty	\<HALL\>	2-306
Lid, girl	\<BRICKHEAD\>	2-070
Lidd, child	\<ONION\>	2-498
Lidde, woman	\<GILBERT\>	2-263
Liddia	\<WARD\>	R-215
Liddy,girl	\<HALL\> \<RUMSEY\>	2-286
Liddy	\<McCOMAS\>	2-438
Limus, boy	\<BROWN\> \<BROWNE\>	2-055
Linda, girl	\<HALL\>	2-276
Lint, girl	\<JOLLEY\>	2-350
Linta, girl	\<HOPKINS\>	2-313
Lintey, baby girl	\<BARTON\>	2-037
Lisa, wife of Jack	\<McCOMAS\>	2-454
Lisha, boy	\<RIGDUN\>	R-028
London	\<MORGAN\>	2-463
London, man blacksmith	\<McCOMAS\> \<ONION\>	2-454
Lordon, man	\<HENLEY\>	R-189
Lordon, man	\<WELLS\>	R-189
Louisa	\<KITLEY\>	2-381
Lovor	\<WORTHINGTON\>	R-159
Luc, woman	\<WATTERS\>	R-148
Lucy, girl	\<BIDDLE\>	2-012
Lucy, girl	\<HALL\>	2-274
Lucy, girl	\<HALL\> \<WHITE\>	R-167
Lusey, girl	\<ROBINSON\>	R-007
Lyd	\<HOLLAND\>	2-324
Lydda, woman	\<McCOMAS\>	2-460
Lydia, girl	\<GILES\> \<WATERS\>	2-237
Lydia,girl	\<HALL\> \<RUMSEY\>	2-286
Lydia	\<ONION\>	2-498
Major	\<GREEN\>	2-252
Manuel, boy	\<HALL\>	2-276
Manuel	\<HOLLAND\>	2-324
Margaret, girl of Hager	\<HALL\>	2-274
Margerret, girl	\<HOPKINS\> \<HUSBAND\>	2-321
Marget, child of Judgath	\<KIMBLE\>	2-369
Margret, girl	\<CRAWFORD\> \<GORRAL\>	2-100
Maria	\<DENNY\>	2-166
Mariah	\<GRIFFITH\>	2-258
Mariah, woman	\<HALL\>	2-288
Mariah, house wench	\<LEE\>	2-384
Mary, alias Pug	\<GREEN\>	2-252
Mary, aged	\<HAWKINS\>	2-292
Mary, young child	\<HOPKINS\>	2-313
Mary, woman	\<MILES\>	2-446
Mary, girl	\<MITCHEL\>	R-199
Mary, woman	\<MITCHELL\>	2-418
Mary, wife of London	\<MORGAN\>	2-463
Mary	\<SHEREDINE\>	R-045
Mary, girl	\<WHEELER\>	R-199
Matilda, woman	\<BIDDLE\>	2-012
Medarah, boy of Hannah	\<HALL\>	2-274
Meriah, wife of Robert	\<JOHNS\>	2-326
Mettway, child	\<LYTTLE\>	2-394
Micah, boy	\<HALL\>	2-274
Michael	\<MORGAN\>	2-411

Name	Owner	Ref
Michael, servant man	TRUELOVE	2-220
Mike	<MORGAN>	2-463
Mike, boy	<WORTHINGTON>	R-255
Milcah	<HALL>	2-276
Milcah	<PACA>	2-513
Milley	<HALL>	2-288
Minggo, man	<NORRIS>	2-493
Mingo	<HALL>	2-276
Mingo, man	<RIGDON>	R-034
Mingoe, man	<JOHNS> <RIGBIE>	2-348
Mint, girl	<THOMPSON>	R-132
Minty	<HALL>	2-306
Miriah, girl	<McCOMAS> <ONION>	2-454
Mirtilla	<HALL>	2-286
Mitway, boy	<WORTHINGTON>	R-146
Moll, woman	<GARRETTSON>	2-223
Moll, woman	<HALL>	2-274
Moll, girl	<HALL>	2-274
Moll, woman	<HALL> <WHITE>	R-167
Moll, child of Judgath	<KIMBLE>	2-369
Moll, girl <LEE>	<WEBB>	2-384
Moll	<OSBORN>	2-494
Morea	<GILES>	2-237
Moses, boy	<CRAWFORD>	2-100
Moses	<RUFF>	R-040
Murriah, young	<HOPKINS>	2-318
Murrier, woman	<BROWNE> <THOMPSON>	2-055
Murrier	<LUSBY>	2-401
Nace	<HALL>	2-306
Nace	<PACA>	2-513
Nan, woman	<DAUGHERTY>	2-149
Nan	<DAY>	2-150
Nan, girl	<GALLION>	2-215
Nan	<HOLLAND>	2-324
Nan <LEE>	<MORGAN>	2-384
Nan, man	<LEE>	2-384
Nan, girl	<MITCHEL> <WHEELER>	R-199
Nan, woman	<MOORE> <THORPE>	R-114
Nan <McGOWAN>	<NEVILL>	2-487
Nan, daughter of Tom	<WHEELER>	R-199
Nance, girl	<DAY>	2-171
Nance, girl	<ONION>	2-498
Nanny, woman	<RIGDON>	R-034
Nat, boy	<BRYARLY>	2-076
Nat, young	<BRYARLY>	2-076
Nat	<MAXWELL>	2-426
Nathan, boy	BRADFORD	2-055
Natt <LEE>	<WILSON>	2-384
Neamy, girl	<HALL>	2-274
old Ned, man	<ALLENDER> <WANE>	2-005
Ned, boy	<ALLENDER> <WANE>	2-005
Ned, boy	<BROWNE> <THOMPSON>	2-055
Ned, boy	<CRAWFORD>	2-100
Ned, fellow	<DREW> <NELSON>	2-174
Ned, boy	<HALL>	2-274
Ned	<HANSON>	2-316
Ned, boy	<HOPKINS>	2-305
Ned	<LYON>	2-389
Ned	<MATHEW>	2-444
Ned	<MORGAN>	2-463
Ned <NEAL>	<WHEELER>	R-152
Ned, waggon driver	<WEBB>	R-205
Neff, son of Nanny	<RIGDON>	R-034
Nell	<DAY>	2-150
Nell	<HALL>	2-306
Nell, girl	<HOPKINS>	2-321
Nell	<LYON>	2-389
Nell, girl	<RIGBIE> <RUMSEY>	R-008
Neo, boy	<GIBSON> <WHEELER>	R-199
Neo, man	<ONION>	2-498
Neo, boy	<OSBORN>	2-494
Nero	<GILES>	2-219
Nesbitt, daughter of Dorcas <HALL>	<RUMSEY>	2-286
Ness	<WORTHINGTON>	R-255
Nessey, man	<LINGAN>	2-391
Oliver, boy	<BAKER>	2-024
Pall	<WORTHINGTON>	R-159
Paraway	<GRIFFITH>	2-258
Paris	<JAY>	2-368
Pat, girl	<DOWNING> <WELLS>	R-189
Patience, girl	<BAKER>	2-024
Patience, girl <COPELAND>	<HOLLIS>	2-301
Patience, woman	<HALL>	2-286
Patience	<PACA>	2-513
Patience, woman	<RUMSEY>	2-286
Patt	<DORSEY>	2-426
Patt	<MAXWELL>	2-426
Patty	<MORGAN>	2-463
Paul, boy	<WHEELER>	R-199

Name	Owner	Ref
Peg, wench	<AMOS>	2-001
Peg	<DAY>	2-150
Peg, girl	<HALL>	R-244
Peg, woman	<MOORES>	2-479
Peg, girl	<OSBORN>	2-496
Peg, wife of Shins	<PACA>	2-517
Peg, child of Harry	<WHEELER>	R-199
Peg, girl	<WILMOTT>	R-244
Pegg, girl	<FISHER>	2-202
Pegg	<HALL>	2-274
Pegg, woman	<LINGAN>	2-391
Pegg, girl	<SCAFF><TALBOTT>	R-134
Pegg, girl	<WORTHINGTON>	R-146
Peggy	<MORGAN>	2-463
Peheb, girl	<ONION>	2-498
Perina, girl	<HALL>	2-274
Perry	<HALL>	2-276
Perry	<HALL>	2-296
Peter, man	<DAY>	2-150
Peter, boy	<DELAPORTE>	2-181
Peter, man	<FISHER>	2-202
Peter, boy	<GARRETTSON>	2-230
Peter, son of Lidde	<GILBERT>	2-263
Peter, man	<HALL>	2-274
Peter, boy	<MATHER>	2-436
Peter, boy	<McCANDLESS><RUTH>	R-011
Peter, boy	<ONION>	2-498
Old Peter	<OSBORN>	2-494
Peter	<SHEREDINE>	R-045
Peton	<KIMBLE>	2-369
Pheby, girl	<WATTERS>	R-148
Pheeby	<WILLSON>	R-180
Philis	<KITLEY>	2-381
Phill, young	<BRYARLY>	2-076
Phill	<HALL>	2-276
Phillip, boy	<HOLLIS>	2-301
Phillip, advanced in years	<MORGAN>	2-463
Phillis, wench	<BAKER>	2-024
Phillis, wife of Tony	<BOND>	2-040
Phillis, woman	<CROOKS>	2-085
Phillis, girl	<HALL>	2-276
Phillis	<McCOMAS>	2-438
Phillis, girl	<ONION>	2-498
Phillis	<PACA>	2-513
Phoebe	<DAY>	2-150
Poatswain, man	<WORTHINGTON>	R-146
Polidare	<GILES>	2-219
Poll, girl	<DREW>	2-155
Poll	<DREW>	2-184
Poll, girl	<FISHER>	2-202
Poll, girl	<GARRETTSON>	2-223
Poll	<GILES>	2-237
Poll, daughter of Diner	<HALL>	2-286
Poll, girl	<JOLLEY>	2-350
Poll, girl	<ONION>	2-498
Poll	<SCOTT>	R-107
Poll	<SMITH>	R-107
Poll	<WILLSON>	R-180
Poll, girl	<WORTHINGTON>	R-146
Pollidore, man	<JOHNS><RIGBIE>	2-348
Polly, woman	<JOHNS><RIGBIE>	2-348
Pompay, man	<WORTHINGTON>	R-146
Pompey	<GILES>	2-219
Pompey, boy	<HAWKINS>	2-292
Pompey, child	<OSBORN>	2-494
Pompey	<PACA>	2-513
Pompey, man	<RIGBIE><RUMSEY>	R-008
Pompy, young	<HOPKINS>	2-318
Poppy	<RUFF>	R-040
Prescilla, female	<DALE>	2-142
Prianna	<RUFF>	R-040
Primes	<WARD>	R-260
Primus	<HALL>	2-276
Prina	<MORGAN>	2-463
Prince	<MAXWELL>	2-426
Prince	<WORTHINGTON>	R-255
Prinor	<HOLLAND>	2-324
Pris, daughter of Diner	<HALL>	2-286
Priscilla	<MORGAN>	2-411
Priscilla	<RUFF>	R-040
Priscilla, girl	<TALBOTT>	R-134
Priss	<DREW>	2-174
Priss, girl	<HALL>	R-244
Priss	<HANSON>	2-316
Priss	<MORGAN>	2-463
Priss, girl	<WILMOTT>	R-244
Priss, girl	<WORTHINGTON>	R-146
Priss, girl	<WORTHINGTON>	R-255
Pug	<GREEN>	2-252
Rachael, girl	<HALL><TOLLEY>	2-288
Rachael, girl	<HAWKINS>	R-191
Rachael	<HOLLAND>	2-324

Name	Owner	Ref
Rachael, house wench	<LEE>	2-384
Rachael, girl	<WELLS>	R-191
Rachael	<WILLSON>	R-180
Rachal, wench	<SMITH>	R-090
Rachel	<CRETIN>	2-116
Rachel, girl	<DAY>	2-150
Rachel, girl	<DAY>	2-171
Rachel, woman	<DORSEY>	2-153
Rachel, girl	<GARRETTSON>	2-223
Rachel, wife of Davy <GIBSON>	<WHEELER>	R-199
Rachel	<LUSBY>	2-401
Rachel, girl	<MEAD> <MURPHY>	2-440
Rachel, girl	<McCANDLESS> <RUTH>	R-025
Rachel	<NEAL>	R-152
Rachel <PACA>	<PHILLIPS>	2-517
Rachel, girl	<RUTH>	R-011
Rachel	<WARD>	R-215
Rachel	<WHEELER>	R-152
Rachel, girl	<WHITE>	R-167
Rachel, woman	<WHITE>	R-167
Rachel. servant	<WHITE>	R-167
Rachell, girl	<HALL>	2-286
Rachell	<McGOWAN> <NEVILL>	2-487
Rachiel, girl of Judah	<HALL>	2-274
Ralph, boy	<WHEELER>	R-199
Rebecka	<MORGAN>	2-463
Rilla	<MORGAN>	2-463
Robert	<JOHNS>	2-348
Robin, man	<GALLION>	2-215
Roger, boy	<ARMSTRONG> <BRYARLY>	2-045
Roger	<JAMISON>	2-335
Root	<RUTH>	R-011
Rose, girl	<BOND>	2-014
Rose, girl	<ONION>	2-498
Ruth, girl	<ONION>	2-498
Sabina, daughter of Hanna	<RIGDON>	R-034
Sal	<MAXWELL>	2-426
Sal	BROWN	2-324
Sal	GWINN	2-324
Sall, girl	<BAKER>	2-059
Sall, girl	<DREW>	2-155
Sall, girl	<GIBSON> <WHEELER>	R-199
Sall, girl	<GREEN>	2-261
Sall, girl	<HALL>	2-296
Sall	<McCOMAS>	2-454
Sall	<ONION>	2-498
Sall, girl	<THORPE> <WILLMOTT>	R-114
Sall, wife of Tom	<WHEELER>	R-199
Sall, girl	<WHITAKER>	R-193
Sall	<WORTHINGTON>	R-255
Sam <AMOS>	<McCOMAS>	2-438
Sam	<CRETIN>	2-116
Sam	<DAY>	2-150
Sam, boy	<GALLION>	2-266
Sam	<GILES>	2-237
Sam, boy	<HALL>	2-274
Sam, boy of Hannah	<HALL>	2-274
Sam	<HALL>	2-276
Sam	<KITLEY>	2-381
Sam, boy	<LEE>	2-384
Sam	<LYON>	2-389
Sam, lad	<LYTTLE>	2-394
Sam	<MATHEWS>	2-469
Sam, man	<MAXWELL>	2-474
Sam	<MORGAN>	2-463
Sam <McGOWAN>	<NEVILL>	2-487
Big Sam	<ONION>	2-498
Sam, boy	<ONION>	2-498
Sam	<OSBORN>	2-494
Sam	<PRESBURY>	2-521
Sam, lad	<RUFF>	2-394
Sam	<RUTH>	R-011
Sam	<THORPE>	R-114
Sam, boy	<WATTERS>	R-148
Sam	<WILLMOTT>	R-114
Sampson	<HALL>	2-276
Sampson	<HALL>	2-306
Sampson	<ONION>	2-498
Samson	<DAY>	2-150
Samson, man	<McCOMAS>	2-438
Samson	<McCOMAS>	2-454
Samuel, boy	<BIDDLE>	2-012
Samuel, young child	<HOPKINS>	2-313
Samuel	<SHEREDINE>	R-045
Santy	<HOLLAND>	2-324
Santy, age 13	<LUSBY>	2-401
Sarah, woman	<DAY>	2-171
Sarah, girl	<HALL>	2-276
Sarah	<HALL>	2-288
Sarah, girl	<HAWKINS>	2-292
Sarah, young	<HOPKINS>	2-318
Sarah	<JOHNS>	2-348
Sarah, daughter of Tom	<WHEELER>	R-199
Sarah, woman	<WILLSON>	R-180
Sarah	<WILLSON>	R-180

Name	Owner	Ref
Saune	<WILLSON>	R-180
Sauney	<RUFF>	R-040
Scipia	<GILES>	2-219
Seasor	<HANSON>	2-316
Sebaboye, child of Hagor	<KIMBLE>	2-369
Sesor	<WORTHINGTON>	R-159
Sharp, young	<HOPKINS>	2-318
Sharper, blacksmith	<HALL>	2-276
Sharper	<HALL>	2-306
Sharper, young	<HOPKINS>	2-298
Shedrach, boy	<DAUGHERTY>	2-149
Shins	<PACA>	2-517
Silvy	<HALL>	2-306
Sim	<DREW>	2-155
Sim, boy	<DREW>	2-158
Simon	<LEE> <PACA>	2-513
Sip, boy	<GALLION>	2-215
Sohia	<HALL> <RUMSEY>	2-286
Sook, woman	<DUTTON> <WALTHAM>	R-212
Sook, woman	<FISHER> <JOLLEY>	2-202
Sook, girl	<MITCHELL>	2-458
Sophia, girl	<DAY> <WETHERALL>	2-165
Sophia, girl	<LEE> <WEBB>	2-384
Sophia	<PRESBURY>	2-521
Stephen	<HOPKINS>	2-321
Stephen, boy	<MITCHEL> <WHEELER>	R-199
Stephney	<HALL>	2-276
Steven, boy	<RIGDUN>	R-028
Steven, boy	<RUTH>	R-011
Suck	<BAKER>	2-024
Suck, woman	<GILES>	2-237
Suck, girl	<HOPKINS>	2-321
Suck	<JOLLEY>	2-350
Suck, girl	<MITCHEL> <WHEELER>	R-199
Suck, wife of Frank	<WHEELER>	R-199
Sucky	<PACA>	2-513
Sue	<HALL>	2-276
Sukey	<WILLSON>	R-180
Sulah	<HALL>	2-286
Susanah, girl	<GILBERT>	2-263
Susanna	<MORGAN>	2-463
Susannah, girl	<HOPKINS>	2-313
Tamer	<BAKER>	2-024
Temperance, woman	<GRAFTON>	2-213
Terry, girl Rachel's daughter <GIBSON> <WHEELER>		R-199
Thamer, woman	<NORRIS>	2-493
Thomas, man	<DAY>	2-171
Thomas, man	<JOHNS> <RIGBIE>	2-348
Thomas, advanced in years	<MORGAN>	2-463
Thomas, servant boy FOX		2-137
Toby, boy	<DAY> <WETHERALL>	2-165
Tom, boy	<BAKER>	2-024
old Tom	<BAKER>	2-024
Tom	<BOYCE>	2-027
Tom	<COWAN>	2-027
Tom, boy	<CRAWFORD>	2-100
Tom	<CRETIN>	2-116
Tom, man	<DAY>	2-150
youngest Tom	<GILES>	2-219
Tom, boy	<GILES> <WATERS>	2-237
Tom, man	<GRAFTON>	2-213
Tom	<HALL>	2-276
Tom	<HALL>	2-296
Tom	<HOLLAND>	2-324
Tom	<LUSBY>	2-393
Tom, girl	<LYTTLE>	2-394
Tom	<MATHEW>	2-444
Tom, boy	<ONION>	2-498
Tom, boy	<OSBORN>	2-494
Tom	<PACA>	2-513
Tom	<RENSHAW>	R-001
big Tom <SCOTT>	<SMITH>	R-107
little Tom <SCOTT> <SMITH>		R-107
Tom	<THORPE>	R-114
Tom	<WARD>	R-260
Tom, man	<WHEELER>	R-199
Tom	<WILLMOTT>	R-114
Tom, boy	<WILSON>	R-157
Tom, fellow	CUDGA	R-132
Tom, son of Tom	<WHEELER>	R-199
Toney, man	<COPELAND> <HOLLIS>	2-301
Toney	<HOLLAND>	2-324
Toney	<NEAL>	R-152
Toney	<WHEELER>	R-152
old Tony	<BOND>	2-040
Tower, man	<JOHNS> <RIGBIE>	2-348
Tower, boy <LEE>	<WEBB>	2-384
Tower	<MORGAN>	2-463
Tower	<WILLSON>	R-180
Triless, boy	<HOLLIS>	2-301

```
Ursulah or Sulah   <HALL>     2-286
Vance    <NEAL> <WHEELER>     R-152
Vi       <HALL> <RUMSEY>      2-286
Vilette, girl      <BAKER>
                   <THOMAS>   2-024
Violett            <ALLENDER>
                   <WANE>     2-005
Violette <HALL> <RUMSEY>      2-286
Wilks              <HALL>     2-306
Will               <DAY>      2-150
Will, boy          <GIBSON>
                   <WHEELER>  R-199
Will               <GREENWELL>
                   <WHEELER>  R-152
Will               <JOLLEY>   2-350
Will, child of Judgath
                   <KIMBLE>   2-369
Will               <OSBORN>   2-494
Will, man          <SCAFF>
                   <TALBOTT>  R-134
Old Will           <SMITH>    R-051
William, man     <HOPKINS>    2-313
William, man       <JOHNS>
                   <RIGBIE>   2-348
William            <RUFF>     R-040
William, boy         HOWE     2-321
William, servant   OLDUM      2-155
Willis, young   <BRYARLY>     2-076
York, son of Chloe
        <ALLENDER> <WANE>     2-005
```

INDEX OF SLAVES BY ASSOCIATED SURNAME

<ALLENDER>, Ceasar	2-005		<BARTON>, Lintey	2-037	
Chloe	2-005		<BIDDLE>, Bash	2-012	
Daniel	2-005		Isaac	2-012	
Dinah	2-005		<BIDDLE>, Lucy	2-012	
Fann	2-150		Matilda	2-012	
black Jack	2-005		Samuel	2-012	
James	2-005		<BLAIR>, Cate	R-011	
Jenny	2-005		<BOND>, Abraham	2-038	(F)
big Joe	2-150		Amey	2-038	(F)
old Ned	2-005		Bell	2-038	
Ned	2-005		Davey	2-014	
Violett	2-005		Dinah	2-014	
York	2-005		Fan	2-014	
<AMOS>, Bess	2-001		George	2-014	
Ignatius	2-001		Guy	2-014	
Peg	2-001		James	2-074	(F)
Sam	2-438		Jane	2-074	(F)
<ANDERSON>, Ben	2-010		John	2-014	
Dinah	2-010	(F)	Letticia	2-074	(F)
Hannah	2-010		Phillis	2-040	
Jim	2-010		Rose	2-014	
<ANDREW>, Jane	R-111		old Tony	2-040	
<ARMSTRONG>, Roger	2-045		<BOWMAN>, Darkis	R-152	(F)
<BAKER>, Archibald	2-059		<BOYCE>, Dembo	2-027	
Barnett	2-024		Tom	2-027	
Beck	2-024		BRADFORD, Abigal	2-055	
Ben	2-024		Chaney	2-055	
Bess	2-024		Jane	2-055	(F)
Betty	2-059		Nathan	2-055	
Ceasor	2-024		<BRICKHEAD>, Cato	2-070	
Coffee	2-024		Clem	2-070	
Darkus	2-059		Lid	2-070	
Dinah	2-024,059		BROWN, Sal	2-324	(F)
Easter	2-024		<BROWN>, Bobb	2-066	
George	2-024		Dipp	2-066	
Isaac	2-059		James	2-066	
James	2-059		Limus	2-055	
Oliver	2-024		Ned	2-055	
Patience	2-024		<BROWNE>, Bob	2-064	
Phillis	2-024		Chance	2-064	
Sall	2-059		Dinah	2-064	
Suck	2-024		Dip	2-064	
Tamer	2-024		Dutches	2-055	
Tom	2-024		Floria	2-064	
old Tom	2-024		Isaac	2-064	
Vilette	2-024		Limus	2-055	
<BARNES>, Ben	2-067		Murrier	2-055	
Bill	2-067		Ned	2-055	
Isaac	2-067		<BRYARLY>, Cisiah	2-076	(F)

[1] (F) Indicates slaves manumitted (freed) in referenced will.

<BRYARLY>, Hannah	2-076 (F)		Peg	2-150
Nat	2-076 (F)		Peter	2-150
Phill	2-076 (F)		Phoebe	2-150
Roger	2-045		Rachel	2-150,171
Willis	2-076 (F)		Sam	2-150
<BRYERLY>, Hager	2-033		Samson	2-150
<BULL>, Bell	2-028		Sarah	2-171
Frank	2-028		Sophia	2-165
<CALBERT>, Ginny	R-157		Thomas	2-171
<CALWELL>, Charles	R-020		Toby	2-165
<CHINWORTH>, James	R-114		Tom	2-150
<CLARK>, Jack	2-082		Will	2-150
<COLEGATE>, Jack	2-082		<DESSAA>, Cathrine	2-176
<COOPER>, Betty	2-261		Celeste	2-176
<COPELAND>, Patience	2-301		<DELAPORTE>, Fany	2-181
Toney	2-301		Fanny	2-181
<COWAN>, Dembo	2-027		Peter	2-181 (F)
Tom	2-027		<DENNEY>, Darkus	2-059
<CRAWFORD>, David	2-100		<DENNY>, Dinah	2-163
Dinah	2-100		Maria	2-166
Gain	2-100		<DORSEY>, Averilla	2-153
Hager	2-100		Beck	2-426
Jane	2-121 (F)		Harry	2-153
Margret	2-100		Patt	2-426
Moses	2-100		Rachel	2-153
Ned	2-100		<DOWNING>, Pat	R-189
Tom	2-100		<DREW>, Abraham	2-155
<CRETIN>, Bett	2-116		Ben	2-184
Joe	2-116		Bill	2-184
Rachel	2-116		Clenas	2-158
Sam	2-116		Clenes	2-155
Tom	2-116		Deck	2-174
<CRISWELL>, Jo	2-120		Dinah	2-155
<CROCKETT>, Ester	2-103		old Easter	2-155
<CROOKS>, Phillis	2-085		Easter	2-184
CUDGA, Tom	R-132		George	2-174
<CUMMINS>, Cloe	2-130		Hager	2-155
<DALE>, Ben	2-142		Hannah	2-155
Dinah	2-142		Hary	2-155
Prescilla	2-142		Jacob	2-174
<DAUGHERTY>, Jean	2-149		yallow Jim	2-155
Nan	2-149		Joe	2-155
Shedrach	2-149		Ned	2-174
<DAVIS>, Dinah	2-100		Poll	2-155,184
<DAY>, Claire	2-171		Priss	2-174
Dark	2-165		Sall	2-155
Fann	2-150		Sim	2-155,158
Fie	2-150		<DUTTON>, Sook	R-212 (F)
Frank	2-150		<EDGAR>, Jo	2-120
Jacob	2-150		<EVATT>, Bill	2-198 (F)
big Jem	2-150		Dark	2-198 (F)
Joe	2-150		Judy	2-198 (F)
Nan	2-150		<FISHER>, Ben	2-202
Nance	2-171		Daniel	2-202
Nell	2-150		Jean	2-202

<FISHER>, Pegg	2-202		Nero	2-219 (F)
Peter	2-202		Polidare	2-219 (F)
Poll	2-202		Poll	2-237
Sook	2-202		Pompey	2-219 (F)
FOX, Thomas	2-137 (F)		Sam	2-237
<GALLION>, Bobb	2-215		Scipia	2-219 (F)
Daniel	2-215		Suck	2-237
Dinah	2-215		youngest Tom	2-219 (F)
Hager	2-215		Tom	2-237
little Jame	2-215		<GORRAL>, Margret	2-100
Joe	2-215		<GRAFTON>, Catharine	2-213
big Jonn	2-215		Temperance	2-213
Jupeter	2-215		Tom	2-213
Nan	2-215		<GREEN>, Abraham	2-252
Robin	2-215		Bet	2-252
Sam	2-266		Betty	2-261
Sip	2-215		Dole	2-252
<GARLAND>, Jacob	2-222		Ester	2-252
<GARRETT>, Ceasor	2-024		Helen	R-152
<GARRETTSON>, Cuff	2-223		Jack	2-261
Cumbo	2-223		James	2-252
Fan	2-223		Jean	2-252 (F)
Grace	2-223		Jean	2-261
Hannah	2-223		Josias	2-261
James	2-230		Kate	2-252 (F)
Jupiter	2-230		Major	2-252
Moll	2-223		Mary	2-252 (F)
Peter	2-230		Pug	2-252 (F)
Poll	2-223		Sall	2-261
Rachel	2-223		<GREENWELL>, Charity	R-152
<GIBSON>, Christian	R-199		Will	R-152
Davy	R-199		<GRIFFITH>, Abigail	2-258
Fan	R-199		little Bill	2-258
Gabriel	R-199		Daphne	2-227
Gin	R-199		Jack	2-258
Neo	R-199		Mariah	2-258
Rachel	R-199		Paraway	2-258
Sall	R-199		GWINN, James	2-324 (F)
Terry	R-199		Sal	2-324 (F)
Will	R-199		<HALL>, Abigail	2-288
<GILBERT>, Betsy	2-263		Abram	R-244
Ester	2-263		Aby	2-288 (F)
Hager	2-215		Augustus	2-286
Jupeter	2-215		Bacchus	2-276
Lidde	2-263		Beck	2-276
Peter	2-263		Belinda	2-306
Susanah	2-263		Bellily	2-306
<GILES>, Cato	2-219 (F)		Ben	2-276,288
Ceesar	2-219 (F)		Betty	2-286
Cissero	2-219 (F)		Bess	2-286
George	2-237		Bill	2-286,288
Grace	2-237		Cass	2-276 (F)
Lancaster Tom	2-219 (F)		Charles	2-286
Lydia	2-237		Corbin	2-306
Morea	2-237		Cudgoe	2-274

<HALL>, Cuff	2-276	Moll	2-274;R-167
Cupid	2-276,306	Nace	2-306
Darkey	2-286	Neamy	2-274
Diamond	2-276	Ned	2-274
Dinah	2-274,276,286;R-167	Nell	2-306
Dinah	2-288 (F)	Nesbitt	2-286
Diner	2-286	Patience	2-286
Doll	2-288	Peg	R-244
Dorcas	2-286	Pegg	2-274
Easter	2-274	Perina	2-274
Elizabeth	2-286	Perry	2-276,296
Emanuel	2-274	Peter	2-274
Fanny	2-286	Phill	2-276
George	2-288	Phillis	2-276
Gill	2-306	Poll	2-286
Gustus	2-274,286	Primus	2-276
Gwin	2-288	Pris	2-286
Hager	2-274,288	Priss	R-244
Hanna	R-244	Rachael	2-288
Hannah	2-274,276,286,288	Rachell	2-286
Harry	2-274	Rachiel	2-274
Isaac	2-274,288	Sall	2-296
Jack	2-286	Sam	2-274,276
Jacob	2-274,296,306	Sampson	2-276,306
Jacque	2-288	Sarah	2-276 (F)
James	2-286	Sarah	2-288
Jane	2-276 (F)	Sharper	2-276,306
Jane	2-286	Silvy	2-306
Jantee	2-288	Sohia	2-286
Jem	2-286,288	Stephney	2-276
Jemmy	2-288 (F)	Sue	2-276
Jen	2-286	Sulah	2-286
Jeney	2-274	Tom	2-276,296
Jenny	2-274	Ursulah	2-286
Jo	2-274,286	Vi	2-286
Joe	2-288	Violette	2-286
Judah	2-274,276	Wilks	2-306
Kate	2-276,296,306	<HANSON>, Fan	2-327
yellow Katre	2-276	Hannah	2-316
Leander	2-274	Ned	2-316
Liberty	2-306	Priss	2-316
Liddy	2-286	Seasor	2-316
Linda	2-276	<HAWKINS>, Cuff	2-292 (F)
Lucy	2-274;R-167	Jerry	2-292 (F)
Lydia	2-286	Jimeney	2-292 (F)
Manuel	2-276 (F)	Mary	2-292 (F)
Margaret	2-274	Pompey	2-292 (F)
Mariah	2-288 (F)	Rachael	R-191
Medarah	2-274	Sarah	2-292 (F)
Micah	2-274	<HENDERSON>, Deck	2-174
Milcah	2-276	<HENLEY>, Lordon	R-189
Milley	2-288	<HITCHCOCK>, Jacob	2-222
Mingo	2-276	<HOLLAND>, Bett	2-324
Minty	2-306	Cass	2-324
Mirtilla	2-286	Dave	2-324 (F)

```
<HOLLAND>, Dinah         2-324           Ceaser            2-368  (F)
  Isaac                  2-324  (F)       Elisha            2-368  (F)
  Jacob                  2-324  (F)       Harriott          2-368  (F)
  Lyd                    2-324            Paris             2-368  (F)
  Manuel                 2-324  (F)     <JEFFRY>, Cance     2-494
  Nan                    2-324          <JOHNS>, Affey      2-348
  Prinor                 2-324            Billie            2-348
  Rachael                2-324            Dinah             2-348
  Santy                  2-324  (F)       George            2-348
  Tom                    2-324  (F)       Jack              2-348
  Toney                  2-324  (F)       Meriah            2-326
<HOLLIS>, Bendow         2-301            Mingoe            2-348
  Fan                    2-494            Pollidore         2-348
  Grace                  2-301            Polly             2-348
  Jack                   2-301            Robert            2-348
  Julia                  2-301            Sarah             2-348
  Patience               2-301            Thomas            2-348
  Phillip                2-301            Tower             2-348
  Toney                  2-301            William           2-348
  Triless                2-301          <JOLLEY>, Beck      2-350
<HOPKINS>, Cassandra     2-321  (F)       Dampiere          2-350
  Cato                   2-318  (F)       Daniel            2-202,350
  Dafney                 2-298            Hanna             2-350
  David                  2-298            Jane              2-350
  Gaberial               2-318  (F)       Joe               2-350
  George                 2-298            Judath            2-350
  George                 2-318  (F)       Lint              2-350
  George                 2-321  (F)       Poll              2-350
  Hannah                 2-313  (F)       Sook              2-202
  Hannah                 2-318  (F)       Suck              2-350
  Harriot                2-321  (F)       Will              2-350
  Isaac                  2-313  (F)     <KIMBLE>, Cas       2-369
  Jane                   2-313  (F)       Darke             2-369
  John                   2-313  (F)       Fill              2-369
  John                   2-318  (F)       Hagor             2-369
  Linta                  2-313  (F)       Jane              2-369
  Margerret              2-321  (F)       Judgath           2-369
  Mary                   2-313  (F)       Marget            2-369
  Murriah                2-318  (F)       Moll              2-369
  Ned                    2-305            Peton             2-369
  Nell                   2-321  (F)       Sebaboye          2-369
  Pompy                  2-318  (F)       Will              2-369
  Samuel                 2-313  (F)     <KITLEY>, Bob       2-381  (F)
  Sarah                  2-318  (F)       Darkey            2-381  (F)
  Sharp                  2-318  (F)       Freeborn          2-381  (F)
  Sharper                2-298            Hannah            2-381  (F)
  Stephen                2-321  (F)       Isaac             2-381  (F)
  Suck                   2-321  (F)       Jack              2-381  (F)
  Susannah               2-313  (F)       Jim               2-381  (F)
  William                2-313  (F)       Louisa            2-381  (F)
<HORNER>, James          2-325  (F)       Philis            2-381  (F)
HOWE, William            2-321  (F)       Sam               2-381  (F)
<HUSBAND>, Margerret     2-321  (F)     <LANCASTER>, Fan    2-327
<JAMISON>, Roger         2-335  (F)     <LEE>, Bett         2-384
<JAY>, Ben               2-368  (F)       Cloe              2-384
```

<LEE>, Dinah	2-384	Aron	2-444
Duke	2-384 (F)	Ned	2-444
Dutchess	2-384	Tom	2-444
Forest	2-384	<MATHEWS>, Charles	2-469
Hagar	2-384	David	2-469
Hannah	2-384	Edmond	2-469
Jenny	2-384	Ferreca	2-469
Jerry	2-384	George	2-469
Kater	2-384	Jacob	2-469
Lamer	2-384	Jim	2-469
Mariah	2-384	Sam	2-469
Moll	2-384	<MAXWELL>, Beck	2-426
Nan	2-384	Nat	2-426
Natt	2-384	Patt	2-426
Rachael	2-384	Prince	2-426
Sam	2-384	Sal	2-426
Simon	2-513 (F)	Sam	2-474 (F)
Sophia	2-384	<McCANDLESS>, Beck	R-011
Tower	2-384	Peter	R-011
<LETANG>, Cathrine	2-176	Rachel	R-025
Celeste	2-176	<McCOMAS>, Amy	2-454
<LINGAN>, Andrew	2-391	Andrew	2-460
Nessey	2-391	George	2-454
Pegg	2-391	Jack	2-454 (F)
<LOGHLIN>, Hagar	R-157	Jack	2-460
<LUSBY>, Grace	2-401 (F)	Jacob	2-438
Hector	2-393 (F)	Jem	2-454 (F)
Jack	2-393 (F)	Jenny	2-454 (F)
Murrier	2-401 (F)	Jim	2-460
Rachel	2-401 (F)	Joe	2-454
Santy	2-401 (F)	Julett	2-454
Tom	2-393	Liddy	2-438
<LYNCH>, Diner	R-111	Lisa	2-454 (F)
Joshua	R-111	London	2-454
<LYON>, Dinah	2-389	Lydda	2-460
Jacob	2-389	Miriah	2-454
Jim	2-389	Phillis	2-438
Lanney	2-389	Sall	2-454 (F)
Ned	2-389	Sam	2-438
Nell	2-389	Samson	2-438 (F)
Sam	2-389	Samson	2-454 (F)
<LYTTLE>, Easter	2-394 (F)	<McGOWAN>, Ann	2-487
Ester	2-394 (F)	Fann	2-487
George	2-394	Nan	2-487 (F)
Hager	2-394 (F)	Rachell	2-487
Han	2-394	Sam	2-487 (F)
Harry	2-394	<McTEE>, Bennet	R-152
Jerry	2-394 (F)	Betty	R-152
Lemon	2-394	Coock	R-152
Mettway	2-394	<MEAD>, Daphne	2-440
Sam	2-394 (F)	Dennis	2-440
Tom	2-394	George	2-440
<MATHER>, Jane	2-436	Grace	2-440
Peter	2-436	Hagar	2-440
<MATHEW>, Amey	2-444	Hannah	2-440

<MEAD>, Rachel	2-440	Priscilla	2-411	
<MILES>, Mary	2-446	Priss	2-463	(F)
<MITCHEL>, Mary	R-199	Rebecka	2-463	(F)
Nan	R-199	Rilla	2-463	(F)
Stephen	R-199	Sam	2-463	(F)
Suck	R-199	Susanna	2-463	(F)
<MITCHELL>, Bob	2-422 (F)	Thomas	2-463	
Cassy	2-418	Tower	2-463	(F)
Isaac	2-458 (F)	<MORRIS>, Bell	2-038	
Jonas	2-418	Jane	2-074	(F)
Mary	2-418	Letticia	2-074	(F)
Sook	2-458	<MURPHY>, Hagar	2-440	
<MOOR>, Nan	R-114	Rachel	2-440	
<MOORE>, Nan	R-114	<NEAL>, Abner	R-152	
<MOORES>, Peg	2-479	Augustus	R-152	
<MORGAN>, Abraham	2-463 (F)	Jack	R-152	
Ann	2-463 (F)	Ned	R-152	
Ben	2-463 (F)	Rachel	R-152	
Benjamin	2-411	Toney	R-152	
Betsy	2-263	Vance	R-152	
Bett	2-463 (F)	<NELSON>, George	2-174	
Bill	2-463 (F)	Ned	2-174	
Bob	2-463 (F)	<NEVILL>, Ann	2-487	
Cate	2-463 (F)	Fann	2-487	
Dutches	2-463 (F)	Nan	2-487	(F)
Ester	2-263	Rachell	2-487	
Fainer	2-463 (F)	Sam	2-487	(F)
Frances	2-463 (F)	<NORRIS>, Affrick	2-493	(F)
George	2-411	Minggo	2-493	
George	2-463 (F)	Thamer	2-493	
Hagar	2-411	OLDUM, William	2-155	(F)
Hannah	2-384	<ONION>, Amia	2-498	
Hannah	2-463 (F)	Amy	2-454	
Hector	2-411	Ben	2-498	
Hester	2-463	Bob	2-498	
Isaac	2-463 (F)	Cass	2-498	
Jack	2-463 (F)	Dick	2-498	
James	2-411	George	2-498	
James	2-463 (F)	Grace	2-498	
Jane	2-411	Isaac	2-498	
Jane	2-463 (F)	Jack	2-498	
Jerry	2-384	Jacob	2-498	
Jerry	2-463 (F)	Jen	2-498	
Joseph	2-463 (F)	Big Jenny	2-498	
Kater	2-384	Jenny	2-498	
London	2-463 (F)	Job	2-498	
Mary	2-463 (F)	Joe	2-454	
Michael	2-411	Julett	2-454	
Mike	2-463 (F)	Landon	2-498	
Nan	2-384	Lem	2-498	
Ned	2-463 (F)	Lidd	2-498	
Patty	2-463 (F)	London	2-454	
Peggy	2-463 (F)	Lydia	2-498	
Phillip	2-463	Miriah	2-454	
Prina	2-463 (F)	Nance	2-498	

<ONION>, Neo	2-498	<PRESBURY>, Andrew	2-521	
Peheb	2-498	Geofray	2-521	
Peter	2-498	Hagar	2-521	
Phillis	2-498	Isaac	2-521	
Poll	2-498	Sam	2-521	
Rose	2-498	Sophia	2-521	
Ruth	2-498	RACO, James	2-324	(F)
Sall	2-498	<RENSHAW>, Dick	R-016	
Big Sam	2-498	Tom	R-001	
Sam	2-498	<RICHARDSON>, Briget	R-020	
Sampson	2-498	Cash	R-020	
Tom	2-498	Charles	R-020	
<OSBORN>, Bess	2-496	Cloe	R-020	
Bridget	2-494	Jack	R-020	
Cance	2-494	Jude	R-020	
Dinah	2-494	<RIGBIE>, Affey	2-348	
Doll	2-494	Billie	2-348	
Fan	2-494	Dinah	2-348	
George	2-496	George	2-348	
Hannah	2-494	Jack	2-348	
Harry	2-496	Mingoe	2-348	
Isaac	2-494	Nell	R-008	
Jack	2-494,496	Pollidore	2-348	
Moll	2-494	Polly	2-348	
Neo	2-494	Pompey	R-008	
Peg	2-496	Thomas	2-348	
Old Peter	2-494	Tower	2-348	
Pompey	2-494	William	2-348	
Sam	2-494	<RIGDON>, Brise	R-034	(F)
Tom	2-494	Davey	R-034	
Will	2-494	Elisha	R-034	
<PACA>, Amynta	2-517	Hanna	R-034	(F)
Bet	2-513 (F)	Mingo	R-034	
Bob	2-513 (F)	Nanny	R-034	
Fan	2-513 (F)	Neff	R-034	
Grace	2-513 (F)	Sabina	R-034	(F)
Hagar	2-513 (F)	<RIGDUN>, Ann	R-028	
Harry	2-517	Lisha	R-028	
Jack	2-513 (F)	Steven	R-028	
Jenny	2-513 (F)	<ROBINSON>, Lusey	R-007	
Jo	2-513 (F)	<RUFF>, Allexander	R-040	(F)
Milcah	2-513 (F)	Ann	R-040	(F)
Nace	2-513 (F)	Benjamin, Jr	R-040	(F)
Patience	2-513 (F)	Benjamin, Sr	R-040	(F)
Peg	2-517	Cyrus	R-040	(F)
Phillis	2-513 (F)	Easter	2-394	(F)
Pompey	2-513 (F)	Ester	2-394,R-040	(F)
Rachel	2-517	Hager	2-394	(F)
Shins	2-517	John	R-040	(F)
Simon	2-513 (F)	Moses	R-040	(F)
Sucky	2-513 (F)	Poppy	R-040	(F)
Tom	2-513 (F)	Prianna	R-040	(F)
<PHILLIPS>, Amynta	2-517	Priscilla	R-040	(F)
Harry	2-517	Sam	2-394	(F)
Rachel	2-517	Sauney	R-040	(F)

<RUFF>, William	R-040 (F)	<TAYLOR>, Diner	R-111	
<RUMSEY>, Betty	2-286	Joshua	R-111	
Bess	2-286	<THOMAS>, Vilette	2-024	
Bill	2-286	<THOMPSON>, Bill	R-132	
Charles	2-286	Clenas	2-158	
Darkey	2-286	Clenes	R-132	
Dorcas	2-286	Dinah	R-132	
Elizabeth	2-286	Dutches	2-055	
Fanny	2-286	Mint	R-132	
Jo	2-286	Murrier	2-055	
Liddy	2-286	<THORPE>, Bine	R-114	
Lydia	2-286	Harry	R-114	
Nell	R-008	James	R-114	
Nesbitt	2-286	Nan	R-114	
Patience	2-286	Sall	R-114	
Pompey	R-008	Sam	R-114	
Sohia	2-286	<THORPE>, Tom	R-114	
Vi	2-286	<TIRE>, Jarret	R-152	
Violette	2-286	<TOLLEY>, Doll	2-288	
<RUTH>, Beck	R-011	Hager	2-288	
Cate	R-011	Rachael	2-288	
Peter	R-011	<TREDWAY>, Diner	R-111	
Rachel	R-011 (F)	Jane	R-111	
Rachel	R-025	Joshua	R-111	
Root	R-011 (F)	TRUELOVE, Michael	2-220 (F)	
Sam	R-011 (F)	<VANCLEAF>, Jenny	2-384	
Steven	R-011 (F)	<VANCLEAVE>, Bett	2-384	
<SCAFF>, Pegg	R-134	<WALLIS>, Dinah	R-185 (F)	
Will	R-134	<WALTHAM>, Sook	R-212 (F)	
<SCOTT>, Dan	R-107	<WANE>, Chloe	2-005	
Poll	R-107	Daniel	2-005	
big Tom	R-107	Dinah	2-005	
little Tom	R-107	black Jack	2-005	
<SHEREDINE>, Aron	R-045	James	2-005	
Jacob	R-045	Jenny	2-005	
Jupiter	R-045	old Ned	2-005	
Mary	R-045	Ned	2-005	
Peter	R-045	Violett	2-005	
Samuel	R-045	York	2-005	
<SMITH>, Dan	R-107	<WARD>, Cate	R-189	
Jacob	R-090	Dido	R-225 (F)	
Jean	R-090	Hannah	R-225 (F)	
Poll	R-107	Jacob	R-225 (F)	
Rachal	R-090	James	R-225 (F)	
big Tom	R-107	Joe	R-225 (F)	
little Tom	R-107	Liddia	R-215	
Old Will	R-051 (F)	Primes	R-260 (F)	
<SMITHSON>, Caesar	R-098 (F)	Rachel	R-215	
<SMITHSON>, Hannah	R-098 (F)	Tom	R-260 (F)	
Jack	R-098 (F)	<WATERS>, Harriot	2-321 (F)	
<TALBOTT>, Jacob	R-134	Lydia	2-237	
Jesse	R-134	Tom	2-237	
Pegg	R-134	<WATTERS>, Cloe	R-148	
Priscilla	R-134	Isabele	R-148	
Will	R-134	Luc	R-148	

<WATTERS>, Pheby	R-148	Rachel	R-152,199
Sam	R-148	Ralph	R-199
<WEBB>, Bett	R-205	Sall	R-199
old yellow Jim	R-205	Sarah	R-199
Moll	2-384	Stephen	R-199
Ned	R-205	Suck	R-199
Sophia	2-384	Terry	R-199
Tower	2-384	Tom	R-199
<WEBSTER>, Becky	R-229	Toney	R-152
Bob	R-221 (F)	Vance	R-152
James	R-229 (F)	Will	R-152,199
<WELLS>, Bobb	R-191	<WHITAKER>, Beck	2-024
Cate	R-189,191	Hannah	R-193
Hannah	R-191	Sall	R-193
Isaac	R-189	<WHITE>, Dinah	R-167
Jack	R-191	Ester	R-167
Jane	R-191	Jesse	R-167
Lordon	R-189	Lucy	R-167
Pat	R-189	Moll	R-167
Rachael	R-191	Rachel	R-167
<WETHERALL>, Dark	2-165	Rachel	R-167 (F)
Sophia	2-165	<WHITEFORD>, Dina	R-203
Toby	2-165	Fann	R-203
<WHEELER>, Abner	R-152	Gess	R-203
Augustus	R-152	Jack	R-203
Beck	R-199	Jean	R-203
Bennet	R-152	<WILLMOTT>, Bine	R-114
Bet	R-199	Harry	R-114
Betty	R-152	James	R-114
Cate	R-199	Sall	R-114
Charity	R-152	Sam	R-114
Christian	R-199	Tom	R-114
Clarke	R-199	<WILLSON>, Adam	R-180
Coock	R-152	Adam	R-180 (F)
Darkis	R-152 (F)	Affee	R-180 (F)
Davy	R-199	Agram	R-180
Fan	R-199	Ben	R-180
Frank	R-199	Betty	R-180
Gabriel	R-199	Bobb	R-180
Gin	R-199	Bristol	R-180 (F)
Hannah	R-199	Charles	R-180
Harry	R-199	Clem	R-180
Helen	R-152	Cloe	R-180
Hester	R-199	David	R-180
Jack	R-152,199	Dinah	R-180
James	R-199	Faney	R-180
Jarret	R-152	Fanney	R-180 (F)
Jerry	R-199	Flora	R-180
Joe	R-199	Hagar	R-180
Mary	R-199	Harry	R-180
Nan	R-199	Henry	R-180
Ned	R-152	Jacob	R-180
Neo	R-199	Jane	R-180
Paul	R-199	Landon	R-180
Peg	R-199	Leanda	R-180

```
<WILLSON>, Pheeby      R-180
   Poll                R-180
   Rachael             R-180
   Sarah               R-180
   Saune               R-180
   Sukey               R-180
   Tower               R-180 (F)
<WILMOTT>, Abram       R-244
   Hanna               R-244
   Peg                 R-244
   Priss               R-244
<WILSON>, Clitus       R-157
   Cloe                2-384
   Dinah               2-384
   Ginny               R-157
   Hagar               R-157
   Natt                2-384
   Tom                 R-157
<WORTHINGTON>,
   Arringe             R-255 (F)
   Ben                 R-146
   Bill                R-255 (F)
   Ceasor              R-146
   Charley             R-255 (F)
   Davey               R-146
   Davey               R-159 (F)
   Harry               R-146
   Harry               R-255 (F)
   Hector              R-159 (F)
   Jim                 R-255 (F)
   Lovor               R-159 (F)
   Mike                R-255 (F)
   Mitway              R-146
   Ness                R-255 (F)
   Pall                R-159 (F)
   Pegg                R-146
   Poatswain           R-146
   Poll                R-146
   Pompay              R-146
   Prince              R-255 (F)
   Priss               R-146
   Priss               R-255 (F)
   Sall                R-255 (F)
   Sesor               R-159 (F)
WRIGHT, John           2-137 (F)
<YORK>, Abraham        R-266 (F)
```

INDEX BY FULL NAME

Name	Ref
ABBIT, Ann	2-074
ACHIN, James	2-212
ADAIR, Robert	2-134;R-197
ADAMS, John	2-031,059
ADY, Jonathan	2-021
William	2-128
AIKEN, Margaret	2-193
ALBERT, Jacob	R-205
Phillip	R-249
ALDERSON, Sarah	2-057
Thomas	2-057
ALLEIN, Jimmy	2-008
William	2-008
ALLEN, Charles	2-449
William	2-303
ALLENDER, Avarilla	2-150
Deborah	2-004
Jane	2-150
John	2-004,005;R-015
Lucenia	2-036
Lucina	2-004,005
Mary	2-150
Nicholas	2-005
Sarah	2-150,171
William	2-150,463
ALLINDER, John	2-004,005;R-010
Lucina	2-004,005,397; R-010,015
William	2-357
ALLISON, James	2-273
AMOS, Anne	2-001
Benjamin	2-001;R-134
Elijah	2-001
Elizabeth	2-001
Frederick	2-462
Hannah	2-082,142
James	2-236;R-134
James Senr.	2-142
John	2-001
Joshua	2-142,236
Martha	2-438;R-037
Mary	2-446
Mordecai	R-037
Robert	2-340
Robert Esq.	2-438
Sarah	2-001
Susannah	2-001
William	2-294,446,490
Zechariah	2-001
AMOSS, Aquilla	2-002
Elizabeth	R-142
Frederick	2-002
George	2-126;R-093
James	2-002,490
Joshua	2-002
Martha	2-002
Mary	2-002
Mordecai Esq.	2-002
Robert	R-103
Robert Esq.	2-031
William	2-002,062
William Jr.	2-062
ANDERSON, Ann	2-010
ANDERSON, Catharin	2-106
Catherine	2-010
Daniel	2-090;R-154
Elizabeth	2-010
George	R-055
Hugh	2-010
James	2-531
ANDREW, Mary	R-111
Sarah	R-111
ANDREWS, Dr. [----]	R-048
Thomas	2-219,280;R-048,167
ANNAN, Daniel	2-009
James	2-009
Peggy	2-009
William	2-009
ARCHER, James	R-011,025
John	2-018,034,104,145, 198,273,296,404,421, 479,513;R-044,087, 107,197,217,229,244
Dr. John	2-116,237,R-011, 025,031,205
John Senr.	2-479
Thomas	R-011
ARLET, Hannah	R-021
Thomas	R-021
ARMIN, Dr. William	2-104
ARMSTRONG, Agness	2-007
David	2-213
Elizabeth	2-007,045
Esther	2-007
Ford	2-439,530
Isabel	2-198
Isabella	2-033
James	2-007
Loving	2-007
Solomon	2-439
ARNOLD, Ephraim	2-530,R-167
William	R-167
ASHLEY, Thomas	2-064,247
ASHMEAD, Samuel	2-033,291
ASHMORE, John	R-028
William	R-028

AYERS, Thomas H.	2-194	William	R-260
AYES, Thomas H.	2-194	BAYER, Sabina HALL	R-228
BAGLEY, William	2-321	BAYLES, Augustine	2-066,396
BAILEY, William	R-066	Daniel	R-197
BAKER, Ann	2-024	John Brown	2-066
Charles	2-024,059;R-007,037	Nathaniel	2-092
Christian	2-024,059	Nimrod	2-066
Gideon	2-493	BAYLESS, Augustine	2-066
Grafton	2-024,059	Samuel	R-062,252
Hannah	2-024	BAYLIS, Samuel	2-128
John	2-024,059	BEAN, John	R-209
Maurice	2-024,059,136	William	R-209
Morris	2-024	BEATTY, Archibald	2-155,174,230
Nathan	2-024,059	BEATY, Ann	2-254
Nicholas Junr.	2-134	Archibald	2-198
Rachel	2-024	William	2-193,198
Theophilus	2-024,498	BEAVER, Charles	R-110
William	2-024,059,325;R-058	BECK, John	2-064
BALDERSTON, Jacob	2-200	Mary	2-359
Martha	2-188	BELL, David	2-035,056
BANKHEAD, Hugh	2-432	George	2-382
BARBEY, John	R-056	James	2-009,034,198
BARCLAY, John	2-206,282	John	2-156;R-129
John Esq.	2-404	Robert	2-035
BARNES, Amos	2-067;R068,195	Sarah	2-035
Bennett	2-067,348	BENCHOOF, Christopher	2-352
Elizabeth	2-079;R-191	BENETT, Zebede	2-494
Ford	2-067	BENFIELD, Dr. [----]	2-142
Garrett	2-067	David	2-031
George Junr.	2-530	Hannah	2-031
Gregory	2-458	Mary	2-031
Hosier	2-067	William	2-031
James	2-079	BENINTON, Henry	R-055
John	2-067;R-242	BENNETT, Caleb	2-099
Joseph	R-242	Elizabeth	2-137
Rebecca	R-195	Jemima	2-099
Richard	2-530	Martha	2-099
Sarah	2-067	Richard	2-335
BARNET, James	2-344;R-161	Robert	2-099
BARNETT, Elizabeth	R-090	BETTY, Archibald	2-155
James	2-085,206;R-083	BIDDLE, Augustine	2-012
Joseph	2-206	Benjamin	2-012
Martha	2-206	Jesse	2-012
BARNS, John	2-122	John	2-012
BARRY, Elizabeth Ann	2-233	Karenhappuch	2-012
BARTIN, Margaret	R-098	Nancy	2-012
BARTON, Alisanna	2-037	Richard	2-012,446
Ann	2-037	BIGGERS, [----]	2-312
Elizabeth	2-037	BILLINGSLEA, Clemency	2-057
James	2-037,191,340,364	James	2-196
John	2-037	John	2-196
William	2-037	Walter	2-057,106
BAY, Hugh	2-051	Walter Junr.	2-404
John	2-051	William	2-196
Nathan	2-400	BILLINGSLY, Sias	R-001

BIRCKHEAD, Ann	2-070		Peggy	2-454
Elizabeth	2-070		Priscilla	2-040
Francis	2-070		Ralph	2-040
Margret	2-070		Sally	2-454
Mathew	2-070		Sally Charity	2-053,071
Nehemiah	2-070		Samuel	2-021,044
Samuel	2-070		Sarah	R-037
Seaborn	2-070		Thomas	2-021,024,040,
Thomas Howell	2-070,165,			044,053,340,454,
	474;R-266			498;R-051,105
BIRUM, Martha	R-079		Thomas Scott	2-014,053
BISHOP, Robert	2-036,037		William	2-021,038,040,071,
BLACK, Jean	2-051			074,336;R-059,061
John	2-051		Zacheus Onion	2-014,053
Lydia	2-088		BONDS, William	2-336
Mary	2-051		BONER, Elizabeth	R-159
BLACKBURN, Robert	2-338		Robert	R-090
BLACKSTON, Elijah	2-115		Sarah	2-198
BLAIR, Jean	R-011,025		William	2-198
Thomas	R-011,025		BOSLEY, Rachel	R-114
BLEANY, Thomas	2-141,399		William	2-037,422
BOARDMAN, Ann	2-018		BOWMAN, Mary Ann	R-152
Catharine	2-018		BOYCE, Ann	2-027
William	2-018		Benjamin	2-391
BOARMAN, Rev. Sylvester	2-126		John	2-027,391
BODKES, Robert	2-123		Roger	2-027,066;R-164
BODKIN, Robert	2-202		BOYER, Amelia	R-008
BODY, Benjamin	2-049		BOYLE, Thomas	2-237,348
BONAR, James	2-271		BRABZON, Grace	2-376
BOND, Alsannah	2-014		BRADFORD, Abigal	2-055
Amelia	2-038,074		Chaney	2-055
Ann	2-038,040,074		Jane	2-055
Barnett	2-040		Nathan	2-055
Buckler	2-038,071,074,498		Sarah	2-438
Charlotte	2-040		BRADIN, Enoch	2-056
Daniel	2-014,053		Robert	2-056
Dennis	2-040,071		Thomas	2-056
Edward Fell	2-021		BRADLEY, Robert	2-282,344
Elizabeth	2-014,038,053,		BRADSHAW, Hester	2-146
	482,485;R-059,061		BRADY, Rose	R-152
Hannah	2-014		BREDIN, Enoch	2-056
Jacob	2-040,082,164,213,		BREWER, William	2-458
	331,482,485,508;R-121		BRIARLY, George	2-389
Jacob Junr.	2-482,508		Nathaniel	2-069
James	2-038,040,071,074		Susannah	2-389
John	2-021,040,044;		BRICE, Christian	2-029
	R-037,105		Elisabeth	2-029
John Jr.	2-190		James	2-029,333
Joseph	R-059,061		Margaret	2-029
Joshua	2-014,038,040,053,071		Mary	2-029;R-001
Martha	2-040		Thomas	2-029;R-001
Nancy	R-134		BRICKHEAD, Thomas Howell	2-474
Nathan	2-044		BRIERLY, Ann	2-017
Pamelia	2-071		George	2-017
Patience	2-014		Margaret	R-205

D-3

BRIERLY, Robert	2-017	Mary	2-049
Thomas	2-017	BRYARLY, Elisha	R-225
BRINLEY, Elizabeth	2-363	Hugh	2-045,076
BROCK, James	2-012	John	2-045,069
BROOKE, Clement	R-068	Margaret	2-045
BROWN, Amelia Freeborn	2-055	Nathaniel	2-069
Ann	2-047	Robert	2-010,045,076;
David	R-150		R-150,260
Elizabeth	2-019,047,066,166	Thomas	2-045,076
Fenton	2-047	BRYERLY, Hugh	2-033
Freeborn	2-034,357	John	2-033
Garrett	2-034	Robert	2-033,479
George	2-166	Sarah	2-479
Hannah	2-019,051	Thomas	2-033
Jacob	2-047;R-229	BUCHANAN, George	2-340
James	2-019	BUCKALOW, John	R-062
Jean	2-051	BULL, Ann	2-016
John	2-019,031,047,051,	Billingslea	2-062
	064,066,230;R-140	Easther	2-060
John Junr.	R-140	Edmond	2-463
John Thomas	2-046,066	Edmund	2-028,082,336;R-221
Joshua	2-046,066	Elisha	2-062
Marget	2-051	Elizabeth	R-056
Martha	2-019	Esther	2-028
Mary	2-019,046,047,066,165	Frances	2-016
Mary Bains	2-092	Hannah	2-016
Peregrine	2-394	Jacob	2-016,028,060,404
Rebekah	2-166	John	2-016,028,060,062,
Robert	2-051		436,463;R-056,221
Sal	2-324	Mary	2-016,028,060
Sara	2-051	Rachel	2-028,062
Sarah	2-046	Richard	2-016,197;R-056
Solomon	2-031	Sarah	2-062,404
Thomas	2-019,046,047,	Susannah	2-028,060,082
	230;R-167	Walter	2-062,404
William	2-047,051,230	William	2-016,062,294
BROWNE, Elizabeth	2-064	BURGES, Joseph	2-053,124
Freeborne	2-055	BURNET, Hannah	R-105
Garrett	2-055	BUSH, Isaac	R-004
John	2-055	BUSSEY, Ann	2-261
John Thomas	2-064	Bennet	2-099,252;R-007
Joshua	2-055,064	Bennett	2-261
Martha	2-064	Clement	2-252
Sarah	2-055,064	Edward	2-030
Thomas	2-055	Edward B.	2-364
Thomas Freeborne	2-055	Jesse	2-340
BROWNING, Ann	2-050	Susana	2-030
Martha	2-050	Thomas	2-030
Perygrine	2-050	BUSSY, Bennet	R-058
Thomas	2-233	BUTLER, Lt. Joseph	2-031
William	2-050	BUTTERWORTH, Benjamin	2-261
Wilson	2-050	CALBERT, Johanna	R-157
BRUCE, John	2-188	CALDER, James	R-167
BRUSEBANKS, Abraham	2-049	John	R-061
Blanche	2-049	CALHOUN, James, Esq.	2-463

CALVERT, James	R-157		CHALK, George	R-103
CALWELL, Samuel	2-001,490;R-020		CHAMBERS, William	2-186
Thomas	R-020		CHANCE, John	2-371
CAMBESS, Jacob	2-019		CHANCEY, Elizabeth	2-249
CAMPBELL, Benjamin	2-096		John	2-249
Hannah	2-096		CHANEY, Richard	2-090
James	2-096		Thomas	2-090
John	2-096		CHAPPELL, William	2-092
John Jr.	2-096		CHASE, Samuel	2-280
Martha	R-150		CHAUNCEY, Benjamin	2-496
Moses	2-271		George	2-327,494
Rebecca	2-331		George Junr.	2-444,517
CANE, Ann	2-081		CHAUNCY, George	2-158,184,311
David Junr.	2-470		George Junr.	2-184
Dennis	2-081		CHEW, Elizabeth	2-463
James	2-081		Richard	R-121
Jsab	2-081		William	2-463
Mary	2-081		CHEYNE, Elizabeth	R-010
Mathew	2-081		Roderick	R-010
CANNEL, Bartholomew	2-432		CHINWORTH, Thomas	R-114
CANNON, William	2-373		CHRESWELL, John	R-090
CARR, John	2-107		CHRISHOLM, Thomas	2-266
John Dyer	2-179		CHRISTIE, Gabriel	R-068,073
Phebe	2-179		Garbiel	2-296
CARRELL, Michael	2-476		Priscilla	2-296,306
CARROL, Martha	2-087		CLARK, Aquila	2-087
CARROLL, Ann	2-084,111		David	2-082,321,404;
Benjamin	2-111			R-103,217
Delilah	2-438		Elinor	2-010
Elizabeth	2-115		Elizabeth	2-082,087;R-034
Hannah	2-084		Francis	R-103
James Junr.	2-084		George	2-082;R-103
James	2-111		James	2-206,282;R-163
John	2-084,136		John	2-010;R-209
Peter	2-111		Rev. John	2-035
CARROLLE, Sarah	R-205		Kesiah	2-037
CARRS, John	2-107		Margrate	R-028
CARTER, Daniel	2-443		Mathew	R-163
Francis	2-186		Rachel	2-082
John	2-186		Robert	2-012,082,087
Zacriall	2-186		Salina	2-082
CARTY, Elizabeth	2-161		Thomas	2-087
Frances	2-161		William	2-082
CARVER, Henry Wells	2-021		CLARKE, David	R-199
CASELDINE, John	2-223		Hanner	2-186
CASH, William	2-373		John	R-167
CASKERY, Francis	2-116		CLEMMENTS, Ann	2-053
CASKREY, Bettsey	2-116		CLENDENHAN, James	R-142
Francis	2-116		CLENDENING, James	2-088
CASSELDINE, John Jr.	2-303		CLENDENON, James	2-309
John Sr.	2-303		CLENDINEN, Adam	2-128
Mary	2-303		David	2-128
CAUSLEY, James	2-137		Elinor	2-128
John	2-137		James	2-106,128,142,309
CAVENER, Mary	2-508		Jane	2-128

CLENDINEN, John	2-076,128	Lydia	2-088
Mary	2-128	Mary	2-088
CLERK, James	2-414	Mathew	2-088
CLERKE, Richard	2-448	Milcah	2-123
COALE, Ann	2-097,110	Nansey	2-123
Anna Junr.	2-110	Robert	R-055,110
Cassandra	2-110	Samuel	2-088
Elizabeth	2-110	Sarah	2-088,123
Francis	2-110	COOLEY, John	2-257
Henry	R-146	COOP, Hannah	2-107
Phillip	2-097,110,237	COOPER, Alexander	R-203,240
Richard	2-110	Anna	R-240
Samuel	R-040	Henry Junr.	2-261
Sarah	2-097,110,219,298	Jacob	2-200
Shipwith	2-097	Mary	2-200,261;R-203,240
Skipwiith	R-146,159	William	2-236
Thomas	2-316	COPE, Hannah	2-107
William	2-045,097,110,313; R-040,045	COPELAND, Frances	2-104,301
		George	2-104
William Jun.	R-046,157	John	2-104
William Shipwith	2-162	Mary	2-104
COCHRAN, Andrew	R-090	Sarah	2-104
William	R-229	COPLAND, Frances	2-009
COCHRON, William	R-229	CORBIN, Temperance	2-254
COGGINS, Sylvester	R-004	CORBIT, James	2-106
COLE, Elizabeth	2-263	John	2-106
James	2-327,422;R-167	Lewis	2-106
Thomas	2-327	Samuel	2-106
William	2-222	William	2-106
COLEGATE, Elizabeth	2-082	CORD, Abraham	2-090
Richard	2-211	Amoss	2-204
COLLINS, Frances	2-164	Ashberry	2-426
Jemima	2-099	Elizabeth	2-247
Robert	2-099	Jacob	2-247
COMBESS, Utey	2-208	COSLEY, James	2-140
COMBEST, Jacob	2-274	John	2-232
Uty	2-208	COSTLY, Jane	R-121
CONAWAY, Michael	2-171	COTTER, John	2-222
CONDRIN, John	2-232	COTTINGHAM, Henry	2-296
CONDRON, Ann	2-389	COULSON, Joseph	R-101
CONN, John	2-510	COUNIGIN, Ann	R-111
Margaret	2-376	Mary	R-111
Robert	2-190,510	COURTNEY, Hanson	2-327
CONNEL, Bartholomew	2-473	Jonas	2-327
CONNELL, Bartholomew	R-064	Thomas	2-327
CONNELLY, Donn	2-126	COVENHAVEN, Hannah	2-111
John	2-126	John	2-124
Mary	2-126	COVENHOVEN, Betsey	2-124
COOK, Agnes	2-088	Gainer	2-124
Alexander	2-463	Hannah	2-124
David	2-261	Jacob	2-124
Esther	2-123	John	2-124
James	2-088,123	COVINTREE, Jean	2-206
Jeaims	2-123	COWAN, Alexander	2-027,391, 498;R-008
John	2-088,123,402		

COWAN, Col. Alexander	2-150		CROCHETT, Benjamin	2-122
Eleanor	2-027		CROCKETT, Benjamin	2-103,122
Hannah	R-154		John	2-103
Roger Boyce	2-027,066		Samuel	2-103
William	2-227		CROOK, Joseph	2-354
COWEN, Benjamin	2-090		Walter	2-354
Elizabeth	2-090,356		CROOKS, Henry	2-085;R-161
John	2-090		James	2-085
William	2-090		Jennet	2-085
COX, Isreal	2-092,109		Margaret	2-085
John	2-002,069,092,		Mary	2-085
	096,109,254,431		Robert	2-085
Mary	2-092,109,153,219		Rosanna	2-085
Mercy	2-092,109		Thomas	2-085
Rachel	2-092,109		William	2-085
Sarah	2-109,407		CROSEN, Elizabeth	2-378
Thomas	2-364		Jane	2-378
William	2-092,109,188,		John	2-378
	346,379;R-223		Martha	2-378
William Jr.	2-092		Samuel	2-378
COYNS, Lies	2-271		William	2-378
CRAIG, Ann	2-118		CROSSMORE, John	R-134
Charles	2-312		CROSSON, Jean	R-161
John	2-118		John	R-161
CRAIGE, John	R-223		Martha	R-161
CRAIL, Margaret	R-064		Samuel	R-161
CRAWFORD, Alexander	2-107,388;		William	R-161
	R-193		CROW, Samuel	R-187
Frances	2-107		CRUIKSHANKS, Avarilla	2-150
Francis	2-107		Robert	2-150
George	2-107		CUDGA, Tom	R-132
Hannah	2-227		CULVER, Ann	2-079
James	2-100,352		Benjamin	2-079
John	2-100		Robert	2-079
Margret	2-107;R-157		CUMANS, John	R-252
Mordecai	2-100,121		CUMMINGS, Charles	R-006
Ruth	2-100		CUMMINS, Cassandra	2-130
Seaborn	2-100		John	2-130
Susannah	2-100,121		CUNARD, Edward	2-510
Thomas	2-107		CUNNINGHAM, Chrispin	2-263;
CREAGH, Pierse	2-462			R-117
CREAL, Margaret	R-136		Clothworthy	2-382
Philip	2-210		Daniel	R-117
Thomas	R-136		George	2-111;R-117
William	2-076		James	R-117
CRETIN, Elizabeth	2-116		Parker	2-111
James	2-116,126		Polly	R-249
John	2-081,116;R-152,244		Sarah	2-111
Patrick	2-116		Thomas	R-117
CRISWELL, Elizabeth	2-120		CUNNUM, William	2-373
Isabella	2-120		CURRY, Abraham	2-471
James	2-120		James	2-012
Mary	2-120		Thomas	2-034
Robert	R-258		CURTIS, Daniel	2-526
William	2-120		CUTHBARN, Wiliam	2-508

DAGG, James	2-120;R-258	James Maxwell	2-171
DAGLE, James	2-085	John	2-140,150,171,354,426
DALE, John	2-142	John Junr.	2-283
Mary	2-142	Martha Gouldsmith	2-171
Nancy	2-142	Mary Gouldsmith	2-171
Richard Colgate	2-142	Mary Ann	2-165
William	2-142	Nicholas	2-150
DALEY, Mary	2-186	Roderick	2-171
DALLAM, Francis	2-415,513	Samuel	2-031,071
John	2-110,305,368,	Sarah	2-150
	517;R-031,097	DE SAUSCARIS, P. Jauna	2-176
Josias William	2-220;R-051	DEACON, Stephen	2-137
Richard	2-110,428,463,	DEAN, Hugh	R-008
	517;R-051,090	DEARMOTT, John	2-399
Col. Richard	2-124	DEAVER, Aquilla	2-167
Sarah	R-051	Hannah	2-167
Winston Smith	R-157	James	2-167
DARLEY, Samuel	2-225	Mary	2-167
DARMOT, John	2-399	Richard	2-167,333
DASHIELL, James	2-027	Sarah	2-167,271
DAUGHERTY, George	2-149,280	DEBRULAR, Benjamin	2-148
John	2-149	Frances	2-178
Mary Ann	2-149	Samelia	2-148
DAVIDSON, Ealce	2-051	DEBRULER, Hannah	R-266
James	R-016	DEELEY, James	2-084
John	R-049	DELAPORTE, Betsy Herbert	2-181
DAVIS, Amos	R-119	Claudius F.F.	2-181
Elijah	2-306	Elizabeth	2-181
Dr. Elijah	2-258	F.	2-176
Elizabeth	2-136	Francis	2-181
John	2-002	Frederick	2-181
Joseph	R-205	Joanna	2-181
Mary	2-005	DEMOSS, John Senr.	2-193
Rebekah	2-487	John Junr.	R-096
Susannah	2-100	DEMSTER, Joseph	2-142
William	2-136	DENISON, Ezra	R-107
DAVISON, James	2-206	DENISTON, Matthew	R-252
John	2-051	DENNING, James	2-261
DAWES, Benjamin	2-146	DENNY, Ann	2-059
Isaac	2-146,164	Elizabeth	R-081
Isaac Junr.	2-146	James	2-163
Mary	2-164	Margaret	2-163,166
Mordecai	2-111	Margret	2-163
DAWNS, Jesse	R-096	Michael	2-059,163,479
DAWSON, Christopher	2-031	Michal	2-166
Margaret	2-076	Rebakah	2-163
Thomas	2-076	Simon	2-163
DAY, Charlotte	2-470	DESSAA, Jean	2-176
Charlotte Elizabeth	2-150	DESRAMEAUX, Mastios	2-176
Edward	2-140,150,171,354	DEVER, Hugh	R-264
Elisha	2-123	DEYERMID, Catharine	2-399
Elizabeth Maxwell	2-171	Mary	2-399
Frances	2-171	DICKSON, Benjamin	2-145
Gouldsmith	2-171	David	2-145
Hannah	2-036	Henry	R-064

DICKSON, Jennet	2-145		Margaret	2-513
John	2-145		Margaret Lee	R-205
Rachel	2-186		Richard	2-513;R-189
Robert	2-145		Richard W.	2-292
DILLON, [----]	2-179		Susanna	R-189
Moses	2-294		DREW, Anthony	2-155,158,184,301
DITTO, William	R-085		Aquilla	2-184
DIXON, Margarett	2-212		Bennett	2-184
Rachel	2-407		George	2-155,158,184,359
DOBBINS, Sarah	R-081		Hannah	2-155
DONAHAY, John	2-414		Henry	2-155,158
DONAHEY, Anne	2-414		James	2-155,158,316
John	2-414		Mary	2-155,158
DONAWIN, Daniel	R-167		Priscilla	2-174,184
DONN, John	R-068		Sarah	2-155,174
DONOVAN, Daniel Senr	2-422		Susan	2-174,184
John	2-327		DRUMMOND, Thomas	2-040
DONTHEY, Thomas	2-498		DU BLOCK, Francois	2-176
DORAN, Catharine	2-141		DULANEY, Daniel	2-092
Edward	2-141		Daniel Esq.	R-068
Francis	2-141		DULEY, James	2-084;R-078
Hugh	2-141		DUNAVON, Margret	R-049
John	2-141		DUNCAN, Jacob	2-457
Margaret	2-141		Jesse	2-124
Margret	2-141		DUNGAN, Jesse	2-124
Mary	2-141		DUNGHAM, Phebe	2-106
Nicholas	2-141		DUNN, Robert	2-411,463
Patrick	2-141,314,341, 443;R-142		DURBAN, Rachel	2-161
			Sinah	2-161
Phillip	2-141		Thomas	2-161
Thomas	2-141		DURBIN, Avarilla	2-134
DORNEY, Mary	2-140;R-121		Cassandra	2-162
Patrick	R-240		Cassandrew	2-162
Thomas	2-140,150,171		Cina Lee	2-161
DORSEY, Ann	2-426		Daniel	2-134,162;R-068
Ann Maxwell	2-474		John	2-162
Edward	2-187		Mary	2-162
Frances	2-426		Samuel	2-162
Frisby	2-187,258		Sinah or Sina	2-186
Greenberry	2-187,223, 247,369;R-195		Thomas	2-134
			DURHAM, Ann	2-159,451;R-098
Greenbury	2-153		Aquilla	2-057,159
J. Hammond	R-079,268		Betsy	2-451
James Maxwell	2-474		Charlotte	2-159
John	2-153		David	2-087
Doc. John	2-153		Eleanor	2-159
John Hammon	R-036		Elizabeth	R-098
John Hammond	2-059,267,474		Elizabeth Senr.	2-451
Leonard	2-153		John	2-507
Mary	2-153		Joseph	2-159
Phrisby	2-504		Lee	2-159
Thomas	2-286		Loyd	2-159
DOUGHERTY, William	2-139		Mordecai	2-144
DOWNING, Constant Priscilla	R-205		Samuel	2-144,159
			Sarah	2-087;R-098

DURHAM, Selah	2-451	Thomas Junr.	2-188
Susannah	2-159	William	2-188,200
Thomas	2-159	ENLOWS, James	2-526
William	2-159	ENSOR, William	2-140
DUTTON, John	2-124,331;R-212	ERWIN, William	2-389
Robert	2-331;R-121	EVANS, Ann	2-194
DUZAN, William Gray	2-139	Evan	2-194
DYER, Aaron	2-179	Griffith	2-194
Elizabeth	2-146,179	John	2-196
Hannah	2-179	Mary	2-194
Hester	2-146	Nathan	2-088
Joanna	2-179	EVATT, John Jr.	2-198
John	2-146	John Senr.	2-198
Joseph	2-146,179	Margaret	2-198
Josiah	2-146	Richard	2-198
Mary	2-146	William	2-198,237,348
Phebe	2-146	EVENS, Nathan	2-088
Rachel	2-146	EVERETT, Edeth	R-212
Thomas	2-146	EVERIT, Hannah	2-059
EAKINS, Margaret	2-193	Samuel	2-059
EDEN, Benjamin	2-197	EVERITT, Ady	2-124
Jeremiah	2-197	EVERTT, Isaac	2-021
Mary	2-197	EWING, John	2-257
Sarah	2-197	Joseph	2-257,265
William	2-197	FALLS, Hannah	R-260
EDGAR, Eliner C.	2-120	FARMER, Gregory	2-092
Mary	2-120	John	R-016
William Criswell	2-120	Samuel	2-092
EDWARDS, James	2-181	FARVET, Henry	2-031
ELLEET, Eleanor	2-090	FAWCETT, Henry	2-031
Edward	R-205	Mary	R-167
Samuel	R-205	FELL, William	2-276
ELLICOTT, Ann	2-188	FIELD, Aaron	2-046
ELLIOT, Agnes	2-190	FINCH, Thomas Jr.	2-092
Eleanor	2-090	Thomas Sr.	2-092
James	2-190	FINNEY, John	2-206
Sarah	2-190	Manassa	2-206
ELLIOTT, Ann	2-191	FISHER, James	2-202;R-191
John	2-190	John	2-202
Kerenhappuch	2-191	Robert	2-202
Thomas	2-031,191	Thomas	2-222
Samuel	2-191	William	2-202
ELLIS, James	2-092	FITZGERALD, John	2-209
John	2-471	FITZHUGH, Col. William	R-229
William	R-191	FLAHARTY, Thomas	R-205
ELY, Ann	R-105	FLANAGAN, Alexander	2-327
Hugh	2-188,200	Edward	2-116
John	2-402	FORD, Aquila	2-211
Joseph	2-188,200	Betty	R-119
Mahlon	2-188,200	Clemency	2-211
Mary	2-402	David	R-095
Rachel	2-188,200	Drusiller	2-186
Ruth	2-188,200	Capt. Joseph	2-031
Sarah	2-200	Joseph	R-126
Thomas	2-188,200;R-105	Mary	2-211

FORWOOD, Hannah	2-346	William	2-220
Jacob	2-066,232,306,396;R-205	GANT, Samuel	2-283
Jacob Esq.	2-327	GARLAND, Catherine	2-232
John	2-016,163,166,346,528;	Frances	2-232
	R-119,136,213,249	Francis	2-222
Samuel	2-166	Henry	2-222
Sarah	2-082,166	James	2-232
William	R-249	GARRETT, Amos	2-134,215,220,
FOSTER, Aaron	2-210,212		247,382,416
Benjamin	2-210	Elizabeth	R-090
Catharine	2-212;R-093	Frances	2-247
Henry	2-210	Francis	R-183
John	2-210;R-093	Jonas	2-274
Margaret	2-210,212	Margaret	2-024,059
Moses	2-210	Martha	2-030
Samuel	2-210	Mary	2-024
William	2-210	Susanna	R-090
FOWLER, Samuel W.	2-469	GARRETTSON, Aquilla	2-223,426
FOX, Thomas	2-137	Elizabeth	2-223,230
FRALEY, Frederick	2-016,144	Frances	2-230,258
FRANKLIN, Thomas	R-114	Freeborn	2-061,223,369
FRAZIER, Alexander	2-027	Freeborn Junr.	2-149
Penelone	2-366	Garret	2-276
Samuel	2-366	Garrett	2-230,249
FREEMAN, Abraham	2-225	James	2-149,502
Avarilla	2-225	Martha	R-167
FRENCH, Benjamin	2-397	Richard	2-223
FRISBY, John	2-204	Sarah	2-230
Mary	2-204	Sophia	2-223
Thomas P.	2-187	Susanna	2-230
Thomas Peregrine	2-204,274	GARRISON, Cornelius	2-014,446
William	2-187,324,469	GASSAWAY, Nicholas	2-470
William Holland	2-204	GAWTHROUP, Elizabeth	2-362
FULTON, Jean	2-273	GIBBENS, Joseph	2-420
Samuel	2-273	GIBSON, Ann	2-254
FYE, Baltis	2-208	Anna	R-203,240
Mary	2-208	Hugh	R-240
GAFFORD, Joseph	2-474	Jacob	R-203,240
GALE, Benjamin	2-233	John Lee Esq.	R-217
James	2-233	John Lee	R-238
Mary	2-233	Mary	R-199
Reason	2-233	William	2-254
William	2-233	GILBERT, Ann	2-265
GALLION, Elizabeth	2-220,266	Charles	2-079,134,234,
Hannah	2-266		256,263,265
Jacob	2-215	Clemency	2-263
James	2-215,220	Elizabeth	2-256,263
Joannah	2-220	Garvis	2-234
John	2-215,220	James Cole	2-265
Martha	2-215,220	Julia	2-265
Mary	2-220	M. Junr.	2-276
Nathan	2-104,215	M. Taylor	2-234
Pheeby	2-215	Martha	2-256,263,265
Rachel	2-215,220,266	Martin Taylor	2-265
Samuel	2-215,268	Mary	2-215,234

GILBERT, Mary Gilbert	2-256		Elizabeth	2-379
Micah	2-234		Hannah	2-257
Michael	2-234,263,271		James	2-379
Michael Junr	2-288,428,436		Joseph	2-257
Parker	2-234		Lawson	2-257
Philip	2-265		Martha	2-379
Phillip	2-234		Mary	2-257
Samuel	2-234		Susanna	R-090
Sarah	2-265		GORSUCH, Mary	R-134
Taylor	2-256		GOUGH, Hannah	2-454
Thomas	2-418		Martha	2-454
William Presbury	2-263		GOULD, William Budd	2-311
GILDEA, Daniel	2-381		GOULDSMITH, W. Presbury	R-068
GILDER, Daniel	2-381		GOVER, E. Gittings	R-018
GILES, Aquilla	2-237		Elizabeth	2-251
Caroline	2-219		Ephraim Gittings	2-251,318
Charlotte	2-219		Gerard	2-251
Edward	2-237;R-167		Mary	2-251
Eliza	R-097		Philip	2-251
Elizabeth	2-219,237		Priscilla	2-251
Hannah	2-219		Robert	2-251,298
Jacob	2-237		Samuel	2-251,298;R-018
Jacob Jun.	R-167		GRAFTON, Aquilla	2-213
James	2-237,296		Cassandra	2-213
Joanna	2-237		Daniel	2-213
Martha	2-268		Margaret	2-213
Nathaniel	2-219,237		Nathaniel	2-213
Sarah	2-219		Prissilla	2-213
Thomas	2-237		Samuel	2-213
William Axtell	2-237		Sarah	2-213
GILL, Elizabeth	R-114		William	2-213
William	R-114		GRANT, Elizabeth	2-413
GILLESPIE, Simon	R-240		GRAVES, Col. Richard	2-397
GILLIS, Robert	R-129		William	2-004
GILMORE, Charles	2-280		GRAY, James	2-285
John	2-263		John	2-231
GITTINGS, Asal	R-111		Samuel	2-236
Elizabeth	R-111		GREEN, Abel	2-164
James	R-111		Benjamin	2-252;R-059,152
Mary	R-111		Cassander	R-098
Thomas	R-111		Clement	2-252
GLADDEN, James	2-167		Edward	R-113
Mary	2-167;R-093		Elenor	R-152
GLASGOW, Elizabeth	2-479		Elizabeth	2-261
James	2-479		Hannah	2-252
GLENN, David	2-198;R-011		Henrietta	2-252
Martha	2-198		Henry	2-261
Robert	2-193		John	2-040,159
GOLDSMITH, Sarah	2-165		Joshua	R-098
GOODWIN, George	2-418		Martha	2-261
GORDON, Jean	R-209		Sarah	2-261
William	R-085		Susannah	2-261
GORRAL, Hannah	2-100		GREENFIELD, Patty	2-496
GORRELL, Ann	2-379		Micajah	R-111
Easter	2-257		William	R-098

GREENLAND, Leonard	R-058
GREENLEAF, [widow]	2-092
GREENWELL, Mildred	R-152
GREME, Auguste	2-176
GRIEST, Isaac	2-416
GRIFFEN, William	2-076
GRIFFITH, Alexander	2-258
Avarilla	2-227
Catharine	2-225
Edward	2-258
Elizabeth	2-225,227
Evan	2-202
Frances	2-227,258
James	2-227
John	2-227
John Hall	2-258
Lewis	2-258
Luke	2-225,258
Martha	2-258,296,306
Mary	2-225,227
Samuel	2-055,225,230, 258,296;R-167
Dr. Samuel	2-258
Samuel Gouldsmith	2-258
Sarah	2-258
William	2-227
GROVES, Abraham	2-267
Asael	2-267
Isaac	2-267
Sarah	2-140,267
William	2-140,267
GRUDER, Jacob	2-435
John	2-435
GUFFEE, Henry	2-085
GUITON, Abraham	2-231
Mary	2-231
GUYON, John	2-446
GUYTON, Abraham	2-231
Edward	2-422
Isaac	2-071,231
Jacob	2-231
John	2-231
Joseph	2-231
Joshua	2-231,422
Mary	2-231
Nathaniel	2-231
Samuel	2-231
Sarah	2-231
Thomas Michell	2-231
GWINN, James	2-324
Sal	2-324
HALE, Sarah	2-031
HALL, Aquila	2-274:R-167
Aquilla	2-249,288,324,426
Aquilla Jun.	R-167
Avarilla	2-276
Barthia	2-276,296
Benedict	2-247,280
Benedict Edward	2-047,247, 268,280,286,288,306, 426,428,R-068,167,183
Charlotte	2-274,280;R-167
Charlotte White	2-286
Christopher	2-350
Cordelia	2-288
Edward	2-274,276,280, 288,296,306;R-167
Elizabeth	2-276,306;R-205
Francis	2-288
Hannah	2-268,286
Henry	2-247
Hetty	2-288
Jacob Junr.	R-062
Dr. Jacob	R-244
James	2-280
James W.	R-073
James White	2-274;R-068
Jane	2-286,379
John	2-208,268,274, 276,280,306;R-068
Col. John	2-276,286;R-167
John Beedle	2-276,296,306
John Carville	2-286
Josias	2-276,296,306,513
Josias Carvil	2-249
Josias Carvill	2-268,286,324
Martha	2-274,280
Mary	2-274,276,280, 296,306;R-244
Milcah	2-247,286
Parker	2-288
Priscilla	2-276
Richard Wilmott	R-244
Sabina	R-228
Sarah	2-288
Sophia	2-268,274,280;R-167
Sydney	2-247
Thomas	2-263,274,280;R-167
Thomas Parry	R-244
William	2-196,247,268,274, 280,288;R-068,167,228
William Wilmott	R-244
HAMBY, William	2-479
HAMMILTON, Jonathan	R-238
Martha	R-081
Robert	R-238
HAMMOND, Larkin	2-219
William	2-219
HAMTON, Elizabeth	2-257
HANNA, Alexander	2-145

HANNA, Rebecca	R-140	Hannah	2-294
William	2-379	James	2-294
HANNAH, Alexander	2-145	Ruth	2-294
Deliverance	2-479	Sarah	2-294
William	2-479	HAYS, Archer	2-130
HANSON, Avarilla	2-225	Ester	R-011,025
Benjamin	2-225,316,327	John	R-011,025
Elizabeth	2-225,327	Joseph	R-011
Hollis	2-316,327	Thomas	R-011
Lewis	2-504	HAZEN, Gen. Moses	2-118
John	2-184,316,327,428,496	HEAPS, Archa	2-443
Mary	2-225	HEDRECK, Charles	2-479
Sarah	2-225,316,327	HENDEL, Hannah	2-137
Semelia	2-316	HENDERSON, Andrew	2-156
Sophia	2-316	Elizabeth	2-285
William	2-496	Frances	R-051
HANWAY, Jesse	2-099	Francis	2-156
HARDY, John	2-257	George	2-174,504
HARE, Daniel	2-356	Hester	2-179
HARGROVE, John	2-401	Nathaniel	2-285
Thomas	2-209	Thomas	R-167
HARPER, James	2-462;R-093	HENDON, Hannah	2-482
HARPLEY, Nathaniel	R-255	HENERY, Elizabeth	2-300
HARRIS, Dorthea	2-273	Isaac	2-300
Elizabeth	2-273	John	2-300
James	2-273;R-049	Mary	2-300
Jean	2-273	Samuel	2-300
John	R-167,180	HENLEY, Frances	R-189
Joseph	2-318;R-255	Joseph	R-146
Margaret	2-298	Lemuel	R-258
Robert	R-193	HENLY, Joseph	R-159
Samuel	2-188	HENRY, Mary	2-300
Sarah	2-273	Samuel	2-300
HARRISON, W. Thomas	R-167	HERBERT, Benjamin	2-263
HARRY, David	2-510	HILL, Aaron	2-290
HASLETT, Moses	R-008	Elizabeth	2-291
HASSETT, Bridgett	2-209	James	R-268,270
HAWKINS, Cassandra	R-191	James Sr.	2-050
Elizabeth	2-092,109	John Green	2-283
John	2-292	Martha	2-283
Luranah	R-191	Mary	2-188,291
Martha	2-136	Marthew or Marther	2-140
Richard	2-092,292	Moses	2-290
Robert	2-136	Richard	2-137,283
Samuel	2-292,463	Sarah	2-290
Sarah	2-100	Stephen	2-163
William	2-136	Thomas	2-140,186
HAY, John	2-153,312,397	William	2-035,291,502;R-150
HAYES, Elizabeth	R-154	HILLEN, Thomas	R-213
John	R-086	HITCHCOCK, Anne	2-222
Rebecca	R-086	Asel	2-314
Thomas	2-194	Charity	2-087
HAYHURST, Ann	2-294	Cordelia	2-389
David	2-294	Elizabeth	2-087
Elizabeth	2-294	Henry	2-222

HITCHCOCK, Isaac	2-314		Elizabeth	2-053;R-020
John	2-314		Frances	2-288
Josiah	2-389		J. Beale	2-498;R-020
Josias	2-222,314		John	2-266
Mary	2-314		John Beale	2-036,426
Nancy	2-314		Leonard	2-266
Randal	2-222,225		Mary	2-186
Sarah	2-314		Sarah	2-053
William	2-314		Thomas Gasway	2-498
HOLLAND, Elizabeth	2-288		HOWE, William	2-321
Frances	2-286,324,413		HOWLETT, Andrew	R-011,025
Francis	2-204		James	R-034
HOLLIS, Amos	2-311,316,327		HUDLY, James	2-126
Avarilla	2-311		HUDSON, James	2-186
Benjamin	2-311		HUGANS, Ann	2-033
Benjamin Osborn	2-327		Jacob	2-033
Catharine	2-311		HUGGINS, Ann	2-045
Clark	2-301,311		James	2-498
Elizabeth	2-301		HUGHES, Amy or Amey	2-271
Martha	2-494		Ann	2-309
William	2-301,311,312,316,494		Aram	2-309;R-117,124
William James	2-311		Charles	2-309
HOLLOWAY, Richard	2-024,136		Elizabeth	2-309
HOOFMAN, Christian	2-408		Esram	R-142
Peter	2-408		George	2-309
HOOPER, Samuel	2-474		Jean	2-309
HOOPMAN, Peter	2-408		John	2-271,309;R-167
HOPE, Richard	2-194		John Hall	2-517
Thomas	2-128,309		John Taylor	R-124
HOPKINS, Ann	2-318		Joseph	2-309
Charles	2-305,321		Margaret	2-309
Elizabeth	2-318,321		Martha	2-309
Epheram	2-318		Mary	2-309
Fanny	2-321		Rowland	2-271
Frances	2-109,305;R-185		Samuel	2-309;R-073
Gerrard	2-109,305,313,321		Samuel Esq.	2-237
Joel	2-321		Sarah	2-309
John	2-318;R-048		Susannah	2-309
Joseph	2-298,318		Thomas	2-309
Joseph Junr.	2-346		Timothy	2-309
Joseph Senr.	2-346;R-146		William	2-271
Rachel	2-305,321		HUGHS, Elizabeth	2-446,482
Samuel	2-305,313,318,321		John Hale	2-162
Sarah	2-313;R-185		John Hall	R-090
William	2-305,321		Nathan	2-504
William Sr.	2-085		HUGHSTON, Elizabeth	2-331
HORNER, Jean	2-325		Jane	2-331
Mary	2-263		John	2-331
Nathan	2-325;R-148		Thomas Waltham	2-331
Nicholas	2-325;R-095		HUNT, Phineas	2-021
Rachel	2-325		Susanna	2-021
HORNEY, Thomas	2-303		HUSBAND, Elizabeth	2-321
HORTON, William	2-479		Joshua	2-109;R-229
HOWARD, Benjamin	2-211		HUSBANDS, Elizabeth	2-305
Blanch	R-020		William	2-237

HUSTON, James	2-007	Samuel	2-368;R-073
Jane	2-007	Stephen	2-368;R-062
HUTCHINGS, Richard	2-014	Thomas	2-368
HUTCHINS, Eleanor	2-446	JEFFERY, Alexander	2-338
Thomas	2-498	Hugh	2-338
HUTCHINSON, Agness	2-282	Robert	2-338
Ann	2-282	Samuel	2-338
Elizabeth	2-282	Thomas	2-338
James	2-282	Martha	2-338
Jean	2-282	Robert	2-494
Jennet	2-282	JEFFRYS, Elizabeth	2-356
Margaret	2-282	JENKENS, John Clark	2-357
Mary	2-088,282	JENKINS, Robert	2-356
HYNSON, Mary	2-150	Samuel	2-463
INGRAM, Arthur	2-271	JERVIS, Ann	2-397;R-015
Olivia	R-090	John	2-159
IRELAND, Isabella	R-107	JEWELLS, Richard	2-210
Rev. John	R-107	JEWETT, Ann	R-229
IRONS, Mary	2-346	John	R-229
JACKSON, Edward	R-101	Thomas	R-229
John	2-122,344	JINKINS, Francis	2-357
JACOB, Grace	R-185	John Clark	2-357
Joseph	R-185	Samuel	2-357
JAMES, Cordelia	2-354	JOHNES, Thomas	R-146
Elizabeth	2-344,508	JOHNS, Aquilla	2-021
Ester	2-344	Hannah	2-021,237
Henry	2-354	Henry	2-348,513;R-195
John	2-344,360	Hosea	2-292
Latis	2-344	Mary	2-251,292
Mary	2-344	Nathan	2-348
Micajah	2-416	Richard	2-348,376
Nathaniell	2-354	Shipwith	R-045
Rachel	2-344,526	Skipwith	2-237
Richard	2-344,378	Susanna	2-376
Sarah	2-344	JOHNSON, Adam	2-359
Sedgwick	2-344	Agnes	2-190
Thomas	2-118,340	Alice	2-336
Walter	2-354	Ann	2-082,333,352,359;R-101
William	2-402	Ann Love	2-528
JAMISON, John	2-273	Archabel	2-061
William	2-335	Archibald	2-070,359
JARRETT, Abraham	2-030,340,364	Barnet	2-333;R-136
Bennett	2-340,364	Barnett	2-336,531
Eli	2-340,364	David	2-366
Elisha	2-340	Elizabeth	2-352
Ellinor	2-340	Ephraim	2-340
Elsha	2-364	Hannah	2-336
Emeline	2-364	Hester	2-082
Jesse	2-314,340,364,446	Isaac	2-352
Martha	2-340	James	2-128,318,333;R-255
Mary	2-340	Jane	R-260
JARVIS, Ann	2-036	John	2-049,333,336,359,
JAY, Elizabeth	2-368		531;R-001,101,129,188
Joseph	2-368	Joseph	2-352,359
Martha	2-368	Joshua	2-336

D-16

JOHNSON, Josiah	2-333		John	2-376
Martha	2-352		John Bond	2-021
Mary	2-082,222,336,352,528		Nathan	2-376
Mechesedec	2-366		Pamela	2-376
Moses	2-366		Thomas	2-021,376
Moses Junr.	2-366		Capt. Thomas	2-021,044
Priscilla	2-366		Thomas Jr.	2-044
Rachel	2-336		William	2-376
Robert	2-336		KELLY, Alexander	2-379
Samuel	2-336		Andrew	2-379
Sarah	2-082,333,366		Robert	2-379
Tabitha	2-366		KEMBERLAND, Bond James	2-090
Thomas	2-029,082,333,		KENARD, Hannah	2-158
	336,352,359,366,384		KENLEY, Daniel	2-202
Thomas Jr.	2-033		KENLY, Daniel	2-374
William	2-128,190,336,		Samuel	R-258
	366,524;R-129		KENNEDY, Ann	2-373
JOHNSTON, Benjamin	R-090		Hannah	2-373
Mary	2-362		John	2-374
William	2-088		Mary	2-373
JOLLEY, Betsey	2-350		Richard	2-374
Cassandra	2-350		Robert	2-373,420
Edward	2-321,350		William	2-373
Elizabeth	2-202,350		KENT, Jesse	R-064
Isabela	2-350		Rachel	R-064
John	2-350		KERNS, Ann	2-064
Nancy	2-350		KEY, Job	2-336
Sally	2-350		KIDD, Hennery	2-371
William	2-350		James	2-371
JONES, Amos	2-021		John	2-371
Aquila	2-363;R-203		Joshua	2-371
Benjamin	2-167,363		Rebekah	2-371
Charles	2-363		William	2-371
Elizabeth	2-373		KIMBAL, [----]	2-274
Ezekiel	2-254		KIMBELL, John	2-208
Frances	2-363		KIMBLE, Francis	2-369
Joseph	2-346		Giles	2-371,502
Obier	2-346		James	2-369
Rachel	2-167,346,363		Margaret	2-369
Rebeckah	2-363		Sarah	2-369
Reubin	2-346		Stephen	2-066,369,371
Robert	2-258		KINGSTON, Nathaniel	2-017
Sarah	2-363		KIRKPATRICK, Hugh	R-264
Stephen	2-363		Moses	R-011
Theophilus	R-187		Sarah	R-011,025
JORDAN, Ellenor	2-236		William	R-011,025
KANADAY, Anna	2-007		KIRKWOOD, Robert	R-142
Mary	2-007		KITELY, Elizabeth	2-115
Sary	2-007		Hannah	2-393
KEEN, Richard	2-374		Mary	2-115
KEIN, Jehu	R-223		Rachel	2-115,381
KELL, Alisanna	2-021,376		KNIGHT, David	2-271
Anna	2-376		Nancy	2-211
Elizabeth	2-376		KRUSON, Garrett	2-374
Isaac	2-376		John	2-374

KRUSON, Mary	2-374	LINGAN, Elizabeth	2-391
Nicholas	2-374	James McCubbin	2-391
LACEY, Elizabeth	2-294	Martha	2-391
Thomas	2-294	Nicholas	2-391
LACKHARD, William	R-051	Susanna	2-391
LAMMOT, Barbara	2-408	Thomas	2-391
Henry	2-408	LION, Priscilla	2-488
Jacob	2-408	Sarah	2-087
John	2-408	LITTEN, Elizabeth	2-402
LAMMOTT, Henry	2-408	Hannah	2-402
LANCASTER, Benjamin	2-021	John	2-402
Benjamin Jr.	2-021	Mary	R-159
Samelia	2-327	Samuel	2-092
LATHAM, John	2-300	LITTLE, George	2-008,174
LATIMORE, John	2-399	Gerge	2-416
LAZZEL, Amos	2-137	James	R-003
LE FAURRE, Feberque	2-176	LITTON, James	2-402
LEACH, James	2-424,493	John	2-525
LEE, Charles	R-159	LOCKHARD, Elizabeth	2-378
Corbin	2-396,513	Frances	2-378
Deborah	2-407	Martha	2-378
Elizabeth	2-384	Samuel	2-378
James	2-384,396,513	Sarah	2-378
James Jun.	2-384	LOCKHERD, Samuel	R-161
Dr. James	2-513	LOCKWOOD, Alisanna	2-021
John	2-150,400	LOGHLIN, Sarah	R-157
Josiah	2-357,384,	LOGUE, Mary	2-166
	411,513;R-159	LONDON, John	2-030
Mary	2-384,400	LONEY, Moses	2-139
Milca	2-396	Ufan	2-139
P. H.	2-463	LONG, John Jr.	2-056
Parker Hall	2-396,513	Mary	2-106
Rachal E.	R-011	Temperance	2-488
Rachel	2-400	LOVE, John	2-028,059,082,261,
Richard	2-513		336,404,524,528;
Samuel	2-384,400,513		R-001,090,118,119
Sarah	R-159	Margaret	2-404,528;R-118
Thomas	2-400	Margaret M.	2-028
LEGO, Alica	2-397	Robert	2-252
Elizabeth	2-397	Thomas	R-114
Mary	2-397	William	2-252
LEGOE, Judah	2-137	LOVETT, Francis PM	2-047
LEPPER, William	2-141	LOWE, Deborah	R-018,046
LESTER, Norris	2-223,359,369	LOWREY, Hannah	2-206
William	2-187,428	John	2-206
LETANG, Fournie	2-176	LUCAS, Thomas	R-111
LETIMORE, John	2-399	LUCKEY, George	2-457
LEWIS, James	2-037	LUCKIE, William	2-356;R-087
Jesse	2-360	LUCKY, Jane	2-009
Rev. John	R-152	William	2-009
Mary	2-364	LUKENS, Jacob	R-064
Polly	2-364	LUSBY, Elizabeth	2-382,393
LIGHTL, Elizabeth	2-394	John	2-382
LINDSEY, Andrew	R-083	Joseph	2-507
Elizabeth	R-083	Milcah	2-382,401

LUSBY, Sarah	2-382,393,401	Joanna	2-436;R-056
Susanna	2-382	Michael	2-436
Susannah	2-393,401	MATHEWS, Ann	2-470
LYNCH, Anthony	2-388	Bennet	2-396;R-244
Elizabeth	R-086	Bennett	2-428,444
John	2-071,338,388	Capt. Bennett	2-428
Mary	2-388;R-111	Carvel	2-324,444,469
Rachel	2-344	Carvil	2-428
Samuel	2-440	Elizabeth	2-470;R-244
LYON, Cassandra	2-389	Fanny	2-444,469
Easter	2-389	Frances	2-428,470
Elijah	2-389	Hannah	2-428
Elizabeth	2-411	James	2-268,276,428;R-167
John	2-389,488	John	2-396,428
Jonathan	2-389	Joseph	2-444
Leonard	2-389	Josias	2-428
Martha	2-389	Leven	2-444
Mary	2-389	Levin	2-225,416,470
Nancy	2-389	Mary	2-428
Priscilla	2-488	Milcah	2-204,428,469
Sarah	2-389	Naomy	2-324
LYONS, Robert	2-378	Neomy	2-428,444,469
LYTLE, Elizabeth	2-477	Rebecca	2-268,428
James	R-096,221	Roger	2-047,324,396,
LYTTLE, Ann	2-394		428,444,469,470
Elizabeth	2-394	William	2-141
Hannah	2-394	MATSON, Thomas	R-187
Jacob	2-394	MATTINGLY, James	R-113
James	2-394;R-188	Joseph	R-113
Nathan	2-394	MAULSBY, John	2-014
MacATEE, Henry	R-034	Sarah	2-074
MacCOMAS, Daniel	2-024,084,	MAXWELL, Elizabeth	2-426,474
	424,438,460	Jacob	2-153,426,440,474;R-079
MacCOMAS, Silina	2-082	James	2-426
William	2-024	Moses	2-426,440,474;R-079
MacNABB, John	2-252	Phebe	2-426
MACON, James	2-007	MAY, James	2-273
MADDEN, James	2-009	McADOO, John	2-120
MADEN, James	R-124	McADOW, John	2-145,338,
MADON, James	2-007		388;R-264
MAGEE, Daniel	2-274	McATEE, George	R-028
David	2-104	McCALLA, Andrew	2-156
Sarah	2-517	Mary	2-156
MANFORDS, Thomas	2-294	McCANDLESS, Alexander	R-011
MARSH, Loyd	2-517	Ester	R-011,025
MARTIN, William	2-374	James	2-056;R-011,025
MASH, John	2-526	Ruthea	R-011
MASON, Ann	2-400	Ruthia	R-025
John	2-400,490	Sarah	R-011,025
Susanna	2-305	William	R-011
Susannah	2-321	McCARTHY, James	2-019
MASSEY, Aquila	2-463	McCARTIE, Jacob Giles	2-439
Aquilla	2-118,200	Sarah	2-439
Isaac	2-118,318;R-031,046	McCLAIN, Patrick	2-223
MATHER, James	2-436	Patrick O.	2-149

McCLAIR, Mary	2-502	McCORD, Ann	2-457
McCLASKEY, Agness	2-142	Arthur	2-457
Joseph	2-142,371	McCORMICK, Elizabeth	2-254
Patrick	2-451	George	2-254
McCLINTICK, Ann	2-472	John	2-137
Mathew	2-472	McCOY, Margaret	R-008
William	2-472	McCRACKEN, David	2-416
McCLINTOCK, Mathew	2-273	Elizabeth	2-416
Susannah	2-273	James	2-416
McCLINTOKE, Mathew	2-421	John	2-416
McCLURE, Francis	2-421	Mary	2-416
John	R-150	McCRACKIN, Mary	R-090
Nathaniel	R-011	McCREERY, Benjamin	2-167
Richard	2-421	McCRERY, Benjamin	2-434
Robert	2-421	McCUBBIN, Ann	2-391
McCOMAS, Aaron	2-424	McCULLOGH, David	R-004
Aaron Junr.	2-449	McCULLOUGH, William	R-150
Alexander	2-462,477	McDANIEL, James	2-103
Amos	2-462	Mary	R-110
Ann	2-424,462	McDONALD, Cornelius	2-156
Aquilla	2-096,462	John	2-156,231;R-129
Benjamin	2-415	McDOUGH, William	2-333
Charilotte	2-449	McELHINNEY, Mathew	R-118
Clemancy	2-462	McELRATH, Joseph	2-198
Daniel	2-002,084,438, 449,460,R-142	McFADIN, Benjamin	2-263
		John	2-282
Edward Day	2-477	McFILTON, Daniel	2-107;R-193
Elizabeth	2-438,449,2-460	McGACLIN, Ceartrin	2-435
George	2-477	Patrick	2-435
Hannah	2-053,424,438,454	McGAW, James	R-023
James	2-053,096,438, 449,462;R-093	Jane	2-178;R-023
		John	R-023
James Preston	2-462	McGAY, James	2-187
John	2-415,449,460	Robert	2-215
Josiah Scott	2-460	McGEAUGH, Elizabeth	R-064
Josias	2-449	James	2-432
Margaret	2-373	McGIRR, Arthur	2-120
Martha	2-438,449,460	McGOUGH, Miles	2-116
Mary	2-424,449,477	McGOVERN, William	2-291
Moses	2-460	McGOWAN, Elizabeth	2-487
Nathaniel	2-449	Capt. James	2-487
Nicholas Day	2-477	Capt. John	2-487
Quilla	2-462	John	2-487
Sarah	2-449	Judith	2-487
Serah	2-462	McGREAUGH, James	2-443
Solomon	2-424	McJILTON, Daniel	2-107;R-193
Susanna	2-454	McKAY, Sarah	R-085
Susannah	2-449	McKESSON, James	2-457
William	2-096,415,424, 449,454;R-051	Sarah	2-457
		McKINLA, Roger	2-193
Zachius	2-454	McKISSON, Sam	R-055
McCOMASS, Daniel	2-431;R-093	McLAUGHLIN, George	R-221
Elizabeth	2-431	James	R-249
Frederick	2-431	John	2-357
William	2-431	John Sr.	R-249

McLAUGHLIN, John Jr.	R-249
McMATH, Mary	2-471
Samuel	2-471
Sarah	2-122,471
William	2-122,471
McMULLEN, John	2-209
McNAIR, Archenbald	2-414
Elizabeth	2-414
James	2-414
Jane	2-414
Jennet	2-414
John	2-414
McQUIRE, Patrick	2-092
McTEE, Elizabeth	R-152
McWILLIAMS, Christian	R-159
MEAD, Benjamin	2-440
Edward	2-440
Elizabeth	2-440
James Junr.	R-117
William	2-440
MEADS, Benjamin	2-283
James Jr.	2-017
MECOUN, Marey	2-516
MEEK, Andrew	R-154
MEGAW, Addam	R-264
MICHAEL, John	2-055,067
MIDDLEMORES, Dr. Josias	R-051
MILES, Aquila	2-446
Cashandrow	2-420
Cassandra	2-434
Elizabeth	2-420
Isaac	2-434
Isuck	2-420
James	2-420,434
Jane	2-434
Jene	2-420
John	2-420;R-113
Joshua	2-014,446
Margaret	2-446
Peter	2-420
Sarah	2-420
Thomas	2-167,420,446
William	2-028
MILLAR, Joseph	2-120
MILLER, Edward	2-476
John	2-476
Joseph	2-292,305,321, 368,476;R-031
Robert	2-312
MILLS, John	R-049
Mary	2-448
Robert	R-049
Susannah	R-049
Thomas	2-448
MITCHEL, Elizabeth	R-199
James	2-414
Kent	2-090;R-167
MITCHELL, Ann	2-418
Aquila	2-418,458
Charlotte	2-458
Clemency	2-458
Edward	2-418,458
Elizabeth	2-422,458
Hannah	2-422,458
James	2-090,458
Kent Junr.	2-134
Kent	2-422,458
Martha	2-418
Mary	2-422,458
Micajah	2-418,458;R-090
Parker William	2-458
Sarah	2-458
Sophia	2-458
Susanna	2-458
Thomas	2-422
William	2-418,458
Winston	2-418
MOLTON, Mathew	2-458
MONAHON, Arthor	2-130
MONEY, Robert	2-451
MONK, Richard	2-394
MONKS, John	R-246
MONTGOMERY, James	2-432
John	R-163,209
Margaret	2-432
Martha	2-432
Thomas	2-432
William	2-363;R-163
MOOBERRY, William	R-093
MOOR, Hannah	R-114
James	R-114
MOORE, Ann	2-404
Charles	2-081
Deborah	R-252
Hannah	R-114
James	2-104,404;R-114
Jason	R-252
John	2-463
Pamela	2-021
William	2-021
MOORES, Daniel	2-479
James	2-479
John	2-479;R-252
MORGAN, Cassandra	2-384,463
Edward	2-411,463
Elizabeth	2-263,411
Ellinor	2-463
James L.	2-463
James Lee	2-513
Margaret	2-463

MORGAN, Martha	2-463	NELSON, Aquilla	2-174
Mary	2-463	Jean	R-011
Robert	2-123,360,402,	John	2-174
	411,463,531	NESBITT, Robert	2-198
Samuel	2-411,463	NEVILL, Rachel	2-487
Sarah	2-463	NICHEAS, James	2-161
Susannah	2-411	NICHOLS, Charlotta	R-085
William	2-352,384,411,463,513	NICLEAS, James	2-161
MORRES, Isreal	R-167	NIGHT, Nancy	2-211
MORRIS, Edward	2-413	NISBITTE, Robert	2-198
Frances	2-413	NORRINGTON, Abraham	2-488
Giles	2-413	Isaac	2-488
Isreal	R-086	John	2-488
James	R-167	Martha	2-488
Jane	2-413	Mary	2-488
John	2-413	Rachel	2-488
Joseph	R-167	Susannah	2-488
Mary	R-167	NORRIS, Abraham	2-482
Michael	2-413	Ann	2-490,493
Richard	2-413	Aquila	2-490
Robert	R-167	Aran or Aron	2-488
Sarah	2-038,071,074	Benjamin	2-482
Susannah	2-071,413	Benjamin Bradford	R-011,021
Thomas	2-413	Benjamin Bradford Esq	2-443
William	2-413	Charles	2-115
William Bond	2-071,074	Christian	2-029,482
MORRISON, Ann	R-238	Edward	2-485,490
Daniel	2-435	Elijah	2-488
James	2-424,435	Elizabeth	2-490,493;R-021
MORRISS, Elin	2-511	Ellenor	2-193
MORRISSON, Matthew	2-363	Hannah	2-488,490
MORROW, Mary	2-059	Henry	2-111,493
MUNK, William	2-516	Henry Davis	2-111
MUNN, John	R-209	James	2-193,485,493
MUNROW, Rebecca	R-040	John	2-096,362,482,490
MURNAHAN, Susanna	R-081	Joseph	2-482
MURPHY, Allice	2-443	Joseph Junr.	2-111
Elizabeth	2-115,443	Martha	2-508
Francis	2-443	Mary	2-485,490
Henry	2-381	Oliver	2-490
James	2-443;R-021	Rebecca	2-115
John	2-443	Sarah	2-482,485,488
Mary	2-440	Susanna	2-362,490
Rachel	2-381	Thomas	2-482
Rose	2-443	William	2-087,446,490
Timothy	2-274	William Junr.	2-314
William	2-055	NORRISS, Abraham Junr.	2-415
MURRAY, Susannah	R-093	Christian	2-336
NEAL, Francis	R-152	NORTON, Nathan	R-101
John	R-152	Sophia	2-069
Joseph	R-152	Stephen	2-069,123,402
Sarah	R-152	NOWLAND, Ben	R-246
William	R-152	O'LEARY, Daniel	2-001
NEIL, Francis	R-217	OLDHAM, Edward	R-134
NEILL, Francis	R-126	Henry	R-134

Name	Reference	Name	Reference
OLDHAM, William	R-129,134	PAGE, Christopher	2-348
OLDUM, William	2-156	PAIN, Barnet	2-525
OLIVER, Robert	2-312	Bever	2-525
ONION, Charity	2-454,498	Elizabeth	2-525
Corbin	2-454,498	Jacob	2-525
Elizabeth	2-454,498	James	2-525
Hannah	2-454,498	Thomas	2-525
John Barrett	2-454,498	William	2-525
Martha	2-498	PARIMAN, John	2-285
Sarah	2-498	PARKER, Ann	2-366;R-058,103
Stephen	2-454,498	Edward	R-058
Susannah	2-498	Elizabeth	R-103
Thomas	2-454	John	2-366;R-007
Thomas Bond	2-454,498	Martin	R-103
William Frances Heat	2-498	PARKS, Ann	R-209
William Francis H.	2-454	Elizabeth	2-440
Zachius	2-498,454	John	R-209
ORR, James	2-142	William	R-209
John Dale	2-142	PARSONS, Isaac	2-431
Mary	2-142	Joseph Dyer	2-179
ORRICK, Nicholas	2-378	Rachel	2-179
OSBORN, Alexander	R-021	PATRICK, James	2-510
Benjamin	2-494,496,502	John	2-510;R-157
Benjamin Junr.	2-327	PATTERSON, Avarilla	2-263, 296,306
Cyrus	2-230,249,444, 494,496,504	George	2-009,263,285, 435;R-167
James	2-008,155,158,184, 312,327,494,496, 502,504;R-040	John	2-031,296
		Robert	R-167
Jane	2-502	Samuel	2-056
John Hanson	2-327	William	2-231
Lawrence	2-504	PEACOCK, Cassandra	2-357
Lennard	2-504	John	2-357
Martha	2-494,496,502,504	Mary	2-357
Mary	2-496,502,504	PEARCE, Cassandra	R-008
Nancy	2-504	Henry Ward	2-237
Samuel G.	2-283	PENDIGRASS, Rachel	2-059
Samuel Groom	2-005,070, 153;R-164	PENIX, John	2-350
		PENROSE, Cassandra	2-247
Samuel Groom Esq.	2-397	Frances	2-247
Semelia	2-327,504	Harriot	2-247
Sharlot	2-504	PERDUE, Mary	2-526
Susanna	2-249	Walter	2-526
Susannah	2-230,504	PERKINS, Reuben	2-418
William	2-165,327,494, 496,502;R-164	Solomon	2-123
		PERRY, John	2-413
OWENS, David	R-049	William	2-408
PACA, Aquila Junr.	2-513	PERVEIL, Gidion	R-159
Aquilla	2-415,517	PETE, David	2-128
Frances	2-517	PHILLIPS, Eliza P.	R-097
James	2-384	James	2-215,517;R-167
John	2-517;R-048	Martha	2-517
Mary	2-517	PHIPPS, Nathanell	R-015
Susannah	2-517	PHIPS, Joseph	2-004
William	2-517;R-097	PIKE, Mary	2-178

PINKNEY, William	2-027	Martin	2-057,211
PINNEY, Charles	2-303	Mary	2-057
PINNITON, Michael	2-247	Sarah	2-040,082,524,528
PITT, Francis Loveill	R-126	Scott	2-057
Francis Lovill	2-359	Walter	2-040
Francis Lovitt	2-047	William	2-028,060,524
PLATOR, Col. George	R-229	PREWETT, Joseph	2-494
PLUNKET, Susey	2-516	PRIBBLE, Clemency	2-057
POCOCK, Daniel	2-037	Stephen	2-057
Jemima	2-037	PRICE, Eleanor	2-111
POLLARD, Rebeckah	2-508	James	R-078
PORTER, William	2-418,458	Stephen Ricketts	R-016
POTEET, Mary	2-488	Veazey	2-191
POUZACY, Jean	2-176	PRICHARD, Obadiah	2-227
POWCOCK, Daniel	R-096	PRIGG, Edward	2-360,463,
POWELL, William	2-158,327		531;R-016
PRAUL, Ens. [----]	2-031	Mary	2-411
PRESBURY, Ann	2-521	Martha	2-411
Barthea	2-521	Samuel	2-531
Clemency	2-506	Susanna	R-191
Elinor	2-511	William	2-360,463,531
Elizabeth	2-506,521	PRINGLE, Mark	R-073
George	2-521	PRITCHARD, Benjamin	2-234,530
George Beedle	2-521	Daniel	2-530
George Gouldsmith	2-181,521	Elizabeth	2-530
Greenbury	2-506	James	2-530
Henry	2-511	James Senr.	2-227
Isabella	2-521	Samuel	2-234,530
James	2-506,511	PUSEY, Elizabeth	2-251
James Tolley	2-521	Sarah	2-092
Joseph	2-506,511;R-148	PUTNAM, Gen. [----]	2-009
Joseph H.	2-057	PUTTEE, Ann	2-508
Martha	2-276	Frances	2-508
Mary	2-391,511,521	Francis	2-508
Sarah	2-506	Isaac	2-508
Sophia	2-521	Lewis	2-508
Thomas	2-137,335	Peter	2-508
Thomas Pycraft	2-122,511	Sarah	2-508
William	2-256,335, 506,511,521	PYLE, John	R-119
		Ralph	R-083
William Robinson	2-506	William	R-136
PRESTON, Ann	2-507;R-028	QUINLAN, Phillip	2-081
Barnard	2-528	QUISTON, Jean	R-011
Barnerd	2-033	Moses M.	R-011
Benjamin	2-057	RABURG, Mary	R-266
Bernard	2-057,082,211,528	RACO, James	2-324
Clemency	2-057	RAE, William	R-215
Corbin	2-060,524	RAINE, Samuel	R-225
Daniel	2-033,528;R-211	RAMPLY, James	2-254
Elizabeth	2-057	Sarah	2-254
James	2-028,057,144,382, 393,404,507,524, 528;R-098	Thomas Johnson	2-254
		RAMSEY, Nathaniel	2-249
		William	2-163
John	2-060,524	REARDON, James	2-049
Martha	2-057	Peggy	R-023

REARDON, Samuel	2-165
REDDILL, John	2-516
REDEN, James	2-439
REED, James	R-025
John	2-158
Thomas	2-457
William	R-011,025
REES, Solomon	R-159
REESE, David	2-179
John	2-064
RELEY, Solomon	2-193
RENSHAW, Abe	2-378
Bennett	R-001
Elizabeth	R-189
Frances	2-082;R-001
Hannah	R-016
Hosia	R-001
James	R-001
Joseph	2-374
Martin	R-001
Mary	2-010,333,336;R-001
Robert	R-001
Salinah	R-001
Silina	2-082
Thomas	R-001,016
RICHARDSON, Benjamin	R-020,021,037,051
Elizabeth	R-020,037
Hannah	R-223
Henry	R-037
Joshua	R-037
Mary	R-037
Nathaniel	R-003
Sally	R-020
Samuel	R-020,037,051
Tabitha	2-219;R-003,045,046
Thomas	R-020
Vincent	R-037
William	R-003,020,037
Winston	R-021
RICHENSON, Benjamin	R-021
Winston	R-021
RICHESON, Benjamin	R-006
RICHEY, John	2-402
RICKETTS, Edward	2-290
John Thomas	R-087
Samuel	2-290,301,354;R-036
Samuel Sen.	R-036
RIDLEY, Mathey	R-073
RIGBIE, Ann	R-008
Anna	R-018,031
Cassandra	R-031
Elizabeth	R-031
Hannah	R-018,046
Henrietta	R-008
James	2-348;R-031,185
James Junr.	R-046
John	R-008
Mercy	R-031
Nathan	2-219,346,348;407;R-008,018,031,045,046,048,180
Col. Nathan	R-008
Nathaniel	2-237
Philip	R-008
Sabina	R-008
Sarah	2-219,237;R-031
Susannah	R-031
RIGDON, Ann	R-028,034
Alexander	2-373,434;R-028,034,113
Baker	R-083
Bencemond	R-028
Benjamin	R-034,113
Elizabeth	R-028
Margret	R-034
Sarah	R-083
Stephen	R-034,113
Steven	R-028
Thomas	R-034
William	R-028,034
RILEY, Barney	2-116;R-023
John	2-193
RILLY, Barney	R-023
Charles	R-023
James	R-023
Jane	R-023
John	R-023
Peggy	R-023
Routh	R-023
William	R-023
RISTEAU, Susannah	R-073
RITCHARDS, James	2-134
ROBERTS, Arramenta	2-335
Billingsley	2-137
Clorinda	R-006
Elizabeth	2-335
Irwin	R-006
John	2-290;R-010
Peter	2-335
Richardson	R-006
Samuel	2-335
Stephen	R-010,015
ROBERTSON, Elizabeth	R-229
ROBINSON, Archabald	R-007
Catharine	2-446
Charity	R-064
Edward	2-340;R-027
Elizabeth	R-007
Ellenor	2-458

ROBINSON, Henry	2-312	RUTH, Ester	R-011,025
Joseph	2-059,076,088	Moses	R-011
Margaret	2-446	Moses Sr	R-025
Margret	R-027	RUTTER, Richard	R-068
Richard	2-099;R-007,027	RYAN, John	2-008,303,312
Temperance	R-007	RYELEY, Bernet	2-116
Thomas	2-076	SANGSTER, Capt. Nehemiah	2-312
Walter	2-300	SAPPINGTON, Mark Brown	2-036
William	2-001,331,335;R-007	Rebecca	2-027
ROBISON, Walter	R-055	SAUNDERS, Elizabeth	2-136,211,
ROCK, Patrick	2-193		393;R-078
ROCKHOLD, John	R-027	James	R-085
RODGERS, John	2-316	Joseph	2-448;R-086
Susannah	2-097	Mary	R-085
ROGENS, Thomas	2-123	Robert	2-111,171,211;
ROGERS, Eleanor	R-068		R-078,164
Joseph	2-357	Thomas	R-086
Thomas	2-123	William	2-407;R-085,086
ROWLS, Ann	2-076	SAUSCARIS, P. Jauna de	2-176
ROWNTREE, Thomas	2-338	SAVORY, William	2-301,440
RUFF, Anna	2-528	SCAFF, Ann	R-066
Catharine	2-106	Benjamin	R-066
Daniel	2-394;R-040,246	Hannah	R-134
Daniel Jr.	R-246	John	R-134
Hannah	R-246	Mary	R-134
Henry	2-016;R-087,246	SCATTIN, John	R-048
Henry Jr.	2-104;R-211	SCOTLAND, Hannah	2-103
Henry Sr.	R-211	SCOTT, Ann	R-059,061
James	R-246	Aquila	R-059,061
John	2-215,359,394,	Aquilla	2-057
	517;R-040,132,246	Benjamin	R-059
Mary	2-436	Cassandra	R-061
Richard	R-081	Clemency	2-057
RUFFCORN, Catharine	2-106	Daniel	2-040;R-242
RUMSEY, Col. Benjamin	2-150	Isabell	2-206
Benjamin	2-268,286,521;R-008	James	R-059,061
Benjamin Jr.	2-286	John	R-066
Charles	R-008	Martha	R-059
Charlotte	2-286	Mary	2-057
Hannah	2-286	Robert	R-066,148
Henrietta	2-286	Robert Junr.	R-066
John	2-005,286;R-008,062	Sarah	2-400;R-066
Martha	2-286	Susanna	2-237;R-107
Mary	2-268,286	Walter	R-066
Sabina	R-008	SEAL, Hannah	2-090
William	R-008	James	2-090
RUSH, George	2-021;R-037	SEDGWICK, Benjamin	2-016
Jacob	2-021	SEWELL, John	2-153
RUSSELL, Andrew	R-004	SHA, Margret	2-193
Hugh	R-004	SHARP, James	2-236
James	R-004	SHAY, Thomas	2-066,258;R-132
John	R-004	SHEARER, Thomas	2-079;R-154
Mary	R-004	SHEREDINE, Cassandra	2-219,237;
Robert	R-004		R-045,046
Thomas	R-004		

SHEREDINE, Daniel	2-219;R-018, 045,046,250	Paca	R-073,097
James	2-198	Rachel Hambleton	2-379
Jeremiah	R-045,046	Ralph	2-463;R-090
Nathan	2-237;R-045,046	Robert	2-196;R-049,083
Upton	R-045	Ruth	R-044
SHERIDINE, James	R-011	Samuel	2-007,472; R-034,048,083
Nathan Rigbie	R-018	Mayr. Samuel	2-374
SHERRIDINE, Daniel	R-062	Sarah	R-044
SHIELDS, James	2-197	Susanna	R-073,097,121
Paul	2-233	Thomas	2-292,404;R-051,090
SIKLAR, Martha	2-035	William	2-021,137,148,237, 249,316,477,498, 517;R-031,051,073, 083,090,087,107,246
SIKLER, Martha	2-035		
SILVER, Garsham	R-044		
SIMS, Alse	R-055		
Andrew	2-457	William Jr.	2-237
Elizabeth	R-055	Dr. William	R-167
Francis	R-055	Winston	2-237;R-021,107
Jean	R-055	Winstone	R-051,073
Margret	R-055	SMITHSON, Archibald	R-098
Mary	R-221	Benjamin	2-057;R-098
Robert	R-055	Daniel	R-098
William	R-055	Mary	2-057;R-098
SINCLAIR, William	2-488	Nathaniel	R-098
SKEVINTON, James	R-188	Sarah	2-057
SKINNER, John	R-010	Thomas	R-098
SLACK, Elizabeth	2-346;R-056	William	2-159;R-098
SLADE, Ezekiel	2-056,462	SMYTH, John	2-051;R-140
William	2-056,462	SNOWDONS, Hannah Moor	2-305
SMALLWOOD, Col. [----]	2-031	SPENCER, Batricks	2-140
SMITH, [----]	2-498	Charity	R-064
Col. Alexander Lawson	2-258	Enoch	R-105
Amos	2-137	Ezra	R-105
Avarilla	2-507	James	2-140;R-064,270
Benjamin	R-044	John	R-064
Catharin	R-048	Mahlon	R-105
Elizabeth	2-111,197,237; R-018,031	Sarah	R-105
		William	2-416;R-064
Frances	R-073,097	Zaccharias	R-064
Hannah	R-090	SPRINGER, William	2-198
Harriott	R-051	SPRUCEBANKS, Abraham	2-019
Hugh	R-090	SPRUSBANKS, Abraham	2-019
Jacob Giles	2-237;R-073	SPRUSEBANKS, Abraham	2-061
James	R-090	Ann	2-061
Jane	2-432	Benjamin	2-061
Jean	R-083	Blanche	2-061
John	2-294;R-051,083,090	Francis	2-061
Capt. John	2-292	Jackson	2-061
John Brown	2-051	Jean	2-061
Joshua	2-394	Martha	2-061
Lyle	R-034,083	Mary	2-061
Martha	2-053,258,292;R-051	STALLINGS, William	R-221
Mary	R-044,090	STALLIONS, Edward	R-081
Nathan	R-051	Elizabeth	R-081
Nathaniel	R-090	Jacob	R-081

D-27

STALLIONS, John	R-081		Thomas	2-150,171,283;R-268
Kent	R-081		STUMP, Hannah	R-101
Mary	R-081		Henry	2-227
Richard	R-081		Herman	R-101
Thomas	R-081		John	2-404;R-090,101,215
STANDEFORD, David	2-493		John Sr.	R-101
STANDIFORD, Ann	R-103		SUTTON, Jonathan	2-316
Bathia	R-027		Samuel	2-090;R-095
David	2-438		SWAN, Catherine	R-093
Edmon	R-096		Elizabeth	R-093
Elizabeth	R-103		Frederick	R-093
Loyd	R-103		Jacob	R-093
William	R-096		John	R-093
STANSBURY, [----]	2-021		Margaret	R-093
Dixon	2-340		SWEENEY, David	2-350
Edmund	2-340		David Jun.	2-350;R-110
STEELE, John	2-513		Harriet	2-200
STEPHENSON, Ann	R-062		SWITZAR, Ann	2-111
George	R-062		SYMS, Jean	R-004
James	R-062		TAIT, Charles	2-451
John	2-356,421		TALBOTT, Edmund	R-134
Jonas	2-149		Elizabeth	R-134
Mary	2-162;R-062		Mary	R-134
Rachel	R-062		Thomas	R-134
William	R-062		TALOR, Nancy	2-186
STERLING, Jane	2-088		TASKER, James	R-031
STEVENSON, Andrew	2-007		TATE, David	2-291
John	2-018		TAYLOR, Amasa	2-371
William	R-062		Abraham	2-139,379;R-126
STEWART, Elizabeth	2-230		Aquila	R-126
George	R-079		Asa	2-371
James	2-230;R-058		Ashberry	2-187
John	R-079		Benett	R-126
Mitchel	R-126,195,229		Bethia	R-103
Mitchell	2-047		Charles	R-027,103
Samuel	2-111,267		George	2-197;R-126
Sarah	2-389;R-058		Isabella	R-126
STILES, George	R-087		James	2-413;R-027
John	R-087		John	2-030
Joseph	2-009;R-087		Mary	R-111
STOKES, Ann	R-068		Robert	2-371
Clare	R-068		Thomas	2-237
John	R-068		William	2-525;R-101
Joseph	R-217,244		THOMAS, Anna	R-119
Mary	R-068		Benjamin	R-113
Robert	R-167		Betty	R-119
Robert Young	R-068		David	R-110,118,119,260
Sarah	R-068		Eleanor	2-364
William	R-068		Francis	R-113
William Brooks	R-068		Giles	2-076
STOVINGTON, [widow]	2-010		Hannah	R-119
STREET, John	2-123		Henry	R-118,119
STRICKLING, Elizabeth	R-121		Isaac	R-110
Sarah	R-121		James	R-110,118,119
STRONG, Nathaniel	2-331		John	R-083,110,118,119,136

THOMAS, Joseph	R-113		Kathern	R-086
Martha	R-110		Mary	R-111
Mary	2-360;R-110,113		Sarah	2-225
Owen	R-110		Thomas	R-111,117
Rebecca	R-110		TRICE, Frances	R-249
Rhoda	2-024		Hermon	R-249
Sarah	R-119		Thomas	R-249
Thomas	2-438		TRUELOVE, Michael	2-220
William	R-136		TRULOCK, Margret	2-401
THOMPSON, Capt. [----]	2-451		TURK, Ruth	2-194
Ann	2-488		TURNER, Andrew	2-156;R-129
Anna	R-132		Ann	2-156
Aquilla Genl.	2-031		Arabella	R-129
Cassandra	2-488		Catharine	R-129
Cynthia	2-451		Jane	R-140
Daniel	2-010,194		Margaret	R-129
David	2-158;R-132		Martha	R-129
Elizabeth	R-114		Samuel	R-129
Frances	2-488		Sarah	R-129
Hannah	2-368		Thomas	R-129
Henry	R-132		UNDERHILL, Mary	2-231
James	2-416;R-132		VALENTINE, Alexander	2-137
John	2-055,316;R-132		VANCE, Agnes	R-140
Mary	R-132		Alice	R-140
Ruthea	R-011		Andrew	R-140
Sarah	2-055,158;R-132		Eleanor	R-140
Susannah	2-393		John	2-051;R-129,140
THOMSON, Jean	2-338		William	R-140
THORP, Rachel	R-114		VANCLEAF, Elizabeth	2-384
TIERNEY, Patric	2-144		Mary	2-384
TILBROOK, John	2-366		VANCLEAVE, Dr. [----]	2-513
TILLARD, William	2-411		Elizabeth	2-513
TIMMONS, Edward	R-121		Mary	2-513
John	R-121		VANDERGRIFTE, George	2-374
Thomas	R-121		VANHORN, Ezekial	R-048
TIRE, Francis	2-152		Martha	2-137
William	R-152		VANSCYKLE, Elizabeth	2-416
TOLAND, Adam	R-124		VANSICKLE, Henry	2-155
Benjamin	2-126;R-124		VARNEY, James	2-128
Ester	R-124		VERNAY, James	2-106,291
Haly	R-124		VINCENT, Samuel	2-181
Isaac	R-124		VOGAN, George	2-141;R-142
Jacob	R-124		James	R-142
TOLLEY, Cordelia	2-288		Mary	R-142
Edward Carvel	2-167		WALDRON, David	R-242
James	2-288		Phebey	R-242
Martha	2-288		Richard	R-242
TOWNSEND, Joseph	2-294		Susannah	2-018
TOWSON, Dinah	R-114		WALDRUM, Susannah	2-018
TOY, Joseph	2-115		WALER, Marget	2-162
TREDWAY, [----]	R-111		WALKER, James	2-092;R-044,180
Daniel	2-017;R-117		Mary	2-408
Daniel Junr.	R-117		WALLACE, Andrew	R-018
Elizabeth	2-225		Sarah	R-031
John	2-225		WALLIS, Grace	R-185

WALLIS, Jacob	R-189	Walter	2-196
Joseph	R-185,191	William	2-061;R-211
Joseph Jacob	2-097	WAYNE, John	2-031
Thomas	2-292;R-185,189	WEATHERALL, Henry	2-046
WALTHAM, Carlton	R-212	WEBB, Constance Priscilla	
Elizabeth	R-212		2-384;R-205
Thomas	2-171	Elizabeth	2-432;R-142,205
WANE, John	2-005,036;R-015	Margaret	R-205
Lucina	2-005	Margaret Lee	2-384;R-205
Margaret	2-005	Priscilla	2-513
Sarah	2-005	Samuel	R-205
WARD, Ann	R-150,225,260	Samuel Jr.	2-103
Avis	R-215	Sarah	R-205
Cassandra	R-189,215	William	2-033,103,
Charles	R-150		384,513;R-205
Edward	2-225;R-189,215	WEBSTER, Ann	R-229
Elizabeth	R-215,225,260	Cassandra	R-031
James	R-150,225,260	Elizabeth	R-001,229,250
John	R-225	Hannah	R-228
Marget	2-210	Isaac	2-040,233,274;
Margret	R-215		R-018,023,031,056,
Mary	2-225;R-150,215		167,197,229,250,264
Moses	R-150	Isaac Junr.	2-401
Rebecca	R-150	Isaac Lee	R-229,250
Reubin	R-150	James	2-472;R-111,221
Richard	R-189,215,225,260	John Lee	2-139,274,
William	R-225,260		369;R-229
WARE, Mary	2-076	John S.	R-250
Thomas	2-076	John Skinner	R-229
WAREAM, Abraham	R-187	Margaret	R-228
WARFIELD, Henry	2-316	Mary	R-221,228
WARNER, Crowsdale	2-188	Michael	2-137;R-197
Cuthbert	R-185	Richard	2-263,472;R-197
Joseph	2-097,200;R-185	Samuel	2-472;R-197,250,264
Sarah	2-188	Susannah	R-221
WASKEY, Christian	2-115,381	Thomas	R-250
WATERS, Hannah	2-321	WEIR, Elizabeth	2-371
Henry	2-016,357	John	2-371
Joanna Giles	2-237	Sarah	2-508
WATKENS, Amos	R-183	William	2-378
John	R-183	WELLS, Drusilla	R-191
William	R-183	Jane	R-191
WATKINS, Elizabeth	2-194	John	2-123
John	2-194;R-183	Mary	R-191
WATSON, Mary	2-045	Richard	R-189,191
WATTERS, Charles	2-511;R-148	Richard Senr.	R-189
Elizabeth	2-165	Samuel	R-191
Geofrey	2-079	Thomas	R-146
Godfrey	2-196;R-081,211	William	2-384,411;R-189
Hannah	R-148	William Junr.	2-123
Henry	2-350,357;R-211	WELSH, Andrew	2-163
John	R-148	WERAM, Abraham	R-187
Mary	2-325;R-148,211	Cristiana	R-187
Sarah	R-148	WEST, Ann	R-249
Stephen	2-325,493;R-148	Enos	2-010

WEST, Enuch	2-090	Hugh Junr.	R-209
Joseph	R-249	John	R-203
Polly	R-249	Mary	R-209
Thomas	2-010;R-028	Michael	R-203
William	2-525	William	R-209
WETHERALL, Henry	2-070,165,	WHITEHEAD, Nathan	2-137
	506,507,511;	WHITFORD, Robert	R-134
	R-003,164	WIGFIELD, Mathew	2-325
James	2-165,171,496,511;	William	2-325
	R-036,164,246	WILES, Mary	2-411
Katy	2-165	Sarah	2-411
Mary Ann	2-506;R-164	WILEY, Elizabeth	2-198
William	2-165;R-164	Isabel	2-198
WHEELER, Bennett	2-163;	Jane	2-198
	R-199,217	WILGUS, James	2-088
Elizabeth	R-199,217	WILLETT, Ann	R-008,031,046
Francis Ignatius	R-217	Samuel	R-008
Henrietta	R-217,238	WILLIAMS, Abraham	2-340
Ignatius	2-116;R-199,217,238	Christian M.	R-159
Col. Ignatius	2-404;R-217	Enoch	2-021
Joseph	R-199,213,217,238	Isaac	2-194
Josiah	R-213	John	2-237
Josias	R-152,199	Margret	2-100
Mary Ann	R-217	Peter	2-407
Mildred	R-152	William	R-055,229
Monica	R-199,217	WILLIAMSON, [----]	2-391
Susanna	R-152,213	Robert	R-161
Thomas	2-141;R-152,	Sarah	R-161
	199,213,217	WILLITS, Ann	2-407
Treacy	R-217	Cassandra	2-407
WHITACRE, Catharine	2-508	Samuel	2-069,407
John	2-222	WILLMOTT, Hannah	R-114
WHITAKER, Abraham	R-193	John	R-114
Ann	2-232	Mary	R-114
Elizabeth	2-362;R-193	Richard	R-114
George	R-193	Ruth	R-114
Hezekiah	2-303	Sarah	R-114
Isaac	2-046	WILLSON, Cassandra	R-180
John S.	2-362	John	2-411
Josias	R-193	Rachel	R-180
Martha	2-024,059	Samuel	R-180
Rachel	2-362	William	R-180
Susanna	R-193	WILMER, Lambert	2-150,171,
Susannah	2-232		283,474;R-270
Thomas	R-193	WILMORE, Lambert	2-354
WHITE, Col. [----]	R-087	WILMOTT, John	R-244
Margaret	2-166	Richard	2-196,273,388;R-244
Sarah	2-079,493	Ruth	R-244
Sarah Charlotte	R-167	Sarah	R-244
Sophia	2-276	WILSON, Andrew	R-163
Thomas	R-167	Archibald	R-163
Col. Thomas	2-258,268,285	Benjamin	2-100,121;R-157
Rev. William	R-167	Benjamin Kidd	2-251
WHITEFORD, Anna	R-203,240	Catharine	2-179
Hugh	R-203,209,240	Christopher	2-200

WILSON, Elizabeth	2-100,148, 179,265;R-258	George	2-017
		George Hughes	2-031
Henry	2-251;R-223	Sophia	2-017
Hugh	2-371;R-258	WORTHINGTON, Ann	R-255
Isabel	R-163	Charles	R-146,159,255
James	2-123;R-078,163,258	Charles Senr.	R-146
Jean	R-258	Elizabeth	R-255
John	2-097,109,110,121, 179,294,305,313,384; R-031,079,163,229,258	Henry	R-159
		John	2-298;R-146,159
		Joseph	R-255
		Margarett	R-255
John Junior	2-179	Mary	2-298;R-146,159,255
John Senr.	2-506;R-157	Presila	R-159
John W.	R-250	Samuel	R-146,159,255
Joseph	2-305;R-031	Sarah	R-146,159,255
Joseph Jun.	2-352;R-189	WOTTON, Ann	R-081
Lydia	2-079	WRAIN, William	2-204
Margaret	2-434	WRIGHT, Ann	2-038
Mary	2-384;R-258	John	2-137
Peter	2-200,321,368;R-215,255	Sarrah	2-363
Rachel	R-223	Thomas	2-479
Robert	R-258	WYLIE, Nathaniel	R-203
Samuel	2-179,384,513	YARNALL, Mordecai	R-167
Sarah	2-121,206	YATES, Margret	R-212
Thomas	2-062,190	YEATES, Ann	R-212
William	2-053,100,356, 384,448,449,460, 513;R-157,180	YOAKLEY, Mary	2-413
		YOAKLY, John	2-019
		YORK, Edward	2-521;R-266,268
William Junr.	R-157	George	2-148
William Senr.	2-092	Hannah	R-270
William B.	2-476	John	R-270
WINEMAN, John	R-238	Mary	R-266
WOOD, Benjamin	R-154	Oliver	R-268
Elizabeth	2-090;R-154	Sarah	R-268
Hannah	R-154	William	2-148,521
Henry	R-188	YOUNG, [----]	R-068
Hudson	R-195	Agness	R-264
Isaac	R-154	Alexander	R-252,264
James	R-154	Col. Benjamin	R-008
John	R-195	Clare	R-068
Joshua	2-067;R-195	George	2-436
Mary	R-154,195	Hugh	R-264
Moses	R-154	Mary	R-264
Sarah	R-195	Rebecca	R-068
Susanna	R-188	Robert	R-264
Susannah	R-195	Sarah	2-413;R-264
William	2-031,191;R-154		
WOODARD, John	R-152		
WOODMAN, Sarah	2-031,191		
WOODWARD, John	2-336		
WOOLSEY, George	2-130;R-252		
Henry	R-252		
Joseph	2-479;R-252		
Sarah	R-252		
WORSLEY, Ann	2-017		
Charlotte	2-017		